OPEN SOURCE SOFTWARE

Kamatchi K. S.

Sundaravelrani

KHANNA BOOK PUBLISHING CO. (P) Ltd.
4C/4344, Ansari Road, Darya Ganj,
New Delhi, India

Sathyabama Institute of Science and Technology
Jeppiaar Nagar, Rajiv Gandhi Salai,
Chennai, Tamilnadu, India

Dear Readers,

To prevent the piracy, this book is secured with HIGH SECURITY HOLOGRAM on the front title cover. In case you don't find the hologram on the front cover title, please write us to at contact@khannabooks.com or whatsapp us at +91-99109 09320 and avail special gift voucher for yourself.

Specimen of Hologram on front Cover title:

Moreover, there is a SPECIAL DISCOUNT COUPON for you with EVERY HOLOGRAM.

How to avail this SPECIAL DISCOUNT:

Step 1: Scratch the hologram
Step 2: Under the scratch area, your "coupon code" is available
Step 3: Logon to www.khannabooks.com
Step 4: Use your "coupon code" in the shopping cart and get your copy at a special discount
Step 5: Enjoy your reading!

Thanks,
Khanna Publishing House

ISBN: 978-93-55386-33-5

Open Source Software
by **Kamatchi K.S., Sundaravelrani**

First Edition: 2025

To view complete list of books, please scan the QR Code:

Published by:
Khanna Book Publishing Co. (P) Ltd.
CIN: U22110DL1998PTC095547

Visit us at: www.khannabooks.com
Write us at: contact@khannabooks.com

Printed in Bharat.

Preface

The world of software development has evolved significantly over the past few decades, with open-source software (OSS) playing a pivotal role in this transformation. Open-source systems have become the backbone of modern computing, driving innovation, collaboration, and democratizing access to powerful tools. open-source projects empower developers to create, modify, and distribute software freely, fostering a thriving global community of contributors.

"Open Source Systems" is a comprehensive guide aimed at providing both theoretical and practical knowledge of the key components that define open-source systems. The journey through this book begins with an exploration of the legal landscape of open-source software, focusing on critical topics like copyright, licensing, and patents. In particular, we delve into the various open-source licenses, their implications, and how they impact the development process.

Next, we dive into the tools that form the foundation of open-source systems. These include the indispensable Linux operating system, the GNU C Library (glibc), and the wide range of compilers and linkers that enable the efficient compilation and linking of source code into executable programs. The book also covers open-source programming techniques, highlighting best practices and strategies used by the community to foster collaboration, efficiency, and code quality. These programming techniques include version control, code reviews, documentation, and the effective use of open-source development environments and toolchains. Whether you're a seasoned developer or someone new to open-source software, this book will equip you with the knowledge and skills to navigate the open-source ecosystem. By understanding the legal, technical, and practical aspects of OSS, you'll be empowered to contribute to and leverage open-source systems in your own projects.

We hope that this book will serve as a valuable resource for anyone interested in open-source systems, whether for personal development, professional growth, or simply to explore the world of open collaboration. The open-source movement is constantly evolving, and this book aims to give you the foundation to be a part of this exciting and dynamic field.

Happy Reading and Contributing to Open Source!

Contents

♦♦♦

UNIT 1

Overview of Free/ Open Source Software

OVERVIEW OF FREE/OPEN SOURCE SOFTWARE

Free and Open Source Software (FOSS) refers to software that is both free of charge and open-source. It is a broad concept encompassing a wide variety of software projects and licenses. To understand FOSS fully, it's helpful to break down its two key components: "free" and "open source."

1. Free Software

In the context of software, "free" doesn't always mean "zero cost." Instead, it refers to the freedom to use, modify, and distribute the software. This freedom is best explained by the Free Software Foundation (FSF), which defines it as follows:

- **Freedom 0:** The freedom to run the software for any purpose.
- **Freedom 1:** The freedom to study how the program works, and change it to make it do what you wish (access to source code is a precondition).
- **Freedom 2:** The freedom to redistribute copies so you can help others.
- **Freedom 3:** The freedom to distribute copies of your modified versions to others, so the whole community can benefit from your improvements.

So, free software emphasizes freedom, not necessarily the price. It is often available at no cost, but the core principle is the user's ability to freely control the software.

Key Points

- **Not about price:** The term "free software" refers to freedom (libre), not cost (gratis).
- **Access to source code:** The software's source code must be available so users can inspect, modify, and improve it.

2. Open Source Software

"Open Source" refers to software whose source code is made available to the public under an open-source license. This means that anyone can view, modify, and distribute the software. The Open Source Initiative (OSI) defines open-source software as software that adheres to a set of specific criteria, including:

- **Free redistribution:** The software can be freely shared with others.
- **Source code availability:** The source code must be available to users, allowing them to modify it.

- **Derived works:** Modifications and derived works are allowed.
- **Integrity of the author's source code:** Some licenses may require modifications to be distributed under a different name or as a patch to the original software.
- **No discrimination:** Open-source licenses must not discriminate against any person, group, or field of endeavor.

The term "open-source" emphasizes the transparency and community-driven nature of the software development process. The idea is that when the source code is open, a community of developers can collaborate to enhance and improve the software, ensuring more innovation and rapid problem-solving.

Key Points

- **Transparency:** Users can see how the software works and can modify it.
- **Collaboration:** Open-source projects encourage community contributions, allowing for continual improvements.
- **Licensing:** Open-source software is licensed under specific terms that dictate how it can be used, modified, and distributed.

3. Key Characteristics of FOSS

There are several key characteristics that define free and open-source software:

- **Transparency:** The code is open for inspection. This transparency builds trust in the software's security and performance.
- **Community-driven development:** Many open-source projects are maintained and developed by large communities of volunteers and contributors. Users can report bugs, suggest features, or contribute code.
- **Cost-effectiveness:** Because most FOSS is free of charge, it lowers costs for individuals and businesses. Organizations, for instance, avoid paying licensing fees for proprietary software, potentially saving substantial sums of money.
- **Customization:** Users can modify FOSS to suit their own needs, whether for personal, educational, or enterprise purposes. This can include bug fixes, new features, or performance optimizations.
- **Security:** Open-source software can be scrutinized by anyone, which means security vulnerabilities can be detected and patched quickly by the community. However, it also depends on the activity and size of the community involved in the project.
- **Interoperability:** Many open-source projects are designed to work across various platforms, encouraging better integration with other software and systems

4. Licenses in FOSS

A significant aspect of free and open-source software is the license under which it is distributed. FOSS licenses specify how software can be used, modified, and redistributed. Some of the most common types of FOSS licenses are:

- **left Licenses:** These require that any derivative work or distribution of the software must also be open-source and licensed under the same terms. The GNU General Public License (GPL) is the most well-known example of this.

- **Permissive Licenses:** These licenses allow users to use the software in any way they want, including proprietary applications. The MIT License and the Apache License are examples of permissive licenses.
- **Dual Licensing:** Some projects offer dual licensing, meaning they provide both an open-source license and a commercial (proprietary) license. This is often done to generate revenue while allowing the community to benefit from open-source development.

5. Advantages of FOSS

FOSS has many advantages, both for individual users and organizations:

a. For Individual Users

- **No cost:** Most FOSS is free to use.
- **Freedom:** Users can modify software to fit their needs or fix issues themselves.
- **Security:** Open code makes it possible to detect and fix vulnerabilities quickly.
- **Privacy:** FOSS often has fewer hidden trackers or privacy issues compared to proprietary software, since the code is open to inspection.

b. For Businesses and Enterprises

- **Lower total cost of ownership:** Since FOSS does not have licensing fees, businesses can reduce costs significantly.
- Customization: Organizations can tailor the software to meet their specific needs.
- **Avoiding vendor lock-in:** With proprietary software, businesses can become dependent on a single vendor. FOSS avoids this issue because users can change or upgrade the software without vendor restrictions.

c. For Developers

- **Learning:** Developers can learn from studying open codebases.
- **Collaboration:** Developers can contribute to open-source projects, gaining recognition in the community.
- **Innovation:** Open-source software promotes experimentation and the creation of new ideas or tools that benefit everyone.

Examples of FOSS

- GNU/Linux Operating System
- Android
- Mozilla (Firefox)
- Libre/Open Office
- VLC
- GIMP, Blender
- Apache
- MySQL
- PHP, phpMyadmin
- Wordpress, Drupal, Joomla
- Emacs
- Eclipse
- Firebug
- 7-Zip

Fig 1.1: *FOSS*

6. Challenges of FOSS

While there are numerous benefits to FOSS, there are also challenges:

- **Support:** FOSS might lack formal customer support. While community support exists, it might not be sufficient or timely for enterprise users.
- **Documentation:** Some open-source projects might not have comprehensive or high-quality documentation, which can make it difficult for new users or developers to get started.
- **Integration:** In some cases, FOSS might not seamlessly integrate with proprietary systems or other software.
- **Security Concerns:** While transparency is generally a benefit, it also means that vulnerabilities are visible to everyone, including malicious actors. Without an active community, some projects can be vulnerable to exploitation.

7. Popular Examples of FOSS

- **Linux:** A widely used open-source operating system.
- **Firefox:** A popular open-source web browser.
- **LibreOffice:** An open-source alternative to Microsoft Office.
- **VLC Media Player:** An open-source media player that supports a wide variety of file formats.
- **WordPress:** A content management system (CMS) for building websites.
- Git: A version control system used by developers to manage source code.

8. FOSS Communities

FOSS thrives on vibrant, active communities. These communities contribute by:

- **Contributing code:** Developers contribute to the project by writing, testing, and improving the software.
- **Documentation:** Many contributors help by writing and maintaining documentation.
- **Support:** Community members often assist with troubleshooting and providing user support through forums, chat rooms, or mailing lists.
- **Bug Reports:** Users often help identify and report bugs, leading to faster improvements and fixes.

In summary, Free and Open Source Software (FOSS) provides immense value in terms of freedom, security, cost-effectiveness, and innovation. While there are some challenges to consider, FOSS is a growing and thriving ecosystem that empowers both users and developers to shape software in ways that benefit everyone.

DEFINITION OF FOSS (FREE AND OPEN SOURCE SOFTWARE)

FOSS stands for **Free and Open Source Software**, which refers to software that is both:

1. **Free (as in freedom)**: Users have the freedom to run, study, modify, and distribute the software. It emphasizes user control over the software, not just its price. The software's source code must be accessible, enabling users to modify it according to their needs.

2. **Open Source**: The software's source code is made publicly available, allowing anyone to inspect, modify, and distribute it. This encourages collaboration and transparency in the development process.

FOSS is typically distributed under licenses like the GNU General Public License (GPL), MIT License, or Apache License, which govern how the software can be used, modified, and shared.

Definition of GNU

GNU stands for **GNU's Not Unix**, a recursive acronym. It is a free software project launched by **Richard Stallman** in 1983 with the goal of creating a complete operating system that is **free software** (freedom to use, modify, and distribute). The project was created because Stallman believed that software should be free, allowing users to control it instead of being controlled by it.

The **GNU Project** is best known for the development of the **GNU operating system,** which includes key components such as:

- **GNU Compiler Collection** (GCC): A set of compilers for different programming languages.
- **GNU Core Utilities (Coreutils)**: Basic file, shell, and text manipulation utilities.
- **GNU Emacs**: A highly customizable text editor.
- **GNU**: A shell used in many Unix-like systems.

The **GNU General Public License (GPL)**, created by Stallman, is one of the most widely used free software licenses. It guarantees users the freedom to use, modify, and distribute software, but requires any modified versions of the software to also be released under the same license (known as left).

While the GNU Project contributed key components, the Linux kernel (created by Linus Torvalds in 1991) was added to form what we commonly refer to as Linux-based operating systems (e.g., Ubuntu, Debian). Many people mistakenly refer to these systems as Linux, but they are, in fact, GNU/Linux systems, as they combine the Linux kernel with the GNU operating system components. GNU is a free software project aimed at creating a completely free operating system, and it contributed essential components that are now part of many open-source operating systems.

HISTORY OF GNU/LINUX AND THE FREE SOFTWARE MOVEMENT

The history of GNU/Linux and the free software movement is a story of innovation, ideology, and collaboration. It began in the early 1980s and continues to shape the software world today. Here's an in-depth look at the key events and figures that influenced the development of GNU/Linux and the free software movement.

1. The Birth of the Free Software Movement: Richard Stallman and GNU

The free software movement began in the early 1980s, driven by Richard Stallman's vision for software freedom. In 1983, Stallman, a hacker and software developer at the Massachusetts Institute of Technology (MIT), launched the GNU Project (pronounced "Guh-noo"), aiming to create a completely free operating system. His primary goal was to give users freedom over their software, contrasting with the growing trend of proprietary software, where users had no access to source code or the right to modify it.

Key Events

- **1983**: Stallman announced the creation of the GNU Project, which stood for "GNU's Not Unix." This was a recursive acronym that emphasized the project's ambition to create a Unix-like operating system that would be entirely free and open-source.
- **1985**: Stallman founded the Free Software Foundation (FSF) to support the development of free software, promote its use, and defend the principles of software freedom. The FSF aimed to create software that would allow users to freely use, study, modify, and distribute the software.

Stallman also wrote the GNU Manifesto, which laid out the philosophical and practical foundations of the free software movement. He argued that software should be a tool for empowering users, not a proprietary commodity controlled by corporations.

The Key Concept: Left

One of Stallman's major contributions was the development of the GNU General Public License (GPL), released in 1989. The GPL was designed to ensure that any software distributed under it would remain free. It introduced the concept of left, which required any modified versions of the software to also be distributed under the same terms, preserving the software's freedom.

Stallman's left approach allowed users to modify software, but it also required that the modified versions be made available to others under the same open-source license. This created a viral effect: as long as one person or group used the software and its modifications, the software would continue to remain free.

2. The Development of GNU Components

The GNU Project made significant progress in developing various components needed to create a fully functional operating system. These components were designed to be free and open-source, and they include:

- **GNU Compiler Collection (GCC)**: A collection of compilers for different programming languages, including C, C++, and others. GCC remains one of the most important tools for developers in the open-source ecosystem.
- **GNU Emacs**: A highly extensible text editor. Emacs became one of the most popular editors used by programmers and continues to have a large following.
- **GNU Core Utilities**: A set of basic file manipulation and system management tools such as ls, cp, rm, and mkdir.
- **GNU**: A shell program that has become the standard shell in many Unix-like systems.

Despite the development of these essential tools, GNU was missing one key component: a **kernel**.

3. The Creation of the Linux Kernel

In 1991, a Finnish student named Linus Torvalds began work on a new operating system kernel, which would eventually become the Linux kernel. Torvalds was inspired by the limitations of the existing operating systems and wanted to create a free, open-source kernel for personal computers.

Key Events

- **1991**: Torvalds released the first version of the Linux kernel (version 0.01) to the public. Initially, it was a simple kernel that could boot up on a PC, but over time, it evolved into a powerful, robust, and efficient kernel capable of supporting a variety of systems.
- **1992**: Torvalds made the Linux kernel open-source, releasing it under the GPL. This allowed anyone to inspect the source code, modify it, and distribute it.

Torvalds' decision to license Linux under the GPL was a critical moment in the history of free software because it allowed the kernel to be freely used and modified, aligning it with the values of the GNU Project. This move provided the missing piece for a complete free operating system.

4. The Birth of GNU/Linux

When Torvalds created the Linux kernel, it was not a complete operating system by itself. It needed other components to function fully. This is where the GNU Project's software came into play. Many Linux distributions (often referred to as distros) combined the Linux kernel with various GNU utilities and libraries to create a fully functional GNU/Linux operating system.

By the mid-1990s, developers and organizations began bundling the Linux kernel with GNU software, resulting in fully functional open-source operating systems. These systems, now referred to as GNU/Linux, grew in popularity, particularly among developers, educators, and enthusiasts.

Key GNU/Linux Distributions

- **Debian**: One of the oldest and most influential distributions, Debian has served as the foundation for many other distributions, including Ubuntu.
- **Red Hat Linux**: One of the first commercially supported Linux distributions, which eventually evolved into Red Hat Enterprise Linux (RHEL).
- **Slackware**: One of the earliest Linux distributions, known for its simplicity and control over system configuration.
- **Ubuntu**: A more recent and highly popular Linux distribution designed for ease of use. It brought Linux to a broader audience, including non-technical users.

5. Growth of the Free Software and Open Source Movements

As Linux gained traction, the free software movement began to grow, but it also faced challenges. Some developers and companies were more focused on the technical aspects of open-source software rather than the ideological foundations of the free software movement. This led to the development of the open-source movement.

Open Source Movement

In 1998, a group of influential figures, including Eric S. Raymond and Bruce Perens, formed the Open Source Initiative (OSI), which advocated for open-source software from a pragmatic standpoint. They argued that open-source software's technical advantages—such as transparency, collaboration, and cost-effectiveness—were reason enough for its widespread adoption.

The open-source movement did not emphasize the ethical and philosophical underpinnings that the free software movement focused on, but it helped spread the adoption of open-source software in businesses and commercial applications. In contrast, the free software movement remained deeply focused on software freedom as a key principle.

Despite this difference, the two movements largely overlap, and many people involved in open-source projects also support the values of the free software movement. Today, "free software" and "open-source software" are often used interchangeably, although the ideological distinctions remain.

6. Impact and Legacy

The GNU/Linux operating system and the broader free software movement have had a profound impact on the technology industry:

- **Server Industry**: Linux has become the dominant operating system for servers, powering much of the web, including the majority of web hosting providers, cloud services (e.g., Amazon Web Services, Google Cloud), and enterprise environments.
- **Embedded Systems**: Linux is used in a wide range of embedded systems, from smartphones (Android is built on top of the Linux kernel) to automotive systems, Internet of Things (IoT) devices, and more.
- **Software Development**: The free and open-source software model has influenced the way software is developed. Tools like Git (originally developed by Linus Torvalds) and GitHub have transformed the software development workflow and fostered collaboration.
- **Business**: Many businesses, including major corporations like Google, IBM, and Red Hat, have embraced Linux and open-source software. The open-source business model, which offers services, support, and customization, has proven successful for many companies.

The history of GNU/Linux and the free software movement is a tale of vision, collaboration, and persistence. It started with Richard Stallman's philosophical belief in software freedom and led to the creation of the GNU Project, which laid the groundwork for the modern open-source ecosystem. The Linux kernel, created by Linus Torvalds, was the final piece needed to create a free operating system, and together, they formed GNU/Linux, which has grown into one of the most important and widely used operating systems today.

ADVANTAGES OF FREE SOFTWARE AND GNU/LINUX

The advent of free software and GNU/Linux has brought a wide array of benefits to individuals, organizations, and the global technology ecosystem. These advantages span several areas, including freedom, security, cost-effectiveness, flexibility, and community collaboration. Below is an in-depth exploration of these key advantages.

1. Freedom and Control

One of the foundational principles of free software is freedom—specifically, the freedom to use, study, modify, and distribute software. When using GNU/Linux and other free software, users gain control over their systems in ways that proprietary software does not allow. The free software license, such as the GNU General Public License (GPL), ensures that these freedoms are guaranteed.

Key Freedom-Related Benefits

- **Freedom to use**: You can use the software for any purpose, whether personal, educational, or commercial, without restrictions on the number of devices or locations.
- **Freedom to study and modify**: With access to the source code, users can inspect how the software works and make changes to suit their specific needs. For example, if you encounter a bug or want to add a feature, you can do so yourself or have someone else do it.
- **Freedom to share**: Users can freely share the software, whether it's the original or a modified version, with others. This encourages community-driven innovation and ensures that the software remains free and accessible to all.
- **Freedom to contribute**: If you find an issue or want to improve the software, you can contribute code or suggestions, making you an active participant in the development process.

This freedom contrasts with proprietary software, where users are restricted by license agreements, and modifications are often prohibited. With GNU/Linux, users avoid these limitations and gain complete autonomy over their software environment.

2. Cost-Effectiveness

One of the most significant advantages of GNU/Linux and free software is the low cost of acquisition. Most GNU/Linux distributions and free software packages are available at no cost or at a significantly lower price compared to proprietary software alternatives. This makes GNU/Linux an attractive option for individuals, businesses, educational institutions, and governments seeking to reduce costs.

Cost-Related Benefits

- **Zero Licensing Fees**: Unlike proprietary software that often charges for licenses (whether per user or per device), GNU/Linux distributions are available **for free**. This is particularly beneficial for small businesses, nonprofits, and educational institutions that might struggle with the cost of proprietary software.
- **No Hidden Costs**: Many free software applications are completely free to use without any hidden fees for updates or new versions. In contrast, proprietary software often comes with maintenance or subscription costs.
- **Lower Total Cost of Ownership (TCO)**: Although there might be initial costs associated with training staff or adapting to a new system, the lack of licensing fees, the ability to use older hardware, and the no-cost updates significantly reduce the total cost of ownership compared to proprietary solutions.

In many cases, companies using GNU/Linux can save thousands of dollars in licensing fees and software maintenance costs.

3. Security and Stability

Security is a critical aspect of any operating system or software system. GNU/Linux is often considered one of the most secure and stable platforms, particularly in server environments. Several factors contribute to the security and stability of GNU/Linux systems:

Key Security-Related Benefits

- **Open Source Nature**: Because the **source code** is open and accessible to anyone, it can be thoroughly audited and reviewed by security experts and the global community. If vulnerabilities or security flaws are discovered, they can be fixed quickly. This transparency leads to faster bug fixes and more robust security.
- **Community Monitoring**: The **global community** of developers and users actively monitors and contributes to maintaining the security of the system. Many security flaws are discovered and fixed rapidly, often before they can be exploited.
- **Granular User Permissions**: GNU/Linux offers more granular control over user permissions and access control. Unlike some proprietary systems, where users often have more access than necessary, GNU/Linux allows system administrators to control access to system resources.
- **Reduced Malware Risk**: While no system is immune to malware, Linux has historically been less targeted by malware and viruses. This is due to the security design of the operating system, its permissions model, and the fact that fewer desktop users run Linux compared to Windows (making it a less attractive target).
- **Frequent Security Updates**: Most GNU/Linux distributions offer regular security patches and updates. For instance, distributions like Debian, Ubuntu, and CentOS frequently release patches for newly discovered vulnerabilities, ensuring systems remain secure.
- **Stability**: Many GNU/Linux distributions are known for their **stability**, especially server distributions like Debian and CentOS, which are often chosen for critical infrastructure because they can run for extended periods without needing to be rebooted or suffer from instability.

4. Customization and Flexibility

One of the defining features of GNU/Linux is its customizability and flexibility. Unlike proprietary operating systems, where users are typically locked into a specific set of features or a particular user interface, Linux allows users to tailor their environment to suit their specific needs.

Customization-Related Benefits

- **Choice of Distributions**: There are countless GNU/Linux distributions (distros) designed for different use cases and user preferences. For instance:
  - Ubuntu and Linux Mint are popular among desktop users because they are user-friendly.
  - CentOS and Debian are commonly used for servers due to their stability.
  - Arch Linux offers a minimalist, customizable experience for advanced users.
- **Window Managers and Desktop Environments**: GNU/Linux allows users to choose from a wide variety of desktop environments (e.g., GNOME, KDE, Xfce) and window managers (e.g., i3, Openbox), giving users complete control over the look and feel of their interface.
- **Modular Architecture**: GNU/Linux allows users to install only the components they need. This modularity means that it's possible to build highly specialized

systems tailored to particular tasks—whether it's for a minimalist system or a highly optimized server.

- **Powerful Command Line**: For advanced users, the command line interface (CLI) provides immense power and flexibility, enabling users to automate tasks, write scripts, and tweak the system to a high degree.

GNU/Linux allows users to create a computing environment that suits their personal needs, whether that's for development, gaming, media production, or general desktop use.

5. Privacy and Transparency

In an era of growing concerns about privacy, especially with proprietary software that may track user behavior and share personal data with third parties, GNU/Linux offers an appealing alternative.

Privacy-Related Benefits

- **No Hidden Surveillance**: Unlike proprietary software, which often includes data collection or telemetry features, GNU/Linux offers users more control over their privacy. Most distributions do not include such features by default, and if they do, users can often opt-out or disable them.
- **Transparency**: The open-source nature of GNU/Linux means that every line of code can be reviewed, ensuring that no hidden backdoors or surveillance features are included. This transparency builds trust among users who value their privacy.
- **Data Ownership**: With GNU/Linux, users typically retain more control over their data. Unlike proprietary operating systems or applications that might store user data on central servers, users have more control over how and where their data is stored and shared.

By using GNU/Linux, users can take steps toward maintaining a higher level of privacy and control over their personal information compared to proprietary operating systems that may not prioritize privacy.

6. Community Collaboration and Support

One of the most remarkable aspects of free software and GNU/Linux is the strength of its community. The success of many GNU/Linux distributions and free software projects is largely driven by the collaborative efforts of global communities of developers, contributors, and users.

Community-Related Benefits

- **Collaborative Development**: With open-source software, development is not limited to a single company's resources. Thousands of developers from around the world contribute to improving software, fixing bugs, and adding new features. This collaborative environment leads to faster innovation and the rapid evolution of software.
- **Active Support Forums**: The GNU/Linux community has created a wealth of forums, mailing lists, and IRC channels where users can seek help, share tips, and collaborate on troubleshooting. These communities often provide free support from experienced users and developers.

- **Documentation and Tutorials**: The community also contributes to the vast amount of **documentation** and **tutorials** available online, making it easier for new users to get started with GNU/Linux.
- **Open Contribution**: Users can contribute to the community by reporting bugs, offering feature suggestions, and even submitting code changes. This open model fosters a sense of belonging and ownership in the software.

The GNU/Linux ecosystem is built on collaboration, and this sense of community has allowed the free software movement to thrive and expand globally.

7. Reliability and Performance

GNU/Linux systems are known for their reliability and performance, especially in environments that demand stability, such as servers and embedded systems.

Reliability and Performance Benefits

- **Uptime**: GNU/Linux systems are known for their high uptime in server environments. Many Linux-based servers can run for months or even years without needing to be rebooted, making them ideal for critical applications.
- **Efficient Use of Resources**: GNU/Linux is highly efficient in terms of memory and CPU usage. It can run on older or less powerful hardware without sacrificing performance, unlike some proprietary operating systems that demand more resources.
- **Real-Time Performance**: For specialized use cases, such as embedded systems or real-time applications, GNU/Linux offers real-time versions that provide predictable and guaranteed performance.

In summary, GNU/Linux is a stable, reliable, and performant operating system suitable for a wide range of tasks, from everyday computing to specialized industrial applications.

LICENSING – TYPES OF LICENSING

Licensing is a crucial aspect of software development, as it defines how the software can be used, modified, and distributed. When it comes to free and open-source software (FOSS), the licensing structure ensures that software remains free in terms of freedom, allowing users to access, modify, and redistribute the code under defined conditions. Understanding the types of software licenses, especially in the context of open-source and free software, is essential for both developers and users.

What is Software Licensing?

A software license is a legal agreement that specifies the terms under which a user may use, distribute, or modify software. The license also dictates the permissions, restrictions, and conditions that come with using the software. In the case of open-source software, the license is used to ensure that the software's source code remains freely accessible and that users can contribute to and modify the software. However, different licenses vary in terms of how they regulate the use, modification, and redistribution of the software.

Types of Software Licensing

Software licenses are generally classified into two broad categories:

1. Proprietary Licenses (Closed Source)
2. Open Source Licenses (Free Software Licenses)

1. Proprietary Licenses (Closed Source)

Proprietary software is software that is owned by an individual or a company, and the source code is not made available to the public. These types of licenses restrict the user's ability to modify, share, or even examine the source code.

With proprietary software, the user is generally provided with a license that grants them the right to use the software under specific conditions but does not allow for modification or redistribution.

Key Characteristics of Proprietary Licenses

- **No Access to Source Code:** Users cannot view, modify, or distribute the source code of the software.
- **Limited Usage Rights:** Usage is often restricted to specific use cases, platforms, or devices.
- **Paid Licensing:** Proprietary software is often sold via licensing agreements, with recurring costs or upfront payments.
- **No Redistribution:** Redistribution of the software is typically prohibited, except by the license holder.

Examples of Proprietary Licenses

- **Microsoft Windows:** The operating system's source code is not available for public access, and users are restricted to the terms of the Windows license agreement.
- **Adobe Photoshop:** The software comes with a proprietary license that does not allow users to modify or redistribute it.

2. Open Source Licenses (Free Software Licenses)

Open-source software is software that is released under a license that allows users to view, modify, and distribute the software's source code. However, the terms and conditions of how these actions can be performed vary across different open-source licenses. Open-source licenses can be categorized into two broad categories: permissive licenses and left licenses.

A. Permissive Licenses

Permissive open-source licenses are the most flexible type of license. They allow the software to be freely used, modified, and redistributed with minimal restrictions. Generally, the primary condition is that the original right notice and license text must be included when distributing the software or derivatives. The goal of permissive licenses is to encourage broad use, modification, and adoption of the software.

Key Features of Permissive Licenses

- **Freedom to Use and Modify:** Users are allowed to modify and adapt the software for any purpose, including commercial use.
- **Redistribution:** Users can redistribute the software without being required to release the source code of their modifications.

- **Minimal Requirements:** Typically, the only requirement is that the license text and right notice be included in redistributed code or binaries.

Types of software	Commercial	FOSS
Word processing	Microsoft Office	LibreOffice and OpenOffice
Web browser	Internet Explorer	Mozilla Firefox etc.
Music player	Windows Media Player	VLC etc.
Server	Windows Server	Apache, Lighttpd, etc.
Content management system	Dreamweaver	Drupal, Wordpress, Joomla, etc.
Library management system	Liberty, SirsiDynix, etc.	Koha, Evergreen, SLIMS etc.
Database management system	Oracle	MySQL, PostgreSQL, etc.
Operating system	Windows, Macintosh, etc.	Linux (Ubuntu, Red Hat, etc.)

Fig 1.2: *Types of Software*

Common Examples of Permissive Licenses

1. **MIT License:** The MIT License is one of the most popular and permissive open-source licenses. It allows users to freely use, modify, and distribute the software with minimal restrictions. Users must include the original right notice and license in all copies or substantial portions of the software.
   - **Example:** Most software developed in the open-source community, such as the Ruby on Rails framework, uses the MIT License.
2. **Apache License 2.0:** The Apache License 2.0 is a permissive license that allows users to freely use, modify, and distribute software. It also grants users a patent license, which is important for ensuring that users are protected from patent claims when using the software.
   - **Example:** Popular software projects like Apache HTTP Server, Hadoop, and Android use the Apache License 2.0.
3. **BSD Licenses:** The Berkeley Software Distribution (BSD) License is another permissive license that has minimal restrictions. The 2-clause and 3-clause BSD licenses are commonly used in various software projects.
   - **Example:** FreeBSD and OpenBSD are distributed under the BSD License.

Advantages of Permissive Licenses

- **Maximum Freedom:** Users can freely use and modify the software with few restrictions.
- **Commercial-Friendly:** Because there are no left requirements, software can be used in proprietary projects.
- **Wide Adoption:** Because of their flexibility, permissive licenses often lead to widespread adoption of the software.

Disadvantages of Permissive Licenses

- **Loss of left Protections:** Users can modify the software and release it as proprietary software, which could lead to situations where others benefit from open-source software without contributing back to the community.

B. left Licenses

Left is a key concept in the open-source world. Left licenses require that any derivative works based on the original software must also be licensed under the same terms as the original software. This ensures that the freedoms provided by the software are preserved in modified versions and that derivative works are also made open source.

The idea behind left is to prevent the software from being "closed up" by others. Any changes or modifications to the software must be shared with the community under the same open terms.

Key Features of Left Licenses

- **Same License for Derivatives:** Any modified versions of the software must be distributed under the same license as the original, ensuring that the software and its derivatives remain free.
- **Source Code Availability:** Users must provide access to the source code of both the original and modified versions of the software when distributing it.
- **Protects Freedom:** By enforcing left, these licenses ensure that the software remains open and that others can benefit from and contribute to the software in the future.

Common Examples of Left Licenses

1. **GNU General Public License (GPL):** The GPL is one of the most widely used left licenses. It requires that any derivative work based on GPL-licensed software must also be released under the GPL. This license ensures that the software and any modifications are freely available to all users.
   - **Example:** Projects like the Linux kernel, GIMP, and WordPress are licensed under the GPL.
2. **GNU Lesser General Public License (LGPL):** The LGPL is a less restrictive version of the GPL, typically used for libraries. It allows proprietary software to link to the LGPL-licensed library without the need to release the proprietary software's source code. However, any modifications to the library itself must be released under the LGPL.
   - **Example:** The GTK+ toolkit, used in the GIMP and GNOME, is licensed under the LGPL.
3. **Affero General Public License (AGPL):** The AGPL is a stricter version of the GPL that adds the requirement that if the software is used over a network (e.g., a web server), the modified source code must be made available to users of that service.
   - **Example:** MongoDB uses the AGPL license.

Advantages of Left Licenses

- **Freedom Protection:** left licenses ensure that the software and its derivatives remain free, preventing it from becoming proprietary.

- **Encourages Community Contributions:** By ensuring that modifications must also be open-source, left licenses foster an environment where software improvements are shared with the community.
- **Widespread Adoption of Open Source Principles:** left encourages adherence to open-source principles, ensuring the continued sharing of knowledge and software.

Disadvantages of left Licenses

- **Incompatible with Proprietary Software:** Many proprietary companies avoid using left-licensed software because they cannot keep their modifications proprietary.
- **Complex Licensing:** The requirements for left licensing can be seen as restrictive and complex, especially for commercial applications.

3. Other License Types

Besides permissive and left licenses, there are other specialized licenses for specific use cases.

Dual Licensing

Some software projects are offered under two licenses. For example, a project might be available under both a left license (like the GPL) and a proprietary license. The user can choose between using the software under open-source terms or paying for a proprietary license with different terms.

- **Example:** MySQL offers its database software under the GPL for open-source use and a commercial license for proprietary use.

Creative Commons Licenses

Creative Commons licenses are often used for content (like artwork, music, and educational materials) rather than software. However, they are sometimes applied to software documentation.

- **Example:** Documentation for many open-source projects is often released under Creative Commons Attribution (CC BY) licenses.

INTELLECTUAL PROPERTY (IP) RIGHTS

Intellectual Property (IP) refers to legal protections granted to individuals or organizations for their creations, inventions, and innovations in various fields of art, literature, technology, and commerce. IP rights give creators exclusive control over their work, allowing them to protect and profit from their ideas and creations. These protections are granted by law and typically include a variety of rights, each designed to safeguard different aspects of intellectual output. IP is crucial in today's economy as it incentivizes innovation and creativity by ensuring creators can benefit from their work without others exploiting it unfairly. Here's a detailed look at Intellectual Property Rights, including their types, importance, and how they are protected.

What is Intellectual Property (IP)?

Intellectual property is a broad term that covers creations of the mind. These can include inventions, literary and artistic works, designs, symbols, names, and images used in commerce. IP is vital because it allows creators to retain exclusive rights over their inventions or artistic work and prevents others from ing, using, or profiting from it without permission.

IP rights are intended to encourage innovation and creativity by ensuring that creators can benefit from their work. Without such protections, it would be difficult for inventors, authors, artists, and businesses to profit from their ideas.

Types of Intellectual Property Rights

There are several types of intellectual property rights, each designed to protect different kinds of intellectual creations. The most common types are right, trademarks, patents, and trade secrets. Below is an in-depth explanation of each of these categories.

1. Right

Right is a legal right granted to the creator of an original work. It provides the creator with exclusive rights to use, distribute, and reproduce their work for a certain period of time. right protects a wide range of works, including literary works, music, films, software, sculptures, and more.

Key Features of Right

- **Automatic Protection:** right is automatically granted as soon as an original work is fixed in a tangible form (e.g., written, recorded, or digitized).
- **Exclusive Rights:**

  The right holder has the exclusive right to:
  - Reproduce the work
  - Distribute copies of the work
  - Perform or display the work publicly
  - Create derivative works based on the original
- **Duration:** right lasts for a certain period, which varies depending on the country and the type of work. In many jurisdictions, the duration is the life of the author plus 70 years.
- **Fair Use:** Some uses of righted works are allowed without permission under "fair use" provisions (e.g., for criticism, commentary, or research).

Examples of Righted Works

- Books, articles, and poetry
- Software code
- Music and audio recordings
- Movies and TV shows
- Artworks (paintings, sculptures, etc.)

Right's Role in IP

Right ensures that creators have control over their original works and can prevent others from using them without permission, giving creators a way to monetize their creations, particularly in industries like entertainment, publishing, and software development.

2. Trademarks

A trademark is a sign, symbol, logo, word, or combination thereof that distinguishes the goods or services of one company from those of another. Trademarks help consumers identify and differentiate brands in the marketplace.

Key Features of Trademarks

- **Distinctiveness:** Trademarks must be distinctive to ensure that they are capable of identifying the source of the goods or services. A trademark can be a word, phrase, logo, symbol, design, or a combination of these.
- **Exclusive Rights:** The trademark owner has the exclusive right to use the mark in commerce and can prevent others from using similar marks that could cause confusion.
- **Duration:** Trademark protection can last indefinitely as long as the mark is actively used and the renewal fees are paid. Generally, trademarks are registered for 10 years at a time but can be renewed.
- **Protection Scope:** Trademarks protect the identity and branding of a business but do not prevent others from using similar names, logos, or symbols in unrelated fields.

Examples of Trademarks

- The Nike Swoosh logo and the word Nike
- The Coca-Cola logo
- The McDonald's golden arches
- The Apple logo
- Slogans like "Just Do It" (Nike) and "I'm Lovin' It" (McDonald's)

Trademark's Role in IP

Trademarks are vital for businesses, as they help consumers identify the source of a product or service. They protect the company's branding and prevent others from profiting by using similar marks that could cause confusion in the marketplace.

3. Patents

A patent is an exclusive right granted for an invention that provides a new and innovative way to solve a problem or perform a function. Patents allow the inventor to exclude others from making, using, selling, or distributing the patented invention without permission for a limited time.

Key Features of Patents

- **Novelty:** To be patentable, an invention must be new and not have been publicly disclosed before the patent application.
- **Inventive Step:** The invention must involve an inventive step, meaning it must not be obvious to someone skilled in the relevant field.
- **Industrial Applicability:** The invention must be capable of being used in some kind of industry or trade.

- **Exclusive Rights:** The patent holder has the exclusive right to use, sell, or license the invention.
- **Duration:** Patents typically last for 20 years from the filing date, although this can vary depending on the type of invention and the jurisdiction.
- **Patent Infringement:** If someone else uses the patented invention without permission, it constitutes patent infringement, and the patent holder can take legal action.

Examples of Patented Inventions

- The iPhone's design and technology
- Pharmaceutical drugs and their chemical formulations
- Google's search algorithms (specific aspects)
- Tesla's electric vehicle designs

Patent's Role in IP

Patents provide a significant incentive for technological and industrial innovation by allowing inventors to gain exclusive rights to their inventions, thereby enabling them to profit from their ideas for a limited period. They also encourage public disclosure of inventions to foster further technological progress.

4. Trade Secrets

A trade secret refers to confidential business information that gives a company a competitive advantage. Trade secrets can include formulas, processes, designs, instruments, patterns, or any other business information that is not publicly known.

Key Features of Trade Secrets

- **Confidentiality:** Trade secrets must be kept secret and are protected as long as they remain confidential.
- **No Registration:** Unlike patents, rights, or trademarks, trade secrets do not require registration. They are protected through internal business practices, including confidentiality agreements and non-disclosure agreements (NDAs).
- **Exclusive Rights:** The holder of a trade secret has the right to prevent others from disclosing or using the secret without permission.
- **Duration:** Trade secrets can last indefinitely as long as the information remains secret and is not publicly disclosed or reverse-engineered.
- **Legal Protection:** If someone misappropriates or discloses a trade secret, the holder can pursue legal action for trade secret theft.

Examples of Trade Secrets

- The Coca-Cola formula
- The KFC chicken recipe
- Google's search algorithm (in its entirety)
- Apple's product designs and manufacturing processes

Trade Secret's Role in IP

Trade secrets are critical in industries where maintaining the confidentiality of proprietary information can provide a competitive edge. For example, businesses use trade secrets to protect unique formulas, algorithms, and manufacturing processes that could be easily replicated if disclosed.

Importance of Intellectual Property Rights

Intellectual Property rights play a significant role in fostering innovation and protecting the interests of creators, inventors, and businesses. Some key reasons why IP rights are essential include:

1. Encouraging Innovation

By providing exclusive rights over inventions and creations, IP rights incentivize individuals and businesses to invest time, money, and resources into developing new products, services, and technologies. Knowing they can benefit from their work provides motivation for research and development.

2. Promoting Economic Growth

IP rights contribute to economic growth by enabling creators to commercialize their ideas. They allow businesses to profit from their innovations, create jobs, and attract investments. Strong IP protection can lead to a more vibrant and competitive marketplace.

3. Ensuring Fair Competition

IP rights prevent unfair competition by ensuring that others cannot or profit from someone else's work. This allows companies to differentiate their products or services based on unique features, innovations, and branding.

4. Protecting Consumers

Intellectual property helps protect consumers by ensuring that the products and services they purchase meet specific standards and are of a certain quality. Trademarks, for example, help consumers identify reputable brands and avoid counterfeit goods.

COMMERCIAL LICENSE VS. OPEN SOURCE LICENSE

The distinction between commercial licenses and open source licenses is crucial for both software developers and users. These two types of software licenses are fundamentally different in terms of usage rights, restrictions, and business models. Understanding these differences is key to making informed decisions when choosing or using software for both personal and professional purposes.

Let's explore Commercial Licenses and Open Source Licenses in detail, including their definitions, characteristics, advantages, disadvantages, and examples.

1. Commercial License

A commercial license is a type of software license that grants the purchaser the right to use the software under specific, often restrictive, terms for commercial purposes. It is typically associated with proprietary software, which means the software's source code is closed and not available for modification or redistribution by the user.

In a commercial licensing model, the user (often a business or organization) pays a fee to use the software for specific purposes, and in return, the software vendor provides support, updates, and often a warranty or service level agreement.

Key Characteristics of Commercial Licenses

1. **Ownership and Restrictions**: In a commercial license, the software publisher retains full ownership of the software. The user is granted specific rights to use the software but is generally restricted from modifying, distributing, or reverse-engineering the software.
2. **Paid License**: Commercial software is typically sold for a fee. The payment model could be one-time, subscription-based, or based on the number of users or installations.
3. **Limited Modifications and Redistribution**: Users are often prohibited from modifying the source code, redistributing the software, or using it in a way that was not originally intended by the software publisher.
4. **Support and Updates**: In a commercial license, users usually get access to ongoing support, patches, and updates from the vendor. These services may be provided for free or at an additional cost.
5. **Usage Restrictions**: Commercial licenses usually come with specific restrictions on the number of devices or users that can access or use the software, geographic limitations, or specific terms that apply to how the software is used (e.g., for educational purposes only, or for internal use only).

Examples of Commercial Licenses

- **Microsoft Windows**: The operating system is licensed commercially. You purchase a license for each of Windows you install, and you don't have access to the source code.
- **Adobe Photoshop**: Adobe offers its image editing software under a commercial license. Users must pay for the software either on a subscription basis or a one-time fee, and cannot modify or redistribute the software.
- **Oracle Database**: Oracle provides its database software under a commercial license, which includes ongoing support, updates, and security patches.

Advantages of Commercial Licenses

- **Support and Services**: Commercial licenses typically come with support services, training, documentation, and software updates, ensuring that businesses have the resources they need to implement and maintain the software.
- **Security and Stability**: Commercial software often undergoes rigorous testing and is expected to be stable and secure, making it a preferred option for businesses that require guaranteed reliability.
- **Guaranteed IP Protection**: With commercial licenses, businesses can have more confidence that their proprietary software is protected from unauthorized use or modification.

Disadvantages of Commercial Licenses

- **Cost:** Commercial licenses can be expensive, particularly for large organizations that need to license the software for many users or installations.
- **Limited Flexibility**: Users cannot modify the software to suit their specific needs. Businesses have to rely on the vendor for feature requests or bug fixes.
- **Vendor Lock-in**: Relying on commercial software can lead to vendor lock-in, where the business becomes dependent on the software vendor for updates, fixes, and continued service.

2. Open Source License

An open source license is a type of software license that allows users to freely use, modify, and distribute the software. The key feature of open source software is that its source code is available to the public, which allows anyone to inspect, modify, or contribute to it.

Open-source licenses are primarily focused on ensuring that software remains free and open, allowing the community to collaborate on its development and improvement.

Key Characteristics of Open Source Licenses

1. **Free Use, Modification, and Distribution**: Open source licenses allow users to freely use the software for any purpose, modify it to fit their needs, and distribute both the original and modified versions.
2. **Source Code Availability**: The source code of the software is made publicly available, which allows developers to study, modify, and improve the software. This fosters innovation and collaboration within the open-source community.
3. **Community-Driven Development**: Open-source software is typically developed by a community of volunteers and organizations. Changes and improvements are made collaboratively and shared with everyone.
4. **Variety of License Types**: Open-source licenses come in many forms, from permissive licenses (which allow proprietary use) to left licenses (which require that modified versions of the software also be open-source).
5. **No Vendor Lock-in**: Since the source code is open, users are not locked into a specific vendor or proprietary solution. They can modify or change the software as they see fit.

Examples of Open Source Licenses

- **GNU General Public License (GPL)**: This is a left license that requires anyone who modifies and redistributes the software to do so under the same GPL license. This ensures that the software and any derived works remain free.
- **MIT License**: This is a permissive license that allows users to freely use, modify, and distribute the software with minimal restrictions. The only requirement is that the original right notice and license text remain intact.
- **Apache License 2.0**: This permissive license allows users to freely use, modify, and distribute the software, and it also provides an explicit grant of patent rights.
- **Mozilla Public License (MPL)**: This is a weak left license that allows users to use, modify, and distribute the software. However, modifications to the software must

be released under the MPL, while proprietary code can be combined with MPL-licensed software without being required to be open source.

Advantages of Open Source Licenses

- **Cost-Effective**: Open-source software is typically free to use, which makes it a cost-effective option for both individuals and organizations. There are no licensing fees or per-user costs.
- **Flexibility and Customization**: Users can modify the source code to adapt the software to their specific needs, which is ideal for businesses with unique requirements.
- **Community Support**: Open-source software often has strong community support, including forums, online documentation, and user groups that help resolve issues.
- **Transparency and Security**: Since the source code is open, it can be thoroughly examined for security vulnerabilities. Bugs and security issues are often quickly identified and fixed by the community.
- **No Vendor Lock-in**: Open-source software allows businesses and individuals to avoid dependence on a single vendor. They can modify or replace the software as needed.

Disadvantages of Open Source Licenses

- **Limited Official Support**: While many open-source projects have strong community support, official, professional support may be limited or unavailable. For enterprises that need guaranteed support, this can be a disadvantage.
- **Compatibility Issues**: Open-source software may not always integrate well with proprietary software or other tools used by businesses.
- **Potential for Fragmentation**: Some open-source projects can become fragmented, with multiple versions or forks of the same software that might not be compatible with one another.
- **Less Polished User Experience**: While open-source software has matured significantly, some projects may not offer the same level of polish, user interfaces, or features as commercial alternatives.

When to Choose Commercial License vs. Open Source License?

The choice between a commercial and an open-source license depends on several factors, including business needs, budget, and technical requirements:

Choose Commercial License If

- You require guaranteed support, stability, and updates.
- Your software usage involves sensitive business operations, and you want to ensure reliability and vendor accountability.
- You are working with proprietary technologies that need to remain private, and you don't want anyone to alter or distribute the software.
- You prefer out-of-the-box functionality and professional-grade features that might be difficult to replicate with open-source alternatives.

Choose Open Source License If

- You want to save on licensing costs and have a budget-friendly solution.
- You need the freedom to modify and customize the software to fit your unique needs.
- You value community-driven development and want to contribute to or benefit from collaborative software projects.
- You want to avoid vendor lock-in and ensure that the software remains flexible, scalable, and adaptable over time.

Key Differences Between Commercial and Open Source Licenses

Aspect	Commercial License	Open Source License
Source Code Availability	Closed; the source code is not available to the user.	Open; the source code is freely available for modification and redistribution.
Usage Rights	Restricted usage, usually for specific commercial purposes.	Free to use for any purpose, including commercial and non-commercial.
Modification Rights	Generally prohibited or limited.	Users are free to modify the software as needed.
Cost	Typically paid (one-time fee, subscription, or per-user fee).	Usually free, though some open-source projects may offer paid support or services.
Support	Official support is provided (either included or at additional cost).	Typically community-based support, with optional paid professional services.
Redistribution Rights	Redistribution is usually restricted.	Redistribution is permitted under the same license terms.
Flexibility	Less flexible, as users are limited by the terms of the license.	Highly flexible, as users can modify, adapt, and redistribute the software.
Examples	Microsoft Windows, Adobe Photoshop, Oracle Database.	Linux, Apache HTTP Server, Mozilla Firefox, MySQL (under GPL).

CONTRACT AND RIGHT LAW

Right law and contract law are both crucial areas of legal practice, particularly when it comes to protecting intellectual property (IP). While they intersect at various points—especially in the context of software, creative works, and licensing agreements—they each have distinct principles and functions.

1. Basic Principles of Right Law

Right law is designed to protect the creators of original works, ensuring they have exclusive rights to their creations and can control how their works are used. These rights help incentivize creativity by allowing creators to profit from their work and prevent unauthorized use or reproduction.

Key Concepts in Right Law

1. **Definition of Right**: right is a legal right that grants the creator of an original work exclusive rights to its use and distribution. It applies to a variety of creative works, including:
    - Literary works (books, articles, software code)
    - Musical works (songs, compositions)
    - Dramatic works (plays, scripts)
    - Artistic works (paintings, sculptures, photography)
    - Cinematic works (films, videos)
    - Sound recordings
    - Architectural works
    - Software and digital media
2. **Automatic Protection**: right protection is automatically conferred when a work is created and fixed in a tangible medium of expression (e.g., writing a novel, recording a song). There is no requirement for registration, though registration offers certain benefits, such as the ability to sue for statutory damages in court.
3. **Exclusive Rights**: The creator of the work holds several exclusive rights under right law. These rights allow the right holder to:
    - **Reproduce** the work (e.g., making copies)
    - **Distribute** copies of the work (e.g., selling or sharing it)
    - **Publicly perform** the work (e.g., performing music or theater in public)
    - **Publicly display** the work (e.g., showing artwork in a gallery)
    - **Create derivative works** based on the original (e.g., adaptations, translations, remixes)
4. These rights are exclusive to the right holder, meaning others cannot use the work without permission.
5. **Fair Use and Limitations**: right law includes exceptions, such as the fair use doctrine, which allows limited use of righted works without permission in certain cases, such as:
    - Commentary and criticism
    - Parody or satire
    - Teaching, research, or scholarship
6. Other exceptions include public domain, where works no longer have right protection, and licenses, which allow others to use a work under specific conditions.
7. **Duration of right**: right protection does not last forever. The duration varies depending on the type of work and the laws of the country:
    - For works created by individual authors, right typically lasts for the life of the author plus 70 years (in many jurisdictions).
    - For works created by corporations or anonymous works, right typically lasts 95 years from the date of publication or 120 years from creation, whichever is shorter.

- After the right expires, the work enters the public domain and can be freely used by anyone.

2. Contract Law

Contract law governs agreements between parties and is essential in determining the enforceability of promises, obligations, and rights. A contract is an agreement between two or more parties that creates a set of legal obligations. Contract law ensures that these obligations are met and provides legal recourse when a party fails to honor their contractual duties.

Key Principles of Contract Law

1. **Formation of a Contract**: A contract is created when there is:
    - **Offer**: One party proposes an agreement to another.
    - **Acceptance**: The other party agrees to the terms of the offer.
    - **Consideration**: Something of value (money, services, etc.) must be exchanged between the parties.
    - **Intention to Create Legal Relations**: Both parties must intend that the agreement be legally binding.
    - **Capacity**: Both parties must have the legal capacity to enter into a contract (e.g., they must be of sound mind and the legal age).
    - **Legality of Purpose**: The purpose of the contract must be lawful (e.g., a contract to perform illegal activities is not enforceable).
2. **Breach of Contract**: If one party fails to perform their obligations under the contract, it is considered a breach of contract. The non-breaching party may seek remedies, including:
    - **Damages**: Monetary compensation for losses incurred.
    - **Specific Performance**: Court order requiring the breaching party to perform their obligations.
    - **Rescission**: Cancellation of the contract, with both parties returned to their pre-contract positions.
3. **Types of Contracts**:
    - **Express Contracts**: Clearly articulated terms, either written or verbal.
    - **Implied Contracts**: Terms inferred from the parties' conduct or circumstances.
    - **Unilateral Contracts**: One party promises something in exchange for the performance of an act.
    - **Bilateral Contracts**: Both parties make promises to each other.
4. **Enforceability of Contracts**: For a contract to be enforceable, it must meet the legal criteria mentioned above. If any of these criteria are absent (e.g., lack of consideration or legality), the contract may be deemed **void** or **voidable**.

3. Contract and Right Law: How They Intersect

Right law and contract law often intersect when righted works are created, licensed, or transferred. Contracts are used to establish the terms under which righted works can be used, shared, or distributed. Here's how right and contract law work together:

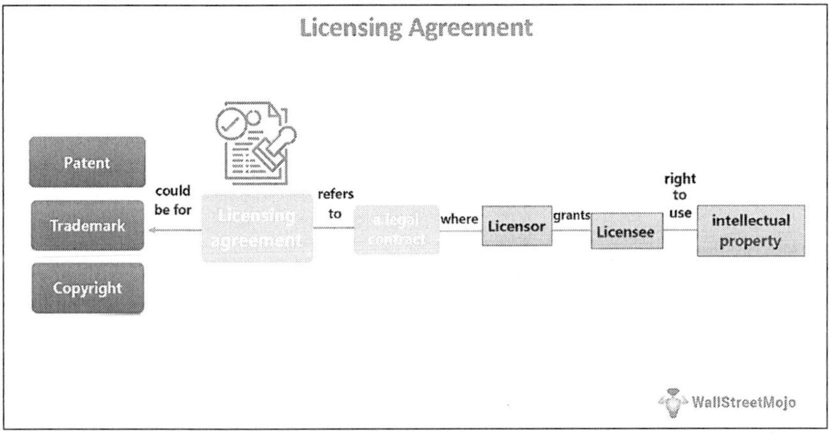

Fig1.3: *Licensing Agreement*

A. Licensing and Right

One of the most common ways that contract law and right law intersect is through **licenses.** A license is a contract that gives someone the permission to use a righted work under certain conditions. Right holders can license their works to others, allowing them to use, reproduce, or modify the work in a specific way.

- **Exclusive License**: An exclusive license grants the licensee (the party receiving the license) exclusive rights to use the righted work, meaning the right holder cannot grant the same rights to anyone else.
- **Non-Exclusive License**: A non-exclusive license allows the right holder to grant the same rights to multiple licensees, so the right holder can license the work to more than one party.
- **Sub-Licensing**: A license agreement may include provisions allowing the licensee to further license the work to others.

In licensing agreements, the right holder and the licensee agree on the terms of use, payment (royalties or flat fees), the scope of the license, duration, and any restrictions on how the work can be used. These agreements are contracts that bind both parties.

B. Assignment of Right

Another way that right law and contract law intersect is when a right holder assigns their right to another party. An assignment is the transfer of ownership of the right from the original creator to another entity, such as a company or individual.

- The assignment must be made in writing to be legally valid, and it transfers all the rights associated with the work (reproduction, distribution, etc.) to the assignee.
- Contracts regarding right assignment typically specify the scope of the assignment, whether it is exclusive or non-exclusive, and whether any compensation or royalties will be paid to the original creator.

C. Work for Hire

In certain circumstances, the creation of a work under an employment agreement or as part of a contract can be classified as a work for hire. In this case, the employer or commissioning party owns the right to the work from the moment of creation, rather than the individual creator.

- **Employee-Related Works**: If an employee creates a work within the scope of their employment, the employer automatically owns the right (unless otherwise agreed upon).
- **Commissioned Works**: If a work is specially ordered or commissioned (e.g., a freelance writer, photographer, or graphic designer), the contract must specify that the work will be a work for hire for the right to automatically transfer to the commissioning party.

The work for hire doctrine can be critical when businesses want to own all rights to creative content, and it must be explicitly stated in the contract between the creator and the company.

D. Right Infringement and Contracts

A contract can also be used to enforce or prevent right infringement. For example, an agreement might include provisions that prohibit the use of righted materials without permission. If a party violates the terms of the contract (e.g., by infringing on the right of the work), the right holder can sue for breach of contract and/or right infringement.

OPEN SOURCE SOFTWARE LICENSING, ISSUES WITH RIGHTS AND PATENTS, WARRANTIES

The landscape of open source software (OSS) is rich with legal considerations, including licensing, right, patents, and warranties. Open-source software presents distinct challenges and opportunities compared to proprietary software, and understanding these issues is critical for both developers and businesses involved in the open-source ecosystem. This section explores the nuances of open source software licensing, right issues, patents, and warranties in the context of open-source software.

1. Open Source Software Licensing

An open-source software license is a legal framework that allows software to be freely used, modified, and shared. However, despite these freedoms, open-source software licenses impose certain conditions, responsibilities, and constraints that users and developers must adhere to.

Key Types of Open Source Licenses

Open-source licenses can generally be divided into two broad categories: permissive licenses and left licenses.

1. **Permissive Licenses:** These licenses are relatively relaxed about how the software can be used, modified, and redistributed. The primary requirement is that the original right notice and license text must be included when redistributing the software. **Examples:**
    - **MIT License:** Permits nearly unrestricted use, modification, and distribution, provided the original license and right notice are retained.
    - **Apache License 2.0:** Similar to the MIT license but includes explicit grants of patent rights from contributors to users.

- **BSD License:** Allows redistribution and modification of the software with minimal restrictions.

2. **left Licenses:** left licenses are more restrictive than permissive licenses. They require that any modified versions or derivative works of the software also be released under the same open-source license. This ensures that the software remains free and open for all users.

   Examples:

   - **GNU General Public License (GPL):** A strong left license that requires any modified version of the software to also be licensed under the GPL.
   - **GNU Lesser General Public License (LGPL):** A more permissive variant of the GPL, which allows linking proprietary code with LGPL-licensed libraries, but still requires modifications to the LGPL-licensed code itself to be open-source.
   - **AGPL (Affero GPL):** Similar to GPL but extends the left requirement to software used over a network (i.e., if the software is accessed via a network, the source code must still be made available).

Key Considerations in Open Source Licensing

- **Source Code Availability:** Open source licenses generally require that the software's source code be made available to users. Some licenses, like the GPL, mandate that any modified versions of the software also make the source code available to the users.
- **Redistribution and Modifications:** Open source licenses dictate how the software can be redistributed, modified, and whether modifications must be made public. For example, the GPL requires derivative works to be licensed under the same GPL license, whereas permissive licenses do not impose such a requirement.
- **License Compatibility:** In some cases, combining code from different open-source projects can be legally complicated if the licenses of those projects are not compatible. For instance, combining GPL-licensed code with software licensed under a more permissive license like the MIT License may be acceptable, but combining two GPL versions may present issues depending on the specific terms.

2. Issues with rights and Patents in Open Source Software

A. right Issues in Open Source Software

In open source, right law plays a critical role in determining the rights of the original authors and contributors. While right protects creators' rights over their works, the open-source model allows others to use, modify, and share the software in specific ways that align with the terms of the open-source license.

1. **Ownership and Contributions:** When multiple contributors contribute to an open-source project, ownership of the software code might be unclear. Typically, contributors retain right over the code they write, but they agree to license their contributions under the project's open-source license.

   In some cases, a contributor agreement is required, where contributors agree to assign their rights to the project or grant certain licenses to the project maintainers.

This ensures that the project maintainers have the rights needed to distribute the software and incorporate changes into the codebase.

2. **left and Derivative Works:** A critical issue in open-source software is left. left licenses, like the GPL, are designed to ensure that any modified versions of the software are also open source. However, this can create legal challenges in understanding what constitutes a derivative work. If a developer modifies the software or combines it with other code, there may be uncertainty over whether the entire work must be released under the same license. The scope of modification can sometimes be difficult to interpret, especially when software is combined with proprietary components or integrated into other systems.
3. **Infringement and Enforcement:** Right holders have the right to enforce their rights by taking legal action against infringement. In open-source communities, this is usually handled in a community-driven manner, with maintainers taking action against violators.

   However, enforcement of right in open-source software can be challenging, especially when contributors are distributed across various jurisdictions with different right laws.

B. Patent Issues in Open Source Software

Patents present a unique challenge for open-source software because they can restrict the use and distribution of software if the software is covered by patents. There are a few key concerns around patents in open-source software:

1. **Patent Infringement:** Open-source software can inadvertently infringe on patents held by others. Even if a piece of software is open-source, its use or distribution could potentially violate a patented technology. This issue is particularly relevant in industries like software development, where many companies hold software-related patents.
2. **Patent Grants in Open Source Licenses:** Many open-source licenses, such as the Apache License 2.0, include explicit patent grants. This means that contributors to the project automatically grant users a license to use any patents that are infringed by the use of the software. The purpose of this is to protect users and developers from patent-related litigation. However, not all open-source licenses provide a clear patent grant. The GPL, for example, does not explicitly address patents, which means contributors could still potentially assert patent rights against users.
3. **Patent Trolls:** Another issue related to patents in open-source software is the potential for patent trolling. A patent troll is a company or entity that acquires patents with the primary goal of suing other companies for patent infringement, often without the intention of creating or using the technology. Open-source projects can be particularly vulnerable to patent trolls, as they often lack the resources to defend against patent litigation.
4. **Patent Encumbrances:** Open-source software could be encumbered by patents, either because a contributor holds patents over the software or because the software integrates patented technologies. This raises concerns about the freedom to operate when using or distributing open-source software.

3. Warranties in Open Source Software

One of the most distinctive features of open-source software is the absence of warranties. Open-source software is typically released "as-is," meaning that the developer or distributor does not offer any guarantees regarding the software's performance, reliability, or security. This can have significant legal implications.

Key Aspects of Warranties in Open Source

1. **Lack of Warranty:** Most open-source licenses include a disclaimer of warranties, meaning that the software is provided without any promises or guarantees. A typical disclaimer might state something like, "The software is provided 'as-is' without warranty of any kind, either express or implied, including but not limited to the warranties of merchantability or fitness for a particular purpose."

   This disclaimer helps protect the developers and maintainers of open-source software from being held liable for any issues, damages, or losses that may result from the use of the software.

2. **Liability for Bugs or Failures:** Since open-source software is often developed collaboratively by volunteers or non-profit organizations, there is usually no commercial entity behind the software to offer formal support or bear the responsibility for issues. This means that users who encounter bugs, security vulnerabilities, or operational failures have limited recourse.

   This is in stark contrast to proprietary software, where the vendor typically provides warranties or customer support.

3. **Support and Patches:** Open-source software generally does not include warranties, but the community or contributors often offer support in the form of forums, documentation, or user-driven bug fixes. However, this support is not guaranteed, and users should be aware that they may need to troubleshoot or patch issues themselves. Some open-source projects may offer paid support or enterprise services (e.g., Red Hat for Linux), which provide formal support and sometimes limited warranties, but this is not typical for most open-source projects.

Summary

The intersection of open-source software licensing, right, patents, and warranties creates a complex legal framework that developers and users must navigate carefully.

- Licensing in open-source software dictates how the software can be used, modified, and redistributed, with various licenses offering different degrees of freedom and restrictions.
- Right ensures that the original creators retain control over their works, but open-source licenses allow others to build upon and redistribute the software under specific terms.
- Patents can complicate the use of open-source software, as they might limit how the software is used, modified, or distributed. Patent grants and patent protections are therefore crucial components of many open-source licenses.
- Warranties are typically non-existent in open-source software, meaning users assume the risk of using the software without guarantees about its performance or security.

Navigating these legal concerns is essential for ensuring that open-source projects are used and distributed correctly while protecting the rights of both creators and users. Developers and businesses involved in open-source software should be aware of these complexities to mitigate legal risks and make informed decisions regarding licensing, contributions, and usage.

FOSS PHILOSOPHY AND TRENDS IN USAGE

The Free and Open-Source Software (FOSS) movement is built on a foundational philosophy that promotes user freedom, collaboration, and transparency in software development. The philosophy of FOSS extends beyond mere access to software—it encourages a culture of openness, community-driven development, and sharing knowledge. FOSS has grown from a niche community of software developers to a dominant force in software development, particularly in the realms of operating systems, development tools, enterprise solutions, and more.

The FOSS Philosophy

The FOSS philosophy is based on several core principles that emphasize the freedom of users and the benefits of collaborative software development.

A. The Four Essential Freedoms (from the Free Software Foundation)

The Free Software Foundation (FSF), a central figure in the free software movement, defines software freedom through four key principles, which form the foundation of the FOSS philosophy:

1. **Freedom 0: The Freedom to Run the Program**

   Users should be able to use the software for any purpose they see fit, without restrictions. Whether it is for personal use, educational purposes, or commercial activities, FOSS ensures that users can run the software in any manner they choose.

2. **Freedom 1: The Freedom to Study How the Program Works**

   The source code of the software must be accessible to users. This freedom allows users to examine the code, understand how the software operates, and even customize it to suit their needs. This principle encourages transparency, enabling users to identify and resolve bugs or vulnerabilities in the software.

3. **Freedom 2: The Freedom to Modify the Program**

   Users have the right to modify the software, add new features, or fix issues. The ability to modify the code fosters innovation and adaptation, allowing the software to evolve based on user needs. This is particularly important for enhancing security, improving performance, and localizing the software to different languages or regions.

4. **Freedom 3: The Freedom to Distribute Copies of the Program**

   Users can share the software with others, either in its original form or after modification. This freedom is a key component of collaboration in the open-source community, allowing others to benefit from and contribute to the software. This fosters a sense of collective responsibility and creates an ecosystem where knowledge is shared freely.

B. Collaboration and Community

One of the central tenets of FOSS is collaboration. FOSS projects are often developed by communities of developers and contributors who work together to create software. Collaboration involves:

- **Peer Review:** Open-source code is typically reviewed by multiple contributors, ensuring high-quality and secure software.
- **Transparency:** All aspects of the development process, from decision-making to code changes, are open for everyone to see. This openness promotes accountability and trust within the community.
- **Diversity of Contributions:** Anyone can contribute to an open-source project, regardless of their background or geographic location. This creates an environment where diverse ideas and approaches can flourish, leading to innovative and robust solutions.

C. Ethical and Political Aspects

FOSS also has an ethical and political dimension. Many proponents of the movement argue that software should be a common good that benefits everyone and not be monopolized by proprietary companies. The ethical aspect focuses on:

- **User Freedom:** Users should retain control over the software they use. FOSS advocates oppose proprietary software that restricts users' ability to modify, distribute, or even understand the software.
- **Avoiding Vendor Lock-In:** Proprietary software can create a situation where users are dependent on a single company for support and upgrades, which can limit innovation and drive up costs. FOSS, on the other hand, offers the freedom to switch between different solutions without losing access to data or functionality.
- **Privacy and Security:** Open-source software allows anyone to inspect the code for security vulnerabilities or privacy concerns. This openness often results in more secure software, as bugs and vulnerabilities can be identified and fixed by anyone in the community.

D. Sustainability and Innovation

FOSS also supports sustainability through collaborative development. Because many open-source projects are community-driven, they do not rely on traditional funding models, such as advertising or subscription fees. Instead, they are sustained through community contributions, donations, and support from organizations that benefit from the software.

Innovation is fostered by the community-driven approach to development. Since there are fewer constraints on how the software can be used or modified, it allows for rapid innovation, experimentation, and adaptation. Open-source software often leads to groundbreaking new tools and technologies.

Trends in FOSS Usage

Over the years, FOSS has evolved from being the domain of hobbyists and activists to becoming a mainstream force in the software industry. Many of the largest companies in the world now use open-source software, and several major FOSS projects have become critical infrastructure in the digital world. Below are some key trends in the usage of FOSS:

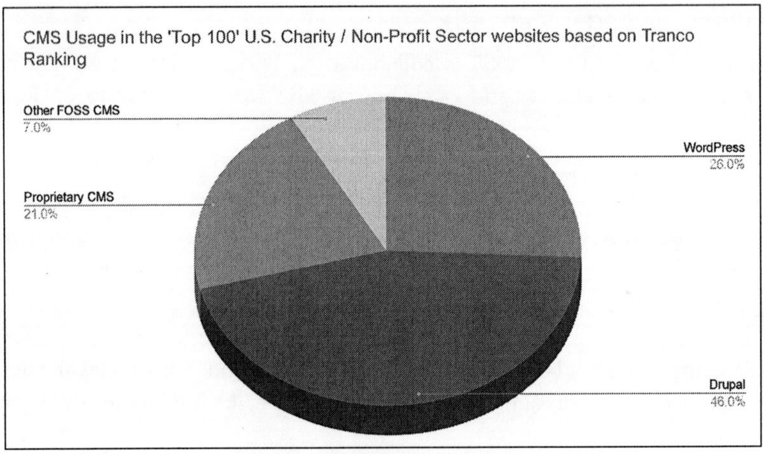

Fig 1.4: *Trends in FOSS*

A. Widespread Adoption in Enterprises

One of the most significant trends is the adoption of FOSS in enterprise environments. Many companies now rely on open-source software for critical infrastructure, such as:

1. **Operating Systems:** Linux has become the de facto standard for server environments. It's widely used by data centers, web hosting companies, and cloud service providers (e.g., Google, Amazon, Facebook).

   The Android operating system, based on Linux, has become the most popular mobile operating system globally, demonstrating how FOSS can be commercially successful.

2. **Development Tools:** Many development tools are open-source, including compilers, IDEs (Integrated Development Environments), version control systems (e.g., Git), and build systems. These tools are vital in helping developers create and manage software efficiently.

   Database Systems like MySQL, PostgreSQL, and SQLite are widely used in production environments, offering enterprises powerful, cost-effective alternatives to proprietary databases.

3. **Cloud Computing:** The rise of cloud computing has been heavily influenced by FOSS. Cloud infrastructure software such as OpenStack (for building private clouds), Kubernetes (for container orchestration), and Docker (for containerization) are open source and widely used in enterprises for managing cloud resources.

   Infrastructure as Code (IaC) tools such as Terraform and Ansible help organizations automate and manage their infrastructure in an open-source environment.

B. Increased Support from Large Tech Companies

Large technology companies have embraced FOSS both as a way to foster community-driven development and as a strategic tool to influence the technology landscape:

- **Google, Microsoft**, and **IBM** are some of the biggest contributors to open-source projects. In fact, Microsoft, a company once known for its opposition to FOSS, now actively contributes to and supports open-source software (e.g., GitHub, VS Code, and Linux on Azure).

- **Red Hat,** a prominent enterprise-focused open-source company, was acquired by IBM in 2019, reinforcing the viability of open-source business models.

This support has led to the increased corporate adoption of FOSS tools, with organizations using these tools to build their technology stacks while also contributing back to the open-source community.

C. Focus on Security and Transparency

One of the major benefits of FOSS is transparency. With the source code available to anyone, vulnerabilities can be spotted and fixed quickly by a wide range of contributors. This has led to an increasing focus on the security advantages of open-source software:

- **Security:** Open-source projects tend to be more secure than proprietary alternatives, as a larger community can identify and patch security flaws faster.
- **Auditing and Compliance:** Organizations can audit open-source software for compliance with internal security standards or regulatory requirements (e.g., GDPR, HIPAA).
- **Security-First Development:** With the growing importance of cybersecurity, many open-source projects emphasize secure coding practices and offer frequent security updates.

D. Open Source in Emerging Technologies

As new technologies emerge, open-source software is playing a key role in their development and deployment. Some notable examples include:

1. **Artificial Intelligence and Machine Learning:** Open-source tools like TensorFlow, PyTorch, and Scikit-learn are widely used in AI and machine learning development. These tools allow researchers and companies to build powerful AI models and contribute to the growing ecosystem.
2. **Blockchain and Cryptocurrency:** Many blockchain projects are built on open-source code. Notable examples include Ethereum (which supports decentralized applications) and Bitcoin (which supports cryptocurrency). Open-source blockchain technologies have enabled decentralized finance (DeFi) and blockchain innovation.
3. **Edge Computing and Internet of Things (IoT):** Open-source technologies like EdgeX Foundry (for edge computing) and ThingSpeak (for IoT) are enabling developers to create and deploy applications at the network edge, furthering the adoption of IoT devices.

E. The Rise of Open-Source Licenses and Compliance Tools

As open-source software becomes more pervasive, compliance tools and license management systems are gaining popularity. Companies that use open-source software need to ensure they comply with the various licenses governing the software they use:

- **License Compliance:** Tools such as FOSSA, WhiteSource, and Black Duck help companies manage their open-source license obligations and ensure they comply with the terms of various open-source licenses.

- **License Proliferation:** With more FOSS projects being developed, the number of available licenses has grown, creating the need for companies to track and comply with a growing number of license types.

THE POTENTIAL OF FOSS: GLOBAL AND INDIAN PERSPECTIVES

Free and Open Source Software (FOSS) has become a transformative force in the global software ecosystem. It challenges traditional software development models by emphasizing collaboration, transparency, and user freedom. FOSS offers immense potential not only on a global scale but also in specific regions, such as India, where it aligns with the country's technological, economic, and socio-political aspirations. Let's explore the potential of FOSS from both global and Indian perspectives.

1. Global Potential of FOSS

The global potential of FOSS is vast, touching various aspects of technology, economics, and society. FOSS has the power to shape industries, improve digital inclusion, foster innovation, and enhance software security. Here's how:

A. Technological Advancements and Innovation

1. **Fostering Innovation:** Open-source development is inherently collaborative. Anyone can contribute to improving the software, which accelerates innovation. This is evident in fields like artificial intelligence (AI), machine learning (ML), cloud computing, and blockchain, where open-source software has become the foundation for cutting-edge solutions.

   Projects like TensorFlow, PyTorch, Kubernetes, and Ethereum have driven significant advancements in AI, cloud infrastructure, and decentralized technologies, making innovation accessible to a broader audience.

2. **Cross-Collaboration Across Borders:** Open-source projects are often global collaborations. Contributors from all over the world can work on a single project simultaneously. This cross-border cooperation promotes diversity of thought, faster problem-solving, and the rapid spread of technological advancements.

   The success of platforms like GitHub and GitLab enables collaboration across borders, fostering a global community of developers and organizations.

B. Reducing Costs for Businesses and Governments

1. **Cost-Efficiency for Businesses:** FOSS solutions can significantly reduce costs for businesses, especially small and medium enterprises (SMEs). Rather than investing in expensive proprietary software, companies can use open-source alternatives without paying licensing fees.

   For example, companies can leverage Linux for servers, MySQL for databases, and Apache for web servers—high-quality, open-source software that can cut operational costs while still offering enterprise-level features.

2. **Governments and Public Sector Adoption:** Many governments globally have adopted FOSS as part of their digital strategy to reduce dependency on proprietary software vendors, ensure transparency, and safeguard data privacy. Countries like Germany, France, Brazil, and South Korea have integrated FOSS into public

institutions, with large-scale adoption of software like Linux, OpenOffice, and LibreOffice. These initiatives have resulted in substantial cost savings while promoting digital sovereignty.

3. **Digital Sovereignty:** FOSS helps nations reduce their dependence on foreign, proprietary software solutions, enhancing their digital sovereignty. By developing and using open-source tools, countries can avoid the risks associated with vendor lock-ins, such as price hikes, security vulnerabilities, and data privacy concerns.

   With FOSS, countries can control their own technology infrastructure, including ensuring data privacy and compliance with local laws, without being subject to foreign regulations.

C. Security and Transparency

1. **Enhanced Security:** One of the most significant advantages of FOSS is transparency. With access to the source code, anyone can examine and audit the software for security vulnerabilities. This means that bugs and security issues can be discovered and fixed quickly, leading to more secure software.

   Open-source projects like OpenSSL, GnuPG, and Linux have benefited from contributions by a global community of security experts, helping to address vulnerabilities more rapidly than proprietary systems.

2. **Resilience Against Surveillance and Censorship:** FOSS is a powerful tool for fighting surveillance and censorship. Open-source encryption tools like Signal and Tor provide secure, private communication channels for users globally. These tools empower individuals in countries with authoritarian regimes or surveillance-heavy environments to protect their privacy.

   Similarly, open-source operating systems like Tails and Qubes OS are designed to prioritize privacy, enabling users to avoid surveillance while maintaining secure digital environments.

2. The Potential of FOSS in India

India presents a unique context for the adoption and potential of FOSS, driven by its demographic diversity, rapid digital transformation, and emphasis on affordable technology. Below are the key drivers of FOSS's potential in India:

A. Bridging the Digital Divide

1. **Affordable and Accessible Technology:** India is home to one of the world's largest populations, and many regions still lack affordable access to proprietary software. FOSS offers an affordable alternative that can help bridge the digital divide.

   By using FOSS, individuals, educational institutions, and small businesses can access world-class software without the need for expensive licensing fees. For example, LibreOffice, a free alternative to Microsoft Office, can be widely adopted in schools, colleges, and government offices, promoting digital literacy.

2. **Government Initiatives and Policies:** The Indian government has recognized the potential of FOSS as a means to enhance digital inclusion. The National Policy on Software Products (2019) promotes the development and use of open-source software for creating solutions that meet national needs.

Digital India initiatives focus on making government services more accessible and inclusive, and FOSS plays a critical role in creating low-cost, scalable solutions for digital governance and e-governance platforms.

Initiatives like Bharat Operating System Solutions (BOSS), an open-source Linux distribution, are part of India's strategy to reduce reliance on foreign proprietary software.

3. **Empowering Rural India:** In rural and underserved areas, where infrastructure and resources are limited, FOSS can be a game-changer. For example, e-learning platforms that use open-source tools can bring educational resources to rural schools and colleges at minimal cost.

   Projects like Khadi Digital Literacy and FOSS-based agricultural applications help empower farmers and rural communities with knowledge and resources that improve their livelihoods.

B. Innovation and Start-Up Ecosystem

1. **Boosting India's Start-Up Ecosystem:** India has a vibrant start-up ecosystem, and FOSS plays a crucial role in driving innovation at a low cost. Start-ups can leverage open-source frameworks, platforms, and tools to rapidly develop their products and services without spending huge sums on software licenses.

   India's software development community is increasingly contributing to open-source projects, building innovative solutions that cater to local and global markets. For example, Moodle (an open-source learning platform) and Akamai (a cloud computing solution) have been successful in leveraging open-source technologies.

2. **Contribution to Global Open Source Projects:** Indian developers are increasingly contributing to major open-source projects. Initiatives like Google Summer of Code (GSoC) have motivated Indian students to actively engage with global open-source communities, creating a pool of skilled developers who contribute to cutting-edge projects.

   Open-source contributions from Indian developers have brought attention to India as a global hub for FOSS talent, further positioning the country to drive innovation in the FOSS ecosystem.

C. Localized Solutions for India's Unique Needs

1. **Customization and Localization:** FOSS allows for the customization of software to suit India's specific needs. For instance, local language support is crucial in a linguistically diverse country like India. Open-source projects can be tailored to support regional languages, ensuring that the technology is accessible to more people. Indian software companies are already creating localized open-source solutions in areas like e-Governance, banking, healthcare, and agriculture. Projects such as IndiaStack, a collection of APIs for digital infrastructure, and Aadhaar's open-source components, show how FOSS can be leveraged to create large-scale national platforms.

2. **FOSS in Education and Research:** Indian universities and research institutions are increasingly adopting FOSS for teaching and research purposes. Open-source tools like R, Python, MATLAB, and SageMath are widely used in academic

settings, providing students and researchers with powerful tools without the financial burden of proprietary software licenses.

D. Government and Private Sector Collaboration

1. **Public-Private Partnerships:** Collaboration between the Indian government and private companies is essential for advancing the adoption of FOSS. Initiatives like NASSCOM and C-DAC (Centre for Development of Advanced Computing) are helping to promote open-source technologies in both the private and public sectors.

   FOSS has a growing presence in smart city projects, banking systems, and e-governance initiatives across India. By collaborating with FOSS communities, the government can ensure that solutions are cost-effective, scalable, and transparent.

FOSS LICENCES

FOSS (Free and Open Source Software) licenses are legal frameworks that allow software to be freely used, modified, and distributed. These licenses ensure that the software is open, meaning that users can inspect, alter, and share the software's source code. FOSS licenses aim to protect both the freedom of software users and the rights of contributors.

There are several popular types of FOSS licenses, each with different rules regarding how the software can be used, modified, and distributed. Here's an overview of the most common FOSS licenses:

1. GPL (General Public License)

- **Versions:** GPLv2, GPLv3
- **Key Characteristics:**
  - Strong left: Any software that is derived from GPL-licensed code must also be released under the GPL if it's redistributed.
  - Modifications to the code must also be made available under the same license.
  - Ensures that the freedoms to use, modify, and distribute the software are maintained in all copies of the software, including derivatives.

2. MIT License

- **Key Characteristics:**
  - **Permissive:** The MIT License allows you to use, modify, and distribute the software with minimal restrictions.
  - The only condition is that the original license and right notice must be included in all copies of the software or substantial portions of it.
  - It's widely adopted due to its simplicity and permissiveness.

3. Apache License 2.0

- **Key Characteristics:**
  - **Permissive:** Like the MIT License, it allows for free use, modification, and distribution.

- Provides an explicit grant of patent rights from contributors to users.
- Modifications and redistributed versions of the software must include a of the license and a notice of changes made.
- Protects against patent claims by contributors.

4. BSD License (Berkeley Software Distribution)

- **Versions:** BSD 2-Clause, BSD 3-Clause
- **Key Characteristics:**
  - **Permissive:** It's a permissive license, similar to MIT, allowing for modification, distribution, and private use.
  - The 3-Clause BSD License includes a non-endorsement clause that prevents the use of the name of the project or its contributors for promotional purposes without permission.

5. Creative Commons (CC) Licenses

- **Key Characteristics:**
  - While not typically used for software, CC licenses are often used for media, content, or documentation.
  - It allows creators to choose permissions for sharing, remixing, and attribution.
  - The most common CC licenses include Attribution (CC BY), ShareAlike (CC BY-SA), and Non-Commercial (CC BY-NC).

6. LGPL (Lesser General Public License)

- **Key Characteristics:**
  - **Weak left:** Unlike the GPL, the LGPL allows you to link to the library from proprietary software without having to license the entire software under the GPL.
  - It is often used for libraries or frameworks that are used in both open-source and proprietary software.

7. MPL (Mozilla Public License)

- **Key Characteristics:**
  - A weak left license.
  - Allows proprietary and open-source code to coexist in the same project, but any modifications to the MPL-covered code must be shared under the same MPL license.
  - Often used for projects like Firefox.

8. Eclipse Public License (EPL)

- **Key Characteristics:**
  - Permissive and a weak left license.
  - You can modify and distribute the software, but modifications to the original EPL-covered code must be released under the EPL.
  - Common in the Eclipse Foundation's projects.

9. AGPL (Affero General Public License)

- **Key Characteristics:**
    - Strong left like the GPL but with a special clause about network use.
    - If the software is used over a network (e.g., a web application), the source code of any modifications must be made available to users, even if it's not distributed.
    - Often used for server-side applications.

10. Public Domain (CC0)

- **Key Characteristics:**
    - The software is effectively placed into the public domain with no right restrictions.
    - Users are free to do anything they want with the software, including modification and redistribution.
    - No attribution is required.
- **Key Concepts:**
    - **left:** A principle where modified versions of the software must also be distributed under the same license.
    - **Permissive Licenses:** These licenses allow users to freely use, modify, and redistribute the software with fewer restrictions, even in proprietary projects.
    - **Weak left:** A form of left that applies only to the original code or to specific components (e.g., libraries), not to the entire project.

GNU

The GNU General Public License (GPL), Affero General Public License (AGPL), Lesser General Public License (LGPL), and Free Documentation License (FDL) are prominent free and open-source software (FOSS) licenses that ensure freedom for users and developers while providing specific rules and conditions on how software can be used, modified, and redistributed.

These licenses are part of the GNU project and, in general, ensure that software remains open and accessible.

1. GNU General Public License (GPL)

The GPL is one of the most widely used licenses for FOSS projects, created by Richard Stallman for the GNU Project. It aims to ensure that software remains free and open by applying a strong form of left. This means that any derivative work based on GPL-licensed code must also be distributed under the GPL license.

Key Features of GPL

- **Strong left:** Any software derived from GPL-licensed software must be released under the same GPL license. This includes software that modifies the original code or integrates with it (e.g., libraries).

- **Source Code Availability:** The source code must be made available to users when distributing the software. If you distribute a modified version, you must also provide the source code of your modifications.
- **Commercial Use:** The GPL allows the software to be used for commercial purposes. The key is that if the software is redistributed or modified, it must comply with the same license.

Implications

- **Sharing and Modifying:** GPL ensures that all modifications are shared with the community and remain open.
- **Compatibility:** GPL-licensed code cannot be combined with code under incompatible licenses without violating the terms of the GPL. This can make it harder to integrate with proprietary software.

FOSS Example

- **Linux Kernel:** The Linux kernel is licensed under the GPL, which has allowed it to thrive as an open-source project while ensuring contributions remain open.

2. Affero General Public License (AGPL)

The AGPL is a derivative of the GPL with an important addition: it addresses the use over a network. This license was created to close a loophole where companies could modify GPL-licensed software and use it on a server without sharing the source code, as long as they didn't distribute the modified version.

Key Features of AGPL

- **Network Use Requirement:** If you modify AGPL-licensed software and use it on a server, you must make the source code of the modified software available to users who interact with it over the network.
- **Stronger left:** Like the GPL, modifications must be released under the same AGPL license.
- **Commercial Use:** Commercial use is allowed, but any derivative works must also be open-source if the software is made available over a network.

Implications

- **Open-source for Network Services:** The AGPL was designed to ensure that web-based applications (SaaS) remain open source. If a company modifies AGPL-licensed software for their server-side applications, they must release the source code of the modifications to their users.

FOSS Example

- **MongoDB:** MongoDB switched from the GPL to the AGPL to ensure that users who provide MongoDB as a service are required to contribute any modifications back to the community.

3. Lesser General Public License (LGPL)

The LGPL is a weaker version of the GPL, primarily designed for libraries. It allows proprietary software to link to LGPL-licensed libraries without requiring the entire proprietary program to be open-sourced.

Key Features of LGPL

- **Weak left:** If you modify the LGPL-licensed library, you must release the modified version under the LGPL. However, proprietary software can link to the library without having to release its source code.
- **Dynamic Linking Exception:** If a proprietary program dynamically links to an LGPL library, the proprietary program doesn't have to be licensed under the LGPL.
- **Source Code Availability:** The modified library's source code must be available when distributed.

Implications

- **Flexibility in Use with Proprietary Software:** LGPL enables proprietary software to use open-source libraries without forcing the proprietary software to be open-sourced, making it a popular choice for libraries.

FOSS Example

- **GTK+ (used by GNOME):** A graphical toolkit for creating graphical user interfaces, which is licensed under the LGPL. Many proprietary applications can use GTK+ without exposing their proprietary source code.

4. Free Documentation License (FDL)

The FDL is a license used primarily for documentation, designed by the Free Software Foundation (FSF).

It allows the content to be freely used, modified, and distributed, with the goal of ensuring documentation remains freely available.

Key Features of FDL

- **Left for Documentation:** Like GPL, the FDL ensures that modified documentation is distributed under the same license.
- **Transparency:** Modifications to documentation must be made available, and derivative works must also be distributed under the FDL.
- **Inclusion of Sections:** Certain sections of the documentation can be marked as "invariant," meaning they cannot be modified or removed.

Implications

- **Protecting the Integrity of Documentation:** The FDL ensures that the documentation remains free and open, but with some restrictions to protect critical sections from modification or removal (e.g., the license notice).

FOSS Example

- **GNU Manuals and Documentation:** Much of the documentation for GNU software is licensed under the FDL.

Implications of These Licenses for FOSS Development

1. **Freedom vs. Control:** GPL and AGPL ensure that modifications remain open-source, fostering a culture of collaboration and transparency.

   LGPL strikes a balance between freedom and allowing proprietary applications to use open-source libraries without making the whole project open.

   FDL ensures that documentation remains open and freely available, although it may require protecting specific sections.
2. **Compatibility and Combining Licenses:** GPL is incompatible with other licenses, especially proprietary licenses, because of its strong left nature. Mixing GPL and proprietary software can be challenging.

   LGPL and AGPL offer more flexibility, especially for integrating with proprietary codebases, but still ensure contributions back to the community when changes occur.
3. **Community and Contribution:** FOSS licenses encourage a vibrant community of contributors, as the licenses ensure that modifications benefit the community. The GPL and AGPL, in particular, guarantee that improvements made to software will be shared back with others.

REVIEW OF COMMON PROGRAMMING PRACTICES AND GUIDELINES FOR GNU/LINUX AND FOSS

The GNU/Linux and FOSS (Free and Open Source Software) communities place a strong emphasis on maintainable, reliable, and efficient code. When contributing to or maintaining projects in these ecosystems, there are well-established guidelines and practices that help ensure consistency, readability, and ease of collaboration. Below is a review of these common practices and guidelines.

1. Adherence to Coding Standards

- **Consistency is Key:** Code readability and consistency are paramount in the FOSS community. This allows contributors to easily understand and modify the codebase, even if they are new to the project.

GNU Coding Standards

- The GNU Coding Standards are a set of guidelines for writing code that is used in the GNU project. These standards emphasize:
  - **Naming conventions:** Functions, variables, and constants should have clear, descriptive names, and naming should be consistent across the project.
  - **Indentation and Formatting:** Consistent indentation is crucial. Most GNU projects use 2 or 4 spaces per indentation level (never tabs).
  - **Line Length:** Lines should be limited to 80 characters to avoid horizontal scrolling and to improve readability in various editors and tools.
  - **Braces:** In the GNU style, opening braces { are placed on the same line as the functioan definition or control structure, not on a new line.

    Example:

    ```
    int sum(int a, int b)
    ```

```
{
    return a + b;
}
```

- **Linux Kernel Coding Style:** The Linux kernel coding style also has its own guidelines that are slightly different from the GNU style, particularly regarding indentation (using 8 spaces for indentation) and bracket placement.

2. Documentation and Commenting

Effective documentation helps others understand the software's functionality, design decisions, and usage. It's also crucial for onboarding new developers into the project.

Inline Comments

- Comments should be used to explain the *why* behind complex or non-obvious code, rather than the *what*. Ideally, they should be concise, relevant, and placed above the code they describe.
- Avoid obvious comments; for instance, don't comment on trivial code like i++ unless it's part of a larger context.

Function Documentation

- Each function or method should have documentation describing:
    - Purpose of the function.
    - Arguments it takes.
    - Return values.
    - Side effects (e.g., modifying global variables, I/O operations).
    - Examples of usage when necessary.

    Example:

```
Function: sum
Calculates the sum of two integers.
a: The first integer.
b: The second integer.
returns: The sum of a and b.
int sum(int a, int b)
{
    return a + b;
}
```

External Documentation

README files should provide basic information about the project, such as:

- Project description.
- How to install and use the software.
- License information.
- Any special requirements or dependencies.

- **Man Pages:** For command-line tools, man pages are standard in the GNU/Linux ecosystem. They provide detailed information about how to use commands, options, and arguments.

Doxygen or Sphinx for Auto-Documentation

These tools help automatically generate documentation from comments within the code, typically used for larger FOSS projects that require detailed documentation (e.g., libraries).

3. Version Control and Collaboration

Using version control systems (VCS), particularly Git, is an essential practice in FOSS development. It allows for tracking changes, collaborating with other developers, and maintaining the history of a project.

Best Practices for Version Control

- **Frequent Commits:** Commit changes frequently to track progress and reduce the risk of losing work. Each commit should represent a logical unit of work.
- **Descriptive Commit Messages:** Write clear, descriptive commit messages that explain *why* the change was made. Follow a format like:

  <Type>: <Short Description>

  <Longer Description (if necessary)>
- **For example:** Fix: resolve issue with memory leak in buffer handling.
- **Branching:** Use feature branches for each task or bugfix. This allows developers to work on features or fixes without interfering with the main codebase (usually the master or main branch).
  - **GitFlow** is a popular branching model that defines different types of branches for features, releases, and hotfixes.
  - **Pull Requests (PRs):** Before merging, use pull requests to facilitate code review. This helps ensure that only high-quality code is added to the main repository.

Code Reviews

- **Peer Review:** Code reviews are a standard practice in most FOSS projects to ensure quality, readability, and maintainability. It's a collaborative process where one or more developers review a piece of code before it's merged.
- Tools like GitHub, GitLab, or Bitbucket facilitate code review processes by offering features for inline comments and discussions.

4. Testing and Continuous Integration (CI)

Ensuring the quality and stability of code is critical in FOSS development. Writing tests and using continuous integration tools are common practices to catch bugs early and improve the reliability of the software.

- **Unit Testing:** Unit tests should be written for any significant piece of logic. These tests ensure that individual components of the software work as expected.

  Frameworks like Google Test (C++), JUnit (Java), pytest (Python), and Mocha (JavaScript) are often used in FOSS projects.

- **Automated Testing:** Use Continuous Integration (CI) systems like Travis CI, Jenkins, or GitHub Actions to automatically run tests whenever code is pushed to the repository. This ensures that new changes don't break existing functionality.

  Test Coverage: Aim for high test coverage (ideally >80%) to ensure most parts of the software are tested.
- **Static Analysis:** Static code analysis tools (e.g., Clang Static Analyzer, Cppcheck, SonarQube) can automatically identify potential bugs, code smells, and maintainability issues.

5. Licensing and Legal Compliance

Proper licensing is essential for FOSS projects to ensure that contributors understand their rights and obligations.

- **License Headers:** Every file should have a license header indicating the project's overall license (e.g., GPL, MIT). This helps ensure that contributors are aware of the terms under which the code is released.

  Example:

  ```
  /* right (C) 2025 <Author Name>
   * This file is part of the Project.
   * Project is free software: you can redistribute it and/or modify
   * it under the terms of the GNU General Public License as published by
   * the Free Software Foundation, either version 3 of the License, or
   * (at your option) any later version.
   * Project is distributed in the hope that it will be useful,
   * but WITHOUT ANY WARRANTY; without even the implied warranty of
   * MERCHANTABILITY or FITNESS FOR A PARTICULAR PURPOSE. See the
   * GNU General Public License for more details.
   */
  ```
- **Contributor License Agreement (CLA):** Some projects use Contributor License Agreements (CLA) to clarify the terms under which contributions are made. This ensures that the project is protected from future legal issues regarding right.

6. Community Guidelines and Etiquctte

Community involvement is central to FOSS projects. Respectful communication and collaboration are essential for maintaining a healthy environment.

- **Code of Conduct:** Many projects include a Code of Conduct, which sets guidelines for respectful and inclusive behavior within the community.
- **Contribution Guidelines:** Provide clear contribution guidelines that explain how others can contribute to the project. This might include:
  - How to fork, clone, and set up the repository.
  - How to submit pull requests.
  - How to report bugs or request features.

Intentionally left blank!

UNIT 2

Linux

LINUX OS INSTALLATION AND HARDWARE CONFIGURATION

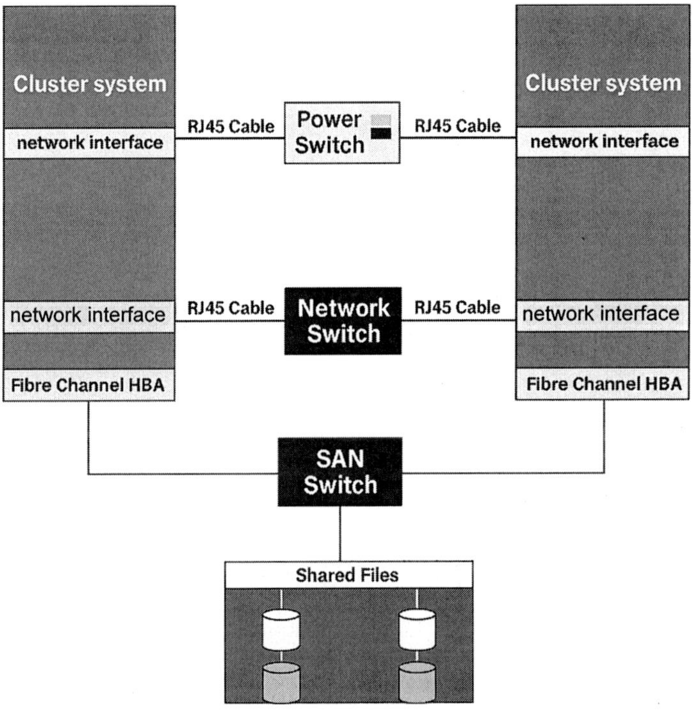

Fig 2.1: *Linux OS Installation and Hardware Configuration*

Installing a Linux operating system (OS) and configuring the associated hardware requires a combination of understanding the Linux environment, hardware compatibility, and system configuration. This process involves selecting the appropriate Linux distribution (distro), configuring the installation settings, and ensuring that hardware components such as storage devices, display, network interfaces, and peripherals are correctly recognized and configured.

1. Choosing a Linux Distribution (Distro)

The first step in installing Linux is choosing a distribution. Linux is modular, and many distros cater to different user needs. Some popular options include:

- **Ubuntu:** A beginner-friendly distribution based on Debian, widely used on desktops and servers.
- **Debian:** Known for stability and used as a base for many other distros.
- **Fedora:** A cutting-edge distro sponsored by Red Hat, known for using the latest software.
- **CentOS / RHEL:** Enterprise-oriented distros based on Red Hat, ideal for servers.
- **Arch Linux:** A minimalist and rolling-release distro, popular with advanced users.
- **Linux Mint:** A user-friendly distro based on Ubuntu, with a familiar interface for Windows users.

2. Preparing for Installation

Before beginning the installation, ensure you have the following:

- **A bootable installation medium:** This could be a USB flash drive, DVD, or a network installation. You can create a bootable USB drive using tools like Rufus (Windows) or dd (Linux).
- **System Requirements:** Confirm that your hardware meets the minimum requirements for the Linux distribution you are installing. Common requirements are:
  - At least 2GB of RAM (4GB or more is recommended for a smoother experience).
  - At least 20GB of disk space (more if you plan to install many applications).
  - A compatible graphics card, CPU, and network adapter.

3. Linux Installation Process

Here are the general steps for installing Linux on your system:

Step 1: Boot from Installation Medium

- Insert the bootable USB drive or DVD into the computer.
- Restart the computer and access the BIOS or UEFI settings (typically by pressing F2, F10, Del, or another key during startup).
- In the BIOS/UEFI, set the boot order to prioritize booting from the USB or DVD.
- Save the changes and exit the BIOS. The system should now boot into the Linux installer.

Step 2: Language and Keyboard Layout Selection

- The installer will prompt you to select your preferred language and keyboard layout. Choose the appropriate options for your location and language preferences.

Step 3: Disk Partitioning

- Partitioning is the process of dividing your hard drive into sections where the OS and data will be stored. Most modern Linux installers handle partitioning automatically, but advanced users may choose to customize the partitions.
  - **Root partition (/):** The main partition where the OS is installed.

- Swap partition: Acts as virtual memory. While Linux can run without it, it's recommended to have a swap partition, especially if you have limited RAM.
- **Home partition (/home):** Optional but recommended. Stores user files separately from system files, making upgrades or reinstallations easier.

- You can choose between automatic partitioning (easier) or manual partitioning (more control). Manual partitioning allows you to define the size and type of each partition (e.g., ext4, XFS).

Step 4: Filesystem Selection

- **EXT4** is the most common filesystem used in Linux and is often the default. It is a journaled filesystem that offers good performance and reliability.
- **XFS:** A high-performance filesystem, commonly used in enterprise environments.
- Btrfs: A newer filesystem with advanced features like snapshots, but less widely used.
- **Swap Space:** If you are using a swap partition, this is typically formatted as swap.

Step 5: Setting Up User Accounts

- You will be asked to create a root password (administrative account) and a user account for regular usage. The root account allows full control over the system, while the user account has limited permissions to prevent accidental system damage.
- Some distributions may also allow setting up the system for automatic login, which logs in a user automatically on startup.

Step 6: Network Configuration

- If you're using a wired connection (Ethernet), this is typically configured automatically.
- For wireless connections, you will need to select your Wi-Fi network and enter the password.
- Some distributions support static IP or DHCP configurations during installation, though these can always be changed after the installation.

Step 7: Install the Bootloader (GRUB)

- The GRUB bootloader is essential for managing operating systems. It will allow you to select the OS to boot if you're dual-booting with another operating system (like Windows).
- In most cases, the installer will automatically install GRUB to the Master Boot Record (MBR) or EFI partition (for UEFI systems).

Step 8: Installing the System

- Once all settings are configured, the installation process will begin. This can take anywhere from 15 minutes to an hour, depending on your hardware and the distro you are installing.

Step 9: Reboot the System

- After installation is complete, you will be prompted to reboot. Don't forget to remove the installation media (USB or DVD) to avoid booting from it again.

4. Post-Installation Setup

Once the Linux system is installed, there are a few important steps to complete the configuration:

Step 1: Update the System

- After booting into the Linux OS for the first time, it's essential to update the system to the latest version of packages and security patches. You can use the following commands:

  For Debian/Ubuntu-based systems:
  sudo apt update

  sudo apt upgrade

  For Fedora:
  sudo dnf update

  For Arch Linux:
  sudo pacman -Syu

Step 2: Install Additional Software

- Depending on your needs, you can install additional software (such as browsers, office suites, or media players) using the system's package manager.
  - **Ubuntu/Debian:** apt install <package-name>
  - **Fedora:** dnf install <package-name>
  - **Arch:** pacman -S <package-name>

You can also install software from external repositories or by compiling from source.

Step 3: Hardware Drivers and Configuration

- **Graphics Drivers:** Modern Linux distributions typically come with open-source graphics drivers (like nouveau for NVIDIA cards), but proprietary drivers may offer better performance, especially for gaming or professional applications.
  - For NVIDIA cards, you can install proprietary drivers using:

    On Ubuntu/Debian:
    sudo apt install nvidia-driver

    On Fedora (using RPM Fusion repository):
    sudo dnf install akmod-nvidia
- **Wi-Fi Drivers:** Most Linux distros come with drivers for common Wi-Fi chipsets. If your Wi-Fi is not recognized, you may need to install additional drivers for your specific chipset.

Step 4: Configure Peripheral Devices

- **Printers:** Use tools like CUPS (Common Unix Printing System) to configure printers. Most Linux distributions offer a graphical interface for configuring printers, such as System Settings in GNOME or KDE's System Settings.

- **Audio:** Linux typically uses PulseAudio or PipeWire for managing audio. If you're having trouble with audio, you may need to configure it using tools like pavucontrol (PulseAudio Volume Control).
- **External Devices (USB, etc.):** Linux generally supports a wide range of external devices (USB drives, external hard drives, etc.) out of the box, but some peripherals, like webcams or certain Bluetooth devices, may require additional drivers.

Step 5: Configure Network Settings

- **Ethernet:** Typically auto-configures with DHCP.
- **Wi-Fi:** You can manage your Wi-Fi networks through the network manager in your desktop environment or through terminal-based tools like nmcli.
- **Static IP Configuration:** You can set static IPs via the network settings in the graphical interface or by editing configuration files like /etc/network/interfaces (for older systems) or /etc/netplan/*.yaml (for modern Ubuntu systems).

5. Advanced Hardware Configuration

Some hardware may require advanced configuration:

Step 1: UDEV Rules

- UDEV is the device manager for Linux. It allows you to define custom rules for how devices are handled. For example, you might want a specific USB device to always be mounted in a particular directory or trigger a script when a device is plugged in.

Step 2: ACPI Configuration (Advanced Configuration and Power Interface)

- ACPI settings may be necessary for configuring power management, especially on laptops. If you encounter issues with sleep, hibernation, or battery management, you may need to tweak ACPI settings or install additional drivers like tlp (a tool for power management).

Step 3: RAID and LVM Configuration

- If you're using RAID (Redundant Array of Independent Disks) or LVM (Logical Volume Manager) for disk management, you'll need to configure these tools during installation or later. Linux provides tools like mdadm for RAID and lvm commands for LVM.

INSTALLING A GNU/LINUX DISTRIBUTION

Installing a **GNU/Linux** distribution (distro) involves several steps, from preparing the installation media to configuring the system after installation. Below is a detailed, step-by-step guide on how to install a GNU/Linux distribution, starting from downloading the right distribution to setting up your system.

1. Selecting the Right GNU/Linux Distribution

The first step is to choose the right **Linux distribution (distro)** for your needs. The selection depends on several factors, such as your experience with Linux, hardware compatibility, use cases (server, desktop, etc.), and personal preferences. Below are some of the most popular distributions and their ideal use cases:

- **Ubuntu**: Great for beginners, widely used for desktops and servers. Offers user-friendly installation and a large support community.
- **Debian**: Known for its stability, often used for servers, and the base of many other distributions like Ubuntu.
- **Fedora**: Cutting-edge distro with the latest software, ideal for developers and tech enthusiasts.
- **CentOS/RHEL**: Enterprise-oriented distros, used in production environments.
- **Arch Linux**: For advanced users who want a minimalistic, highly customizable installation.
- **Linux Mint**: Based on Ubuntu, but with a more Windows-like interface, it's ideal for users transitioning from Windows.
- **openSUSE**: Known for powerful system administration tools, often used in enterprise environments.

2. Preparing for Installation

Before installing a Linux distribution, you need to prepare a few things:

- **A computer with compatible hardware**: Ensure that your computer meets the hardware requirements for the distribution you want to install.
- **Installation medium**: You will need a bootable USB drive or DVD containing the installation files for the chosen distribution. Most distros provide an ISO file that can be burned to a USB drive.
- **Backup your data**: It's always a good idea to back up any important data on your computer before beginning the installation, especially if you plan to overwrite your current operating system.

Creating Bootable Installation Media

- **Using USB**:
  - Download the ISO file for the distribution from its official website.
  - Use tools like **Rufus** (on Windows) or **dd** (on Linux) to create a bootable USB.

    Rufus:

    1. Select the downloaded ISO.
    2. Choose the USB drive.
    3. Click "Start" to create the bootable USB.

    dd (on Linux):

    sudo dd if=/path/to/iso of=/dev/sdX bs=4M status=progress && sync

    - Replace /dev/sdX with the correct drive identifier for your USB stick (e.g., /dev/sdb).

3. Booting from the Installation Media

1. Insert the bootable USB or DVD into the computer and reboot.
2. During startup, enter the **BIOS/UEFI settings** (usually by pressing **F2, F10, Del,** or **Esc** during boot).

3. In the BIOS/UEFI menu, adjust the **boot order** to boot from the USB or DVD drive first.
4. Save the changes and exit. The system should boot into the Linux installer.

4. Installation Steps

Once the computer boots into the installation environment, you'll follow the specific steps provided by the installer for your chosen distribution. The installation process is typically straightforward, and most Linux distributions offer a user-friendly graphical installer.

Step 1: Language and Region Selection

- The installer will prompt you to select the language, region, and keyboard layout for the system.

Step 2: Disk Partitioning

Partitioning is the process of dividing your hard drive into sections that can each hold a specific file system. You'll need to decide how to allocate space between partitions. Modern Linux distributions typically provide an automatic partitioning option for beginners, but advanced users can opt for manual partitioning.

Partitioning Choices:

- **Automatic Partitioning**: The installer will automatically divide the available space on the disk into necessary partitions, including root (/), swap space, and /home. This is the easiest option.
- **Manual Partitioning**: For more control over your system, you can manually partition the disk. This is typically done by selecting the size and type of each partition:
  - **Root partition** (/): The main system partition where the OS and most of the data will be stored.
  - **Home partition (/home)**: Optional but recommended. This separates user data from system files and makes reinstallation or upgrading easier.
  - **Swap space**: Space on the disk used as virtual memory. Typically, it's recommended to allocate 1–2 times your system's RAM.

Partitioning Tools:

- **GParted** (used by many distros during installation) can help you resize, delete, and create partitions if you're doing it manually.

Step 3: Filesystem Selection

Linux supports several file systems. The most common ones are:

- **EXT4**: The default and most widely used file system in Linux.
- **XFS**: A high-performance file system that's good for large data sets.
- **Btrfs**: A modern file system that supports features like snapshots and built-in RAID.

Choose a file system for your root (/) partition. **EXT4** is typically recommended for general use, but if you're working with specialized setups, you might consider other options.

Step 4: Bootloader Installation (GRUB)

The bootloader, typically **GRUB** (Grand Unified Bootloader), is responsible for loading the operating system when the computer starts. The installer will automatically install GRUB unless you are manually partitioning and want to install it elsewhere (for example, if you're dual-booting with Windows).

- **GRUB** should be installed to the **Master Boot Record (MBR)** or the **EFI partition** on UEFI-based systems.
- The GRUB configuration file will allow you to select the operating system to boot into if you have multiple OSes installed (e.g., Windows and Linux).

Step 5: User and Password Setup

During installation, you'll be asked to create:

- **Root password**: This is the administrator account used for system-level tasks (e.g., installing software, configuring system settings).
- **User account**: This is the regular user account for daily activities. You'll be asked to set a username and password.

Most distributions also allow you to enable or disable features like **automatic login** or **full disk encryption** (which encrypts your entire drive to improve security).

Step 6: Timezone and Locale Settings

You'll be prompted to select your **timezone** and **locale** (language and country). This ensures that your system uses the correct time and regional settings.

Step 7: Software Selection

Many installers give you an option to select pre-installed software packages. Some distributions may offer:

- **Minimal installation**: Installs only the essential system files, leaving you to manually install additional software.
- **Desktop environment**: A choice of graphical environments such as **GNOME, KDE Plasma**, or **XFCE**. These environments provide the graphical user interface (GUI) that allows you to interact with the system visually.
- **Additional software**: You may be able to install popular software such as web browsers, office suites, media players, etc., directly during the installation process.

Step 8: Installing the System

Once all configurations are made, the installation process will begin. It typically takes anywhere from 15 minutes to an hour, depending on your system's performance and the software you selected. The installer will the required files to your disk, configure system settings, and set up the bootloader.

5. Post-Installation Configuration

After the installation is complete, you'll need to perform some post-installation tasks to ensure everything works as expected.

Step 1: Reboot and Remove Installation Media

- When the installation is finished, the installer will prompt you to **reboot** your system.
- Make sure to remove the installation media (USB or DVD) before rebooting to avoid booting back into the installer.

Step 2: System Updates

- Once the system has rebooted into your new Linux installation, the first task is to update the system. This ensures that you have the latest security patches and software updates.

  For **Debian/Ubuntu-based** distros:
  sudo apt update

  sudo apt upgrade

  For **Fedora**:
  sudo dnf update

  For **Arch Linux**:
  sudo pacman -Syu

Step 3: Install Additional Drivers

- **Graphics drivers**: Most modern Linux distributions will automatically install open-source graphics drivers (such as **nouveau** for NVIDIA cards or **AMDGPU** for AMD cards), but if you need proprietary drivers, you may need to install them manually. For example: For **NVIDIA**:
  sudo apt install nvidia-driver
  - For **AMD**: The open-source drivers are usually already included, but you may need to install specific firmware or tools.
- **Wi-Fi drivers**: For Wi-Fi cards that aren't supported by default, you may need to install the appropriate driver package.
  Step 4: Install Software
- Install the software that you need for daily use, such as browsers, office suites, and media players. For example:

  Install **Firefox** (web browser):
  sudo apt install firefox

Step 5: Configure System Preferences

- Configure system settings such as:
  - **Display resolution**
  - **Power settings** (especially on laptops)
  - **Keyboard and mouse preferences**
  - **Network settings** (e.g., Wi-Fi, VPN)

Step 6: Backup and Snapshots

- Set up regular backups to prevent data loss.

- Some distributions, like **Ubuntu**, come with **Deja Dup** (backup tool) pre-installed, while **Timeshift** can be used for system snapshots on other distributions (especially useful for restoring the system to a previous state).

6. Final Considerations

- **Dual Boot Setup**: If you want to keep another operating system (e.g., Windows) alongside Linux, you'll need to partition your disk accordingly during the installation and ensure that the bootloader (GRUB) detects both operating systems.
- **Security**: Consider enabling **firewall** and **SELinux/AppArmor** (security tools) to enhance security. You can also install software like **fail2ban** to block malicious activity.
- **Learning Resources**: As you get familiar with Linux, consider exploring documentation (like the **Arch Wiki** or **Ubuntu forums**) to learn more about system configuration and troubleshooting.

BASIC SHELL COMMANDS IN LINUX

The **shell** is a command-line interface (CLI) that allows users to interact with the operating system. It is one of the most powerful tools in Linux, enabling a vast range of tasks from system management to application automation.

In this guide, we'll explore some of the most common and basic shell commands used in Linux for tasks like logging in, managing files, and viewing file contents.

1. Logging Into the Linux System

When you log into a Linux system, you're typically presented with a terminal window or a login prompt, depending on the setup. You interact with the system through this shell interface, where you can run commands.

Login Command

In a typical console environment or over SSH (secure shell), the login command is implicit, as most login managers will ask you for credentials.

However, if you're working on a remote system via **SSH**, the login process will look like this:

ssh username@hostname_or_ip

- **username**: Your system username.
- **hostname_or_ip**: The IP address or hostname of the system you want to access.

  For example:

  ssh user@192.168.1.100

After entering your password, you will be logged into the remote system and dropped into a shell prompt.

2. Listing Files

In Linux, the command used to list files in a directory is ls. This command shows files and directories in the current working directory.

Basic ls Usage

ls

This will list all visible files and directories in the current directory. By default, it doesn't show hidden files (those starting with a dot .).

Using Options with ls

You can use options to modify the behavior of the ls command:

- **-l**: Use a long listing format, which shows additional details like file permissions, owner, file size, and modification date.
  - ls -l
- **-a**: List all files, including hidden ones (those starting with .).
  - ls -a
- **-h**: Show file sizes in human-readable format (e.g., KB, MB, GB).
  - ls -lh
- **-R**: Recursively list subdirectories.
  - ls -R

Example Command

- ls -la /home/user

This would list all files (including hidden) in the /home/user directory in a long format.

3. Editing Files

In Linux, editing files through the command line can be done using a variety of text editors. Two of the most commonly used editors are **nano** and **vim**.

Using nano (Beginner-Friendly Text Editor)

nano is a simple, easy-to-use terminal text editor. Here's how to use it:

nano filename

- This opens the file **filename** in the nano editor.
- If the file doesn't exist, nano will create it.
- After editing, press Ctrl + O to save, then press Enter to confirm the filename. Press Ctrl + X to exit the editor.

Using vim (Advanced Text Editor)

vim is a more powerful and flexible text editor, but it has a steeper learning curve. To open a file in vim:

vim filename

In vim, there are different modes:

- **Normal Mode**: This is the default mode. You can move around the file and delete text.
- **Insert Mode**: To start editing the file, press i to enter insert mode.

- **Command Mode**: Press Esc to go back to normal mode and type commands like :w to save or :q to quit.

Example sequence in vim:

1. Open file: vim myfile.txt
2. Enter insert mode: i
3. Edit the file.
4. Save and exit: Press Esc, then type :wq and press Enter.

4. ing and Moving Files

Linux provides several commands to manage files and directories. Two of the most essential commands for file management are cp () and mv (move/rename).

- **ing Files with cp:** The cp command copies files or directories from one location to another.
  - cp source_file destination_file
- **a file**: To a file from one directory to another:
  - cp myfile.txt /path/to/destination/
- **multiple files**: You can multiple files to a directory by specifying multiple files as the source:
  - cp file1.txt file2.txt /path/to/destination/
- **directories**: To a directory and its contents recursively, use the -r option:
  - cp -r my_directory/ /path/to/destination/

Moving and Renaming Files with mv

The mv command is used for both moving files or directories and renaming them.

mv source_file destination_file

- **Move a file**: To move a file from one directory to another:
  - mv myfile.txt /path/to/destination/
- **Rename a file**: You can rename a file using mv as well:
  - mv oldname.txt newname.txt
- **Move multiple files**: You can move multiple files into a directory:
  - mv file1.txt file2.txt /path/to/destination/

5. Viewing File Contents

Once you have files on your system, you might need to view or examine their contents. There are several commands in Linux to view files, such as cat, less, and more.

Viewing Files with cat

The cat (short for **concatenate**) command is used to display the contents of a file to the terminal.

cat filename

Example: To view the contents of example.txt:

cat example.txt

- **Concatenate Files**: You can also combine the contents of multiple files into one: cat file1.txt file2.txt
- Viewing Files with less and more
  - For large files, cat might be too cumbersome since it displays everything at once. To scroll through a file, use **less** or **more**.
- **less**: Allowsyoutoscrollthroughafileinbothdirections(upanddown).Pressqtoquit. less largefile.txt
- **more**: Similar to less, but only allows scrolling down (forward). more largefile.txt

Other File Viewing Commands

- **head**: Shows the first few lines of a file (by default, the first 10 lines).
  - head filename
- **tail**: Shows the last few lines of a file (by default, the last 10 lines).
  - tail filename
- You can also follow a file in real-time with tail -f:
  - tail -f /var/log/syslog

6. Other Useful Basic Commands

- **pwd**: Print the current working directory.
  - pwd
- **cd**: Change the current directory.
  - cd /path/to/directory
- **mkdir**: Create a new directory.
  - mkdir new_directory
- **rmdir**: Remove an empty directory.
  - rmdir directory_name
- **rm**: Remove a file or directory.
  - rm filename # Remove a file
  - rm -r dirname # Remove a directory and its content

Basic Commands

Once you're in the terminal, you can start typing commands. Here are some common ones:

- **pwd** (Print Working Directory): Displays the current directory you are in.

  $ pwd

  /home/username
- **ls** (List): Lists the contents of the current directory.

  $ ls

  Documents Downloads Pictures Music
- **cd** (Change Directory): Navigate to a different directory.

  $ cd Documents

- **mkdir** (Make Directory): Create a new directory.

  $ mkdir new_folder
- **touch**: Create a new empty file.

  $ touch newfile.txt
- **rm** (Remove): Delete a file or directory.

  $ rm file.txt

  $ rm -r foldername # Removes a directory and its contents
- **cp** (): files or directories.

  $ cp source.txt destination.txt
- **mv** (Move or Rename): Move or rename files and directories.

  $ mv oldname.txt newname.txt
- **cat** (Concatenate): Display the content of a file.

  $ cat file.txt

3. Running Programs and Commands

- **Running Applications**: You can run any installed application or program by typing its name (e.g., firefox, gnome-calculator).

  $ firefox
- **Running with sudo**: Some commands need superuser privileges to run. Use sudo to execute commands with administrator rights.

  $ sudo apt update

  $ sudo apt install curl
- **Background Processes**: You can run a program in the background by appending an ampersand (&) to the command.

  $ gedit & # Opens gedit in the background
- **Piping and Redirection**
  - **Piping (|)**: You can chain commands using the pipe symbol (|) to pass the output of one command as input to another.

  $ ls | grep "Documents"
  - **Redirection (>, >>)**:

    > redirects the output to a file, overwriting it.

    >> appends the output to a file.

    $ echo "Hello, world!" > hello.txt # Overwrites the file $ echo "This is a new line" >> hello.txt # Appends to the file
- **Input Redirection** (<): Redirects input from a file into a command.

  $ sort < file.txt

5. Process Management

Viewing Running Processes: Use ps or top to view running processes.

- **ps**: Shows a snapshot of current processes.

  $ ps aux

- **top**: Shows an interactive list of running processes.

  $ top
- **Killing Processes**: If a process becomes unresponsive, you can terminate it using kill.

  $ kill PID # Replace PID with the process ID

  $ kill -9 PID # Forcefully kill the process
- **Background Jobs**: Use & to send a process to the background, and jobs to list all background jobs.

  $ some_command & # Run a command in the background

  $ jobs # List background jobs
- **Foreground Jobs**: Use fg to bring a background job to the foreground.

  $ fg %1 # Brings job number 1 to the foreground

6. Environment Variables

Environment variables hold system-wide values that affect the way processes run. Common environment variables include PATH, HOME, and USER.

- **Viewing Environment Variables**:

  $ echo $PATH
- **Setting Environment Variables**:

  $ export VAR_NAME=value
- **Viewing Current User**:

  $ whoami

7. Text Editors

You can edit files directly from the shell using text editors like **Nano**, **Vim**, or **Emacs**.

- **Nano**: Simple, user-friendly text editor.

  $ nano file.txt # Open file.txt in nano editor
- Use **Ctrl + X** to exit, **Y** to save changes, and **N** to discard.
- **Vim**: More advanced editor with a steeper learning curve.

  $ vim file.txt

Press **Esc** to enter command mode, and :wq to save and exit.

8. Package Management

Ubuntu uses the **APT** (Advanced Package Tool) system to install, update, and manage software packages.

- **Updating Package List**:

  $ sudo apt update
- **Upgrading Installed Packages**:

  $ sudo apt upgrade
- **Installing Packages**:

  $ sudo apt install package_name

- **Removing Packages**:

  $ sudo apt remove package_name

- **Search for Packages**:

  $ apt search package_name

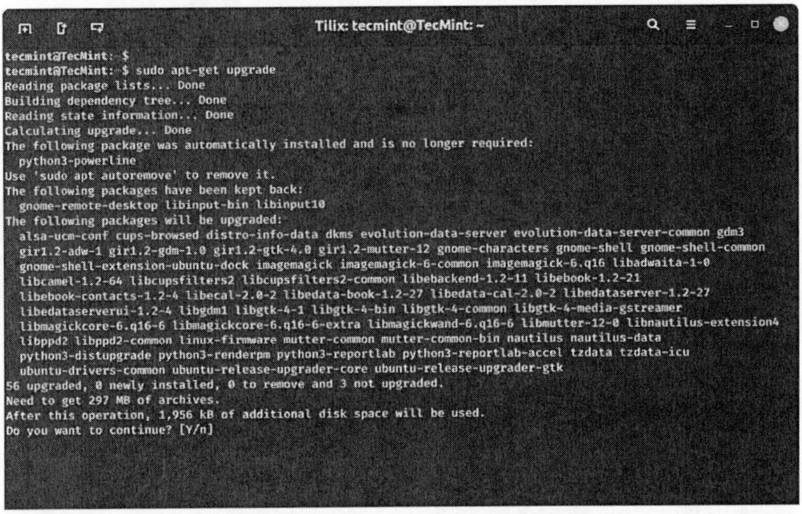

9. Scripting in

scripting allows you to automate tasks by writing a series of commands in a text file and executing them.

- **Creating a Script**: Create a script using a text editor (e.g., nano or vim).

  $ nano script.sh

- **Make the Script Executable**:

  $ chmod +x script.sh

- **Run the Script**:

  $ ./script.sh

10. Help and Manual Pages

If you're unsure about a command, you can get more information by using the man (manual) command or the --help flag.

- **Using man**:

  $ man ls # Displays the manual for the `ls` command

- **Using --help**:

  $ ls --help # Displays help for the `ls` command

Summary

The **Ubuntu shell** (or terminal) is a powerful interface for interacting with the operating system. Learning how to use it efficiently can significantly improve your ability to manage files, run programs, automate tasks, and troubleshoot your system. Understanding common commands, environment variables, text editors, and package management are foundational skills that will help you navigate and control your Ubuntu system with ease.

FILE AND DIRECTORY MANAGEMENT COMMANDS

1. **pwd** - Print working directory
   - Displays the full path of the current directory.

     $ pwd
2. **ls** - List directory contents
   - Lists files and directories in the current directory.

     $ ls
3. **cd** - Change directory
   - Navigates to a different directory.

     $ cd /path/to/directory
4. **mkdir** - Make directory
   - Creates a new directory.

     $ mkdir new_directory
5. **rmdir** - Remove empty directory
   - Deletes an empty directory.

     $ rmdir empty_directory
6. **rm** - Remove files or directories
   - Deletes files or directories. Use -r for directories.

     $ rm file.txt

     $ rm -r folder_name
7. **touch** - Create a new empty file
   - Creates a new empty file.

     $ touch newfile.txt
8. **cp** - files or directories
   - Copies files or directories.

     $ cp source.txt destination.txt

     $ cp -r source_folder destination_folder
9. **mv** - Move or rename files or directories
   - Moves or renames files or directories.

     $ mv oldname.txt newname.txt

     $ mv file.txt /path/to/new/location/
10. **cat** - Concatenate and display file content
    - Displays the contents of a file.

      $ cat file.txt
11. **less** - View file contents interactively
    - Allows scrolling through the contents of a file. $ less file.txt

12. **head** - View the beginning of a file
    - Displays the first 10 lines of a file.
      $ head file.txt
13. **tail** - View the end of a file
    - Displays the last 10 lines of a file.
      $ tail file.txt
14. **find** - Search for files
    - Searches for files within a directory based on various criteria.
      $ find /path/to/search -name "file.txt"
15. **locate** - Find files by name
    - Quickly finds files by their name.
      $ locate filename
16. **tree** - Display directory structure as a tree
    - Lists directories and files in a tree-like structure.
      $ tree
17. **du** - Disk usage
    - Displays the disk usage of files and directories.
      $ du -sh *
18. **chmod** - Change file permissions
    - Changes the permissions of a file or directory.
      $ chmod 755 file.txt
19. **chown** - Change file owner and group
    - Changes the owner or group of a file or directory.
      $ chown user:group file.txt
20. **stat** - Display file or file system status
    - Shows detailed information about a file.
      $ stat file.txt

Process Management Commands

21. **ps** - View running processes
    - Displays information about active processes.
      $ ps aux
22. **top** - Display running processes in real time
    - Shows an interactive list of processes with resource usage.
      $ top
23. **htop** - Interactive process viewer (needs to be installed)
    - Enhanced version of top for better process management.
      $ htop
24. **kill** - Terminate a process by PID

- Sends a signal to terminate a process.
  $ kill PID

25. **killall** - Kill processes by name
   - Terminates all processes with a specified name.
     $ killall process_name
26. **bg** - Resume a job in the background
   - Resumes a paused job and runs it in the background. $ bg %1
27. **fg** - Bring a background job to the foreground
   - Brings a background job to the foreground.
     $ fg %1
28. **jobs** - List background jobs
   - Lists jobs running in the background.
     $ jobs
29. **nice** - Set process priority
   - Starts a process with a specified priority (niceness).
     $ nice -n 10 command
30. **renice** - Change the priority of a running process
   - Changes the priority of a running process.
     $ renice -n 10 -p PID

System Information Commands

31. **uname** - Display system information
   - Displays information about the kernel and system architecture.
     $ uname -a
32. **df** - Display disk space usage
   - Shows available and used disk space for all mounted filesystems. $ df -h
33. **free** - Display memory usage
   - Shows the amount of free and used memory in the system.
     $ free -h
34. **uptime** - Show how long the system has been running
   - Displays how long the system has been running, along with the load average.
     $ uptime
35. **who** - Show who is logged in
   - Displays the users currently logged into the system.
     $ who
36. **top** - Display system processes and resource usage
   - Provides a live, dynamic view of running processes.
     $ top
37. **dmesg** - Display boot and system messages
   - Shows kernel-related messages from the system's buffer.
     $ dmesg

38. **lscpu** - Display CPU architecture information
   - Shows detailed information about the CPU architecture.

     $ lscpu
39. **lsblk** - List information about block devices
   - Displays a list of all block devices (disks, partitions, etc.).

     $ lsblk
40. **lsusb** - List USB devices
   - Displays information about connected USB devices.

     $ lsusb
41. **lspci** - List PCI devices
   - Displays information about the PCI devices on the system.

     $ lspci

Networking Commands

42. **ping** - Send ICMP echo request to check network connectivity
   - Tests the connection to a network host.

     $ ping google.com
43. **ifconfig** - Configure network interfaces
   - Displays or configures network interface settings.

     $ ifconfig
44. **ip** - Network interface management
   - Used to show and manipulate network interfaces.

     $ ip addr show
45. **netstat** - Show network connections, routing tables, etc.
   - Displays network statistics and information about active connections.

     $ netstat -tuln
46. **curl** - Transfer data from or to a server
   - Transfers data using various network protocols like HTTP, FTP.

     $ curl http://example.com
47. **wget** - Download files from the internet
   - Downloads files from the web via HTTP, HTTPS, or FTP.

     $ wget http://example.com/file.zip
48. **scp** - Secure files between hosts
   - Copies files securely between hosts on a network.

     $ scp file.txt username@remote:/path/to/destination

Package Management Commands

49. **apt update** - Update package lists for repositories
   - Updates the local package index to ensure you can install the latest packages.

$ sudo apt update

50. **apt upgrade** - Upgrade installed packages

   - Upgrades all installed packages to their latest versions.

     $ sudo

FILE CREATION, EDITING, AND VIEWING

- **Create an empty text file:**
  touch filename.txt
- **Open and edit a file using nano:**
  nano filename.txt
- **Open and edit a file using vim:**
  vim filename.txt
- **Open and edit a file using gedit (GUI text editor):**
  gedit filename.txt
- **View file contents:**
  cat filename.txt
- **View a file page by page:**
  less filename.txt
- **View a file page by page (another tool):**
  more filename.txt
- **Show file with line numbers:**
  nl filename.txt
- **Open the file in vim without editing (read-only):**
  vim -R filename.txt

Searching and Filtering

- **Search for a string in a file:**
  grep "search_term" filename.txt
- **Search recursively in a directory:**
  grep -r "search_term" directory/
- **Search case-insensitively:**
  grep -i "search_term" filename.txt
- **Count occurrences of a string in a file:**
  grep -c "search_term" filename.txt
- **Search and display line numbers:**
  grep -n "search_term" filename.txt
- **Search for a whole word:**
  grep -w "search_term" filename.txt
- **Search for lines not containing a string:**
  grep -v "search_term" filename.txt
- **Display unique lines in a file:**
  sort filename.txt | uniq

- **Find all occurrences of a word using awk:**
  awk '/search_term/' filename.txt
- **Filter lines that match a pattern using sed:**
  sed -n '/search_term/p' filename.txt

Text Transformation and Editing

- **Replace text in a file (in-place):**
  sed -i 's/old_string/new_string/g' filename.txt
- **Replace text in a file without changing the original:**
  sed 's/old_string/new_string/g' filename.txt
- **Remove blank lines:**
  sed '/^\s*$/d' filename.txt
- **Remove leading whitespace:**
  sed 's/^[\t]*//' filename.txt
- **Remove trailing whitespace:**
  sed 's/[\t]*$//' filename.txt
- **Remove both leading and trailing whitespace:**
  sed 's/^[\t]*//;s/[\t]*$//' filename.txt
- **Convert text to uppercase:**
  awk '{ print toupper($0) }' filename.txt
- **Convert text to lowercase:**
  awk '{ print tolower($0) }' filename.txt
- **Prepend a line of text to a file:**
  sed -i '1s/^/This is the first line\n/' filename.txt
- **Append text to the end of a file:**
  echo "new text" >> filename.txt

File Manipulation and Redirection

- **Redirect output to a file (overwrite):**
  echo "Hello, world!" > filename.txt
- **Append output to an existing file:**
  echo "More text" >> filename.txt
- **Create a of a file:**
  cp filename.txt newfile.txt
- **Move or rename a file:**
  mv filename.txt newfilename.txt
- **Remove a file:**
  rm filename.txt
- **Show the size of a file:**
  wc -c filename.txt
- **Count lines in a file:**
  wc -l filename.txt
- **Count words in a file:**
  wc -w filename.txt

- **Show last 10 lines of a file**:
  tail filename.txt
- **Show first 10 lines of a file**:
  head filename.txt
- **View the last N lines of a file**:
  tail -n 20 filename.txt
- **Combine multiple files into one**:
  cat file1.txt file2.txt > combined.txt
- **Split a file into smaller files by line count**:
  split -l 1000 filename.txt part_

Sorting and Comparing

- **Sort the contents of a file**:
  sort filename.txt
- **Sort the contents of a file in reverse order**:
  sort -r filename.txt
- **Sort by a specific column (e.g., column 2)**:
  sort -k 2 filename.txt
- **Compare two files line by line**:
  diff file1.txt file2.txt
- **Compare two files side by side**:
  diff -y file1.txt file2.txt
- **Find differences and suppress common lines**:
  comm file1.txt file2.txt

Advanced Text Processing

- **Extract specific columns from a file** (e.g., CSV):
  cut -d ‘,’ -f 1 filename.txt
- **Join lines in a file into a single line**:
  tr ‘\n’ ‘ ‘ < filename.txt

CHANGING FILE MODES AND PERMISSIONS IN LINUX

In Linux, **file permissions** and **modes** control the access rights to files and directories. Understanding and managing these permissions is essential for system security, user access control, and file management.

1. Understanding Linux File Permissions

In Linux, every file or directory has a set of permissions that define who can read, write, or execute the file. These permissions are defined for three types of users:

- **Owner (User)**: The user who owns the file.
- **Group**: A set of users associated with the file, typically for users with a common purpose.
- **Others**: All other users who are neither the owner nor part of the group.

Each of these categories has three types of permissions:

- **Read (r)**: Permission to view the contents of a file or list the contents of a directory.
- **Write (w)**: Permission to modify the contents of a file or add/remove files in a directory.
- **Execute (x)**: Permission to run a file as a program or script. For directories, it allows you to enter and search the directory.

2. Viewing File Permissions

To view the current permissions of a file or directory, you use the ls command with the -l (long listing) option:

- ls -l filename

Example output:

- -rwxr-xr–

Breakdown of -rwxr-xr--:

- The first character (-) indicates whether the file is a regular file (-), directory (d), or symbolic link (l).
- The next nine characters represent the permissions, broken down into three sets:
    1. **Owner permissions**: rwx (read, write, and execute)
    2. **Group permissions**: r-x (read and execute)
    3. **Other permissions**: r-- (read only)

3. Changing File Permissions Using chmod

The chmod command (short for "change mode") is used to modify file permissions. You can modify permissions in two ways: using **symbolic** or **numeric** modes.

Symbolic Mode

In symbolic mode, you use characters (r, w, x, and +, -, =) to change the permissions.

Syntax: chmod [who][operator][permission] filename

- **who**: Specifies the user category (owner u, group g, others o, or all a).
- **operator**: Specifies the change (+ to add permission, - to remove permission, = to set exactly the given permissions).
- **permission**: The permission you want to set (r for read, w for write, x for execute).

Examples:

- **Add execute permission to the owner**:
  chmod u+x file.txt
    1. **Remove write permission from others**:
       chmod o-w file.txt
    2. **Set the permissions to read and write for the owner, and read-only for the group and others**:
       chmod u=rw,g=r,o=r file.txt
    3. **Add execute permission to everyone (owner, group, and others)**:
       chmod a+x file.txt

4. **Set all permissions (read, write, and execute) for the owner, and read and execute for group and others:**

   chmod u=rwx,g=rx,o=rx file.txt

Numeric (Octal) Mode

In numeric mode, you represent the permissions as a three-digit number. Each permission type has a corresponding value:

- **Read (r)**: 4
- **Write (w)**: 2
- **Execute (x)**: 1

You sum these values for each category of users (owner, group, others). The first digit represents the owner's permissions, the second digit represents the group's permissions, and the third digit represents the others' permissions.

Syntax:

chmod [mode] filename

Where [mode] is a 3-digit number.

Examples: Set permissions to read, write, and execute for the owner, and read and execute for the group and others:

chmod 755 file.txt

1. **Breakdown:**

- 7: Owner can read, write, and execute (4 + 2 + 1 = 7)
- 5: Group can read and execute (4 + 1 = 5)
- 5: Others can read and execute (4 + 1 = 5)

  Set permission s to read and write for the owner, and read-only for group and others: chmod 644 file.txt

2. **Breakdown:**

- 6: Owner can read and write (4 + 2 = 6)
- 4: Group can read (4)
- 4: Others can read (4)

  Set permissions to read, write, and execute for everyone:

  chmod 777 file.txt

3. **Breakdown:**

- 7: Owner, group, and others can read, write, and execute.

4. Changing File Ownership Using chown

The chown (change owner) command is used to change the ownership of a file or directory. You can change both the owner and the group associated with a file.

Syntax:

chown [new_owner][:new_group] filename

- **new_owner**: The username of the new owner.
- **new_group** (optional): The new group to associate with the file.

- **filename**: The file or directory you want to change ownership of.

Examples:

- **Change the owner of the file to john**:
  chown john file.txt
- **Change both the owner to john and the group to admin**:
  chown john:admin file.txt
- **Change the group of the file to admin** (keeping the current owner):
  chown :admin file.txt

5. Changing Group Ownership Using chgrp

The chgrp command is used to change the group ownership of a file or directory.

Syntax:

chgrp new_group filename

Examples:

- **Change the group of the file to admin**:
  chgrp admin file.txt
- **Change the group of a directory and all its files recursively**:
  chgrp -R admin directory/

6. Special Permissions

In addition to the basic file permissions, Linux has **special permissions** that modify how the operating system manages files:

Setuid (Set User ID on Execution)

The **setuid** permission allows a user to execute a file with the permissions of the file's owner, rather than the permissions of the user running the file. This is commonly used for programs that need elevated privileges, like passwd.

- **Symbolic**: chmod u+s
- **Numeric**: Use the **4** as the first digit of the mode.

Example:

chmod u+s /path/to/program

Setgid (Set Group ID on Execution)

The **setgid** permission allows a file to be executed with the permissions of the file's group. For directories, it ensures that new files created within the directory inherit the group of the directory.

- **Symbolic**:
  chmod g+s
- **Numeric**: Use the **2** as the second digit of the mode.

Example:

chmod g+s /path/to/program

Sticky Bit

The **sticky bit** is often used on directories. When set on a directory, it ensures that only the file's owner, the directory's owner, or root can delete or rename files in the directory, even if others have write permissions.

- **Symbolic**: chmod +t
- **Numeric**: Use the **1** as the third digit of the mode.

Example:

chmod +t /path/to/directory

7. Recursively Changing Permissions

You can change the permissions of all files and directories within a directory recursively using the -R flag.

Example:

To set the permissions of all files and subdirectories in /mydir to 755:

chmod -R 755 /mydir

This will apply the permissions to all files and subdirectories in /mydir.

PAM AUTHENTICATION

PAM (Pluggable Authentication Module) is a framework used by Unix-like operating systems to integrate authentication services. It enables the separation of the authentication mechanism from the application, making it modular and flexible. This allows administrators to easily configure authentication methods without modifying application code. Let's break down how PAM works and its components in more detail.

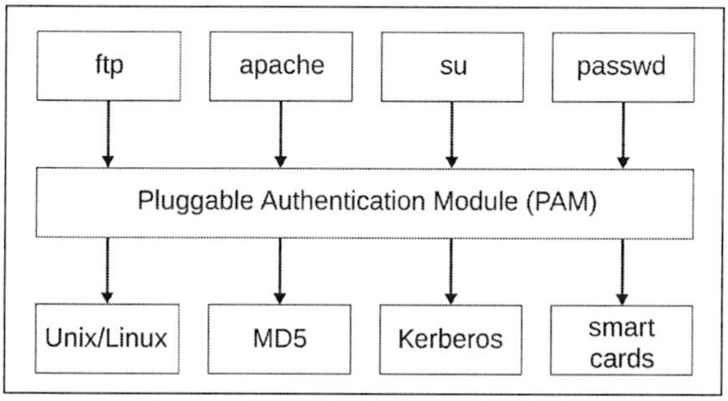

Fig 2.2: Pluggable Authentication Module

1. What Is PAM?

PAM is a standardized interface that allows applications to authenticate users in a system-agnostic way. It acts as an intermediary between applications (like SSH, login, su, etc.) and the underlying authentication mechanisms (like password-based authentication, fingerprint recognition, etc.). PAM provides a way to implement various forms of authentication without having to change the actual application.

2. How PAM Works

PAM operates by using a series of modules, each responsible for a specific aspect of authentication. These modules are loaded dynamically by PAM during an authentication attempt. PAM doesn't dictate how authentication should occur, but it allows administrators to specify the type of authentication via configuration files. Each authentication request goes through a series of stages defined by PAM configuration files. Depending on the configuration, different authentication modules are invoked for different types of checks.

3. Key Components of PAM

There are several key components involved in the PAM framework:

a. PAM Modules

Modules are the core building blocks in PAM. Each module is responsible for one part of the authentication process. Common PAM modules include:

- **pam_unix.so**: The most common module used for traditional UNIX authentication, which checks passwords against local system files like /etc/passwd or /etc/shadow.
- **pam_tally.so**: Used for tracking login attempts, including failed logins, and can lock accounts after a certain number of failed attempts.
- **pam_google_authenticator.so**: Used to enable two-factor authentication via Google Authenticator.
- **pam_ldap.so**: Provides authentication against an LDAP (Lightweight Directory Access Protocol) server.
- **pam_krb5.so**: Used for Kerberos authentication, commonly in enterprise environments.
- **pam_google_authenticator.so**: Supports two-factor authentication using Google Authenticator.

b. PAM Configuration Files

PAM's configuration files determine which authentication modules are invoked during the authentication process. These files are usually located in /etc/pam.d/ and are specific to each service (e.g., /etc/pam.d/sshd for SSH, /etc/pam.d/login for login, etc.). A typical configuration file includes:

- **Service**: Specifies which service the configuration applies to (e.g., sshd, login, sudo, etc.).
- **Module**: Specifies which PAM module to use (e.g., pam_unix.so).
- **Control Flags**: Define how the success or failure of a module affects the authentication process (e.g., required, requisite, sufficient, optional).

c. Control Flags

Control flags determine how PAM handles the success or failure of a module during the authentication process. There are several control flags:

- **required**: The module must succeed for authentication to continue, but even if it fails, other modules will be checked.
- **requisite**: The module must succeed, and if it fails, the authentication process stops immediately with failure.

- **sufficient**: If the module succeeds, authentication is considered successful, and no further modules are checked.
- **optional**: The module is not required, and its success or failure does not impact the overall authentication process.

d. PAM API

The PAM API is a programming interface that applications use to interact with PAM. This interface allows the application to request authentication services, such as verifying passwords, checking access control lists, and more. The API simplifies integrating multiple authentication methods into a single application.

4. PAM Authentication Process

When a user attempts to log in, the PAM system follows a series of steps to authenticate the user. Here's a simplified overview of the process:

1. **Application Request:** An application (e.g., SSH) makes an authentication request through the PAM API.
2. **Service Selection:** PAM identifies the service being invoked (e.g., sshd, sudo, etc.) and loads the appropriate PAM configuration file (e.g., /etc/pam.d/sshd).
3. **Module Execution:** PAM processes each module listed in the configuration file in sequence. Each module may perform different checks such as verifying passwords, using fingerprint scanners, or querying a central authentication service like LDAP.
4. **Control Flags Applied:** The control flags determine what happens after each module's success or failure. If a required module fails, the authentication attempt continues but may ultimately fail if no other modules override this failure. If a sufficient module succeeds, the authentication process will consider the user authenticated and stop checking further modules.
5. **Authentication Result:** Based on the modules' outcome, PAM either grants or denies access. If all required checks pass, the user is authenticated and allowed access.

5. Common PAM Modules and Their Functions

- **pam_unix.so**: Handles traditional UNIX password authentication. It checks the user's password against /etc/passwd and /etc/shadow.
- **pam_ldap.so**: This module allows authentication against an LDAP server, often used in organizations with centralized user management.
- **pam_google_authenticator.so**: Implements two-factor authentication by integrating with Google Authenticator. This can be used as an additional security layer on top of password authentication.
- **pam_tally.so**: Tracks login attempts and can lock accounts after multiple failed login attempts.
- **pam_krb5.so**: Enables Kerberos-based authentication, typically used in environments with centralized authentication (such as Active Directory or MIT Kerberos).

- **pam_pwquality.so**: Ensures password complexity policies are met by requiring passwords to adhere to certain standards (e.g., minimum length, mix of characters).
- **pam_shells.so**: Allows login only if the user's shell is listed in /etc/shells.

6. Advantages of PAM

- **Modular and Flexible**: PAM allows the easy addition of new authentication mechanisms without modifying the application code.
- **Centralized Configuration**: Authentication methods can be configured centrally, allowing for simpler management and consistency across services.
- **Customizable**: It supports various authentication methods, from simple password-based authentication to more complex methods like biometrics, smart cards, or two-factor authentication.
- **Separation of Concerns**: By abstracting authentication away from applications, PAM allows system administrators to change authentication methods without having to alter the applications themselves.

7. PAM Example Configuration (for SSH)

Here is a simple example of what the configuration might look like for SSH authentication, located in /etc/pam.d/sshd:

```
# Authentication section
auth    required    pam_unix.so
auth    requisite   pam_google_authenticator.so
# Account management section
account required    pam_unix.so
# Password management section
password required   pam_unix.so
# Session management section
session required    pam_unix.so
```

In this example:

- **Authentication (auth)**: The system first checks the UNIX password via pam_unix.so, and then checks for Google Authenticator for two-factor authentication.
- **Account (account)**: This section checks account-related restrictions (e.g., expiration).
- **Password (password)**: Manages password changes.
- **Session (session)**: Handles session-related tasks like setting environment variables.

INTRODUCTION TO COMMON SYSTEM CONFIGURATION FILES & LOG FILES

In a Unix-like operating system, configuration files and log files are essential for the system's operation and management. These files serve various purposes such as configuring system settings, managing user permissions, logging events, troubleshooting, and auditing activities. Let's break down the different types of common system configuration files and log files you'll encounter in these systems.

1. System Configuration Files

System configuration files control how the operating system, services, and applications behave. They are generally text files that are stored in standard directories, most commonly /etc, but also in other places depending on the configuration's scope (such as user-specific configurations).

a. /etc/passwd

- **Purpose**: The /etc/passwd file contains essential information about user accounts. It defines user details such as the username, user ID (UID), group ID (GID), home directory, shell, and password information (although passwords are typically stored in /etc/shadow now for security).
- **Example Entry:**

  ruby

  john:x:1001:1001:John Doe:/home/john:/bin/
- **Explanation**:

  john: Username

  x: Placeholder for the password (actual password stored in /etc/shadow)

  1001: User ID (UID)

  1001: Group ID (GID)

  John Doe: GECOS field (full name)

  /home/john: Home directory

  /bin/: Login shell

b. /etc/shadow

- **Purpose**: The /etc/shadow file contains the encrypted password information for users. Unlike /etc/passwd, which is world-readable, /etc/shadow has restricted access because it stores sensitive password data.
- **Example Entry:**

  john:6randomsalt$encryptedpasswordhash:17955:0:99999:7:::
- **Explanation**:

  john: Username

  6randomsalt$encryptedpasswordhash: The password hash (using SHA-512, indicated by 6)

  17955: Last password change date (in days since January 1, 1970)

  0: Minimum number of days between password changes

  99999: Maximum number of days before password must be changed

  7: Number of days before a password expires to warn the user

c. /etc/group

- **Purpose**: The /etc/group file defines the groups on the system and the members of each group. It allows you to assign users to various groups, giving them different permissions.

- **Example Entry:**
  developers:x:1002:alice,bob
- **Explanation:**
  developers: Group name
  x: Placeholder for the password field (not often used)
  1002: Group ID (GID)
  alice,bob: Members of the group

d. /etc/fstab

- **Purpose:** This file defines the disk partitions, mount points, and file systems used by the operating system. It determines which storage devices are automatically mounted during system boot.
- **Example Entry:**
  /dev/sda1 / ext4 defaults 1 1
- **Explanation:**
  /dev/sda1: Device name
  /: Mount point (root file system)
  ext4: File system type
  defaults: Mount options
  1: File system check order
  1: Used by fsck for checking disk health

e. /etc/hostname

- **Purpose:** This file contains the system's hostname (the name of the machine in the network). The system uses this information to identify itself on a network.
- **Example Entry:**
  myhostname

f. /etc/network/interfaces (Debian-based systems) or /etc/sysconfig/network-scripts/ (RedHat-based systems)

- **Purpose:** This file (or directory) contains network configuration settings. In Debian-based systems like Ubuntu, it defines the static or dynamic IP configuration for network interfaces.
- **Example Entry (Debian-based):**
  auto eth0
  iface eth0 inet dhcp

2. Common Log Files

Log files are records of system activities, application events, errors, and other operational data. They are vital for troubleshooting, monitoring, and auditing. Log files are typically stored in the /var/log/ directory in Linux systems.

a. /var/log/syslog (Debian-based systems) or /var/log/messages (Red-Hat-based systems)

- **Purpose**: This file contains general system messages, including boot logs, kernel logs, and system daemons. It's essential for diagnosing system-level issues.
- **Example Entry:**

  Mar 18 15:32:15 myhostname systemd[1]: Starting Daily Cleanup of Temporary Directories...

b. /var/log/auth.log (Debian-based systems) or /var/log/secure (Red-Hat-based systems)

- **Purpose**: This log file records authentication attempts, including successful logins, failed login attempts, and other security-related events such as sudo usage.
- **Example Entry:**

  Mar 18 15:33:15 myhostname sshd[12345]: Accepted password for john from 192.168.1.100 port 22 ssh2

c. /var/log/kern.log

- **Purpose**: This log file records kernel messages. It's crucial for debugging low-level system issues, such as hardware or kernel module problems.
- **Example Entry:**

  Mar 18 15:35:01 myhostname kernel: [12345.678901] eth0: Link is up

d. /var/log/dmesg

- **Purpose**: The dmesg log file contains messages from the kernel ring buffer. It includes information about the boot process, hardware detection, and device initialization.
- **Example Entry:**

  [0.000000] Booting Linux 5.4.0-80-generic...

  [0.678901] ACPI: SSDT 0x00000000B101A000 00035C (v01 DELL CPU1PM 00000001 INTL 20130117)

e. /var/log/cron

- **Purpose**: This file logs events related to scheduled tasks, typically run via cron jobs. It shows when cron jobs were executed or if they failed.
- **Example Entry:**

  Mar 18 15:40:00 myhostname CROND[12346]: (root) CMD (run-parts /etc/cron.daily)

f. /var/log/boot.log

- **Purpose**: This log file records the output of the boot process. It can be useful for diagnosing boot issues and system startup problems.
- **Example Entry:**

  Mar 18 15:30:12 myhostname systemd[1]: Started Journal Service.

g. /var/log/mail.log

- **Purpose**: This log file contains records related to the mail server's operation, including the sending and receiving of email messages.
- **Example Entry:**
  Mar 18 15:30:50 myhostname postfix/smtpd[12347]: connect from unknown[192.168.1.100]

h. /var/log/httpd/ (Apache web server) or /var/log// (web server)

- **Purpose**: These directories contain logs for web server activity. They typically include access logs and error logs, recording details about requests to the server, errors, and other related activities.
- **Example Entry from Apache's access log:**

  192.168.1.100 - - [18/Mar/2025:15:42:11 +0000] "GET /index.html HTTP/1.1" 200 2326

i. /var/log/apt/ (Debian-based systems)

- **Purpose**: These logs contain records of package installations, removals, and updates performed using the APT package manager in Debian-based systems.
- **Example Entry:**

  Log started: 2025-03-18 15:40:00

j. /var/log/ufw.log (Uncomplicated Firewall)

- **Purpose**: This log file records firewall activity when using UFW. It logs allowed or denied network connections based on firewall rules.
- **Example Entry:**

  Mar 18 15:42:12 myhostname kernel: [12456.678901] UFW BLOCK IN=eth0 OUT= MAC=00:1a:2b:3c:4d:5e:00:1f:4e:5d:6c:7f:08:00 SRC=192.168.1.10 DST=192.168.1.20

CONFIGURING NETWORKING

Configuring Networking in a Unix-like system involves setting up how the system interacts with other machines over a network. Networking configuration is essential for both local and remote communications, as well as for enabling various network services like web servers, email servers, file sharing, and more. Proper configuration can ensure that the system is correctly connected to the internet or a local network, and can communicate with other devices securely and efficiently.

Below, I'll break down various methods and files used in configuring networking in Unix-like operating systems, with a focus on Linux. While the process might vary slightly between distributions (such as Debian/Ubuntu and RedHat/CentOS), the underlying concepts are similar.

1. Understanding Networking Components

Before diving into configuration, it's important to understand the fundamental components involved in networking:

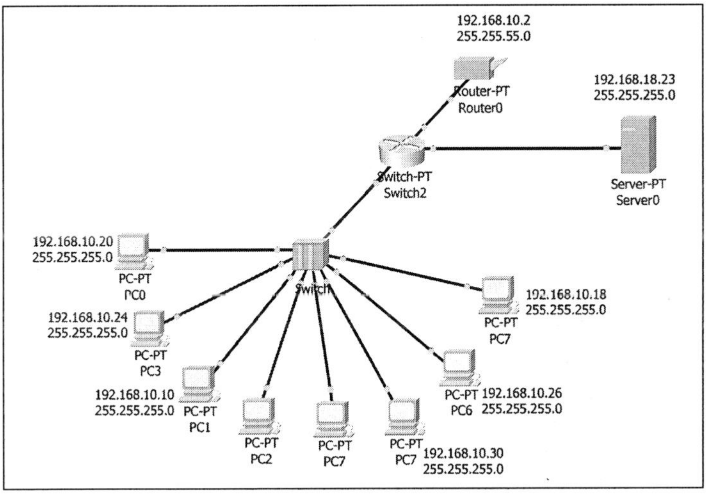

***Fig 2.3:** Configuring Networking*

- **IP Address:** A unique identifier assigned to each device on a network. It can be IPv4 (e.g., 192.168.1.2) or IPv6 (e.g., fe80::abcd:1234:5678:90ef).
- **Subnet Mask:** Defines the network portion of the IP address and the size of the network. For example, 255.255.255.0 defines a subnet with 254 usable addresses.
- **Gateway:** The device that routes traffic from your local network to external networks, typically your router.
- **DNS (Domain Name System):** Resolves domain names (e.g., www.example.com) to IP addresses.
- **Network Interfaces:** Physical or virtual network devices (such as Ethernet eth0 or wireless wlan0) through which the system communicates over the network.

2. Common Network Configuration Files

The specific files used for network configuration can vary depending on the system and distribution, but here are the most common ones.

a. /etc/network/interfaces (Debian/Ubuntu-based systems)

This file is used to configure network interfaces (such as Ethernet or Wi-Fi) on Debian-based systems. It defines static IP settings, DHCP configuration, and other parameters.

Example:

```
# Static IP configuration for eth0 (Ethernet interface)
iface eth0 inet static
  address 192.168.1.10
  netmask 255.255.255.0
  gateway 192.168.1.1
  dns-nameservers 8.8.8.8 8.8.4.4
# DHCP configuration for wlan0 (Wi-Fi interface)
iface wlan0 inet dhcp
```

Explanation:

- **iface eth0 inet static:** Defines that the eth0 interface uses a static IP address.
- **address:** The static IP address assigned to the interface.
- **netmask:** The subnet mask for the network.
- **gateway:** The default gateway for the network.
- **dns-nameservers:** DNS servers to resolve domain names.
- **iface wlan0 inet dhcp:** Configures the wlan0 interface to obtain an IP address dynamically from a DHCP server.

b. /etc/sysconfig/network-scripts/ifcfg-* (RedHat/CentOS-based systems)

In RedHat-based systems (including CentOS, Fedora, and RHEL), network configurations are stored in the /etc/sysconfig/network-scripts/ directory. Each network interface (such as eth0) will have a corresponding configuration file.

Example:

```
# /etc/sysconfig/network-scripts/ifcfg-eth0
DEVICE=eth0
BOOTPROTO=static
ONBOOT=yes
IPADDR=192.168.1.10
NETMASK=255.255.255.0
GATEWAY=192.168.1.1
DNS1=8.8.8.8
DNS2=8.8.4.4
```

Explanation:

- **DEVICE=eth0:** Specifies the network interface (eth0 in this case).
- **BOOTPROTO=static:** Configures the interface to use a static IP address.
- **ONBOOT=yes:** Ensures the interface is started automatically at boot time.
- **IPADDR:** Specifies the static IP address for the interface.
- **NETMASK:** The subnet mask for the interface.
- **GATEWAY:** The default gateway for routing traffic outside the local network.
- **DNS1 and DNS2:** DNS servers to resolve domain names.

c. /etc/hostname

This file contains the system's hostname, which is used to identify the machine on the network.

Example:

```
myhostname
```

- **myhostname:** The name assigned to the system on the network.

d. /etc/resolv.conf

The resolv.conf file defines DNS servers that the system will use for domain name resolution. It is used by applications like ping or curl to resolve domain names into IP addresses.

Example:

nameserver 8.8.8.8

nameserver 8.8.4.4

- **nameserver:** The DNS servers to query when resolving domain names.

e. /etc/hosts

This file maps IP addresses to hostnames. It's used for local name resolution without querying a DNS server. It's typically used for mapping localhost and private network addresses.

Example:

127.0.0.1 localhost

192.168.1.10 myhostname. local

- 127.0.0.1: The loopback address for the local machine.
- 192.168.1.10 myhostname. local: A local machine with IP 192.168.1.10 and hostname myhostname. local.

3. Dynamic Host Configuration Protocol (DHCP)

In many cases, especially for client machines, dynamic IP address allocation is used through DHCP. DHCP automatically assigns IP addresses, subnet masks, gateways, and DNS servers to a client machine without manual configuration.

a. Using DHCP in Configuration

In Debian/Ubuntu, the /etc/network/interfaces file can be configured to use DHCP with the following:

iface eth0 inet dhcp

In RedHat/CentOS, the /etc/sysconfig/network-scripts/ifcfg-eth0 file would have:

BOOTPROTO=dhcp

ONBOOT=yes

b. DHCP Server Configuration

A system acting as a DHCP server (often a router or dedicated server) will have its own configuration file to manage how IPs are assigned to clients. In Linux, dhcpd.conf is the file used to configure the DHCP server (if running isc-dhcp-server or similar software).

Example:

```
subnet 192.168.1.0 netmask 255.255.255.0 {
 range 192.168.1.50 192.168.1.100;
 option routers 192.168.1.1;
 option domain-name-servers 8.8.8.8, 8.8.4.4;
}
```

This configuration provides IP addresses in the range 192.168.1.50 to 192.168.1.100, with 192.168.1.1 as the gateway and Google's DNS servers.

4. Configuring Static IPs

Static IP addresses are manually assigned to network interfaces, ensuring the system always uses the same IP address. This is useful for servers that need a consistent address.

- In Debian/Ubuntu, configure the static IP in /etc/network/interfaces as described earlier.
- In RedHat/CentOS, configure the static IP in /etc/sysconfig/network-scripts/ifcfg-eth0.

For example:

IPADDR=192.168.1.10

NETMASK=255.255.255.0

GATEWAY=192.168.1.1

5. Network Interface Commands

Once the network configuration is set, you can use several commands to manage and check the network status.

- **ip command:** Used to show or manipulate routing, devices, and tunnels.

  Example: ip addr show (shows IP addresses)
- **ifconfig command:** Older tool for configuring network interfaces (though deprecated in favor of ip).

  Example: ifconfig eth0 (shows details for eth0)
- **ping command:** Used to check connectivity to another device.

  Example: ping 8.8.8.8 (ping Google's DNS)
- **netstat or ss command:** Used to display network connections, routing tables, interface statistics, etc.

  Example: netstat -tuln (shows open ports)
- **systemctl command:** Used to manage network services.

  Example: systemctl restart networking (restart networking services in some systems)
- **nmcli command (NetworkManager CLI):** Used on systems that use NetworkManager to configure networking.

  Example: nmcli connection show (list network connections)

6. Configuring Wireless Networking

For wireless networking, configuring interfaces like wlan0 differs slightly from wired interfaces. You can configure the wireless interface through the same network configuration files, but you may also use tools like iwconfig (for wireless settings) or nmcli (if NetworkManager is used).

Example (Debian/Ubuntu):

```
iface wlan0 inet dhcp
   wpa-ssid "your_network_name"
   wpa-psk "your_password"
```

7. Network Troubleshooting Tools

If you encounter network issues, several tools can help diagnose the problem:

- **ping:** Test connectivity.
- **traceroute:** Identify the route packets take to a destination.
- **nslookup or dig:** Query DNS to verify if domain names are being resolved correctly.
- **tcpdump:** Capture network traffic for deeper analysis.
- **netstat:** Display network connections and statistics.

TCP/IP NETWORKING AND ROUTING

TCP/IP (Transmission Control Protocol/Internet Protocol) is the fundamental suite of protocols that drives communication across modern networks, including the Internet. It defines how data is transmitted and routed between different devices across a network, from small local area networks (LANs) to the vast global network of the Internet.

1. Basics of TCP/IP Networking

TCP/IP is a protocol suite that consists of several protocols designed to manage communication over a network. At its core, TCP/IP is divided into four layers, each of which plays a specific role in the process of transmitting and routing data between devices.

TCP/IP Layers

1. Application Layer (Layer 4)

- **Purpose:** This layer handles high-level protocols that are used by applications to communicate over the network. It provides services like email, file transfer, and web browsing.
- **Common Protocols:**
  - HTTP/HTTPS (HyperText Transfer Protocol/Secure) for web traffic.
  - SMTP (Simple Mail Transfer Protocol) for email.
  - FTP (File Transfer Protocol) for file transfers.
  - DNS (Domain Name System) for resolving domain names to IP addresses.

2. Transport Layer (Layer 3)

- **Purpose:** This layer is responsible for end-to-end communication and data integrity. It establishes, maintains, and terminates connections between devices.
- **Key Protocols:**
  - **TCP (Transmission Control Protocol):** A connection-oriented protocol that ensures reliable, error-free transmission of data by establishing a connection between sender and receiver.
  - **UDP (User Datagram Protocol):** A connectionless protocol that sends data without establishing a connection, used when speed is more important than reliability (e.g., video streaming, online gaming).
- **TCP vs. UDP:**
  - TCP guarantees that data is delivered correctly and in order, with error checking and correction mechanisms.

- UDP does not guarantee delivery or order, making it faster but less reliable.

3. Internet Layer (Layer 2)

- **Purpose:** This layer is responsible for logical addressing and routing of data between networks.
- **Key Protocols:**
  - **IP (Internet Protocol):** Provides logical addressing (IP addresses) for devices on the network. There are two versions:
    - **IPv4 (Internet Protocol version 4):** Uses 32-bit addresses, written in dotted-decimal format (e.g., 192.168.1.1).
    - **IPv6 (Internet Protocol version 6):** Uses 128-bit addresses, written in hexadecimal (e.g., fe80::abcd:1234:5678:90ef), to accommodate the growing number of devices connected to the Internet.

4. Link Layer (Layer 1)

- **Purpose:** This layer handles physical addressing, and how data is transmitted on the physical network medium (e.g., Ethernet, Wi-Fi).
- **Key Protocols:**
  - **Ethernet:** A protocol used in wired LANs for communication between devices.
  - **Wi-Fi:** A wireless networking protocol for communication over wireless networks.

How Data is Transferred in TCP/IP

When a device (e.g., a computer) sends data to another device over a network, the process involves several steps:

1. **Application Layer:** The application generates data (e.g., an email or a webpage request).
2. **Transport Layer:** TCP or UDP is used to break the data into smaller segments and add necessary information such as sequence numbers (TCP) or ports (both TCP and UDP).
3. **Internet Layer:** The IP protocol adds the source and destination IP addresses to each segment, allowing the data to be routed across different networks.
4. **Link Layer:** The data is packaged into frames and transmitted over the physical network medium (e.g., Ethernet or Wi-Fi).

Each layer adds its own header (metadata) to the data, which allows the data to be correctly routed, delivered, and reassembled at the destination.

2. TCP/IP Routing

Routing is the process of forwarding data packets between devices on different networks. Routers, which are network devices or software that manage routing, play a crucial role in determining the best path for data to travel from its source to its destination.

How Routing Works

1. **Routing Tables:** Routers maintain routing tables that store information about the paths to various network destinations. These tables are used to determine how to forward packets based on the destination IP address.

   Example Routing Table:

Destination Network	Netmask	Gateway	Interface
192.168.1.0	255.255.255.0	192.168.1.1	eth0
10.0.0.0	255.0.0.0	192.168.1.254	eth1
0.0.0.0	0.0.0.0	192.168.1.1	eth0

   - **Destination Network:** The network that the router will forward packets to.
   - **Netmask:** Defines the size of the destination network (helps the router match the destination network).
   - **Gateway:** The next-hop IP address (usually another router or device on the network).
   - **Interface:** The network interface through which the router sends packets.
2. **Routing Decisions:** When a router receives a packet, it checks the packet's destination IP address and compares it to the entries in its routing table. The router then forwards the packet to the appropriate next hop.
   - If the destination IP matches an entry in the routing table, the router forwards the packet to the corresponding gateway or device.
   - If the packet's destination IP address is not in the router's local network (or subnet), the router forwards the packet to the default gateway (if configured).
3. **Static vs. Dynamic Routing:**
   - **Static Routing:** The routing table is manually configured by network administrators. Routes do not change unless the administrator updates them.
   - **Dynamic Routing:** Routers automatically adjust their routing tables based on network topology changes. Dynamic routing protocols like OSPF (Open Shortest Path First), RIP (Routing Information Protocol), and BGP (Border Gateway Protocol) are used for this purpose.

Routing and IP Addressing

IP Addressing and subnetting are essential concepts for routing.

- **IP Addressing:** Each device on a network must have a unique IP address to be identified by routers and other devices.
- **Subnetting:** Networks are divided into subnets to improve routing efficiency and security. A subnet mask is used to define which portion of the IP address represents the network and which part represents the host.

Example: An IP address like 192.168.1.10 with a subnet mask of 255.255.255.0 means the network portion is 192.168.1 and the host portion is 10. This allows devices on the same network (i.e., 192.168.1.x) to communicate without needing routing.

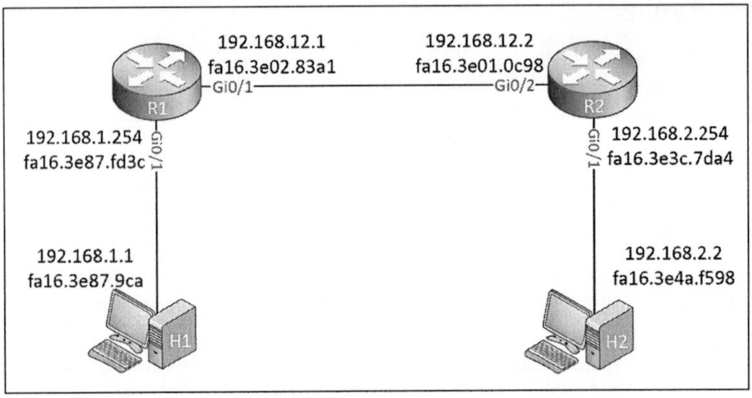

***Fig 2.4:** Routing and IP Addressing*

Types of Routing

1. **Direct Routing (or Directly Connected Networks):**
   - If the source and destination devices are on the same network, the packet is forwarded directly, without the need for routing.
   - This is known as direct routing, and no router is needed.
2. **Indirect Routing (via Routers):**
   - If the source and destination devices are on different networks, routers come into play to forward packets across networks.
   - The packet may pass through several routers before reaching the destination.

Example of Routing in Action

Consider the following network setup:

- **Device A:** IP 192.168.1.2 (on the 192.168.1.0/24 network)
- **Device B:** IP 10.0.0.2 (on the 10.0.0.0/8 network)

If Device A needs to send a packet to Device B, but the two devices are on different networks, the following occurs:

1. **Device A checks its routing table:** It sees that 192.168.1.0/24 is a directly connected network, but 10.0.0.0/8 is not, so it forwards the packet to its default gateway (router).
2. **The router checks its routing table:** The router has an entry for 10.0.0.0/8, so it forwards the packet to the appropriate network interface that connects to the 10.0.0.0/8 network.
3. **Device B receives the packet:** Device B's IP address matches the destination, and the packet is successfully delivered.

CONNECTING TO THE INTERNET

Connecting to the internet involves a combination of hardware, software, protocols, and configuration steps to ensure that a computer or device can communicate with other devices across the internet. This process allows for data transmission between local devices (e.g., computers, smartphones) and remote servers hosting websites, applications, and services.

In this in-depth explanation, we will walk through the different layers involved in connecting to the internet, covering everything from basic network setup to advanced configuration and troubleshooting.

1. Internet Connectivity Overview

To connect to the internet, a device must first establish a connection to a local network, which is in turn connected to an internet service provider (ISP). The process involves several components:

1. **Device:** The machine that wants to connect to the internet (e.g., computer, smartphone).
2. **Network Interface:** The physical or virtual interface used for network communication (e.g., Ethernet, Wi-Fi).
3. **Modem:** A device that converts digital signals to analog signals and vice versa, allowing communication over phone lines, coaxial cables, or fiber-optic cables.
4. **Router:** A device that routes traffic between devices on the local network and external networks (including the internet).
5. **ISP:** Internet Service Provider, which provides access to the broader internet.
6. **Internet Backbone:** The high-speed data highways that interconnect ISPs and provide global connectivity.

2. Types of Internet Connections

There are several types of internet connections, each with its own method of connecting a device to the internet:

a. Wired Connections

1. Ethernet (LAN)

- **Description:** This is the most common method for connecting devices to the internet via physical cables.
- **Setup:** The device (e.g., computer) is connected to a router or modem via an Ethernet cable (e.g., Cat 5, Cat 6).
- **Advantages:** Faster, more stable, and secure compared to wireless connections.
- **Disadvantages:** Limited mobility due to physical cables.

2. DSL (Digital Subscriber Line)

- **Description:** DSL provides internet access over standard telephone lines.
- **Setup:** A DSL modem is connected to the telephone line and the router to provide internet access.
- **Advantages:** Widely available, stable connection.
- **Disadvantages:** Slower speeds compared to fiber-optic connections; performance degrades with distance from the DSL exchange.

3. Cable Broadband

- **Description:** Uses coaxial cables (like cable TV) to deliver high-speed internet.

- **Setup:** A cable modem connects to the coaxial cable, and the router shares the connection with local devices.
- **Advantages:** Faster speeds than DSL, reliable.
- **Disadvantages:** Shared bandwidth with other users in the neighborhood may cause slowdowns during peak hours.

4. Fiber-Optic Internet (FTTH/FTTP)

- **Description:** Provides internet over fiber-optic cables, which offer extremely high-speed connections.
- **Setup:** Fiber-optic cables run directly to the home or office, connecting to a modem or gateway device.
- **Advantages:** Ultra-fast speeds, low latency, high reliability.
- **Disadvantages:** Limited availability in some regions.

b. Wireless Connections

1. Wi-Fi

- **Description:** A wireless local area network (WLAN) standard that allows devices to connect to the internet via a router.
- **Setup:** Devices connect to the router's Wi-Fi network (using radio waves) after entering the correct SSID and password.
- **Advantages:** Convenient, no cables required.
- **Disadvantages:** Slower speeds compared to wired connections, range limitations, and potential security risks.

2. Mobile Broadband (3G/4G/5G)

- **Description:** Internet access via cellular networks (using mobile data).
- **Setup:** A mobile device (smartphone) or mobile hotspot device connects to the network using cellular towers.
- **Advantages:** Available in most locations, especially when traveling.
- **Disadvantages:** Data limits, slower speeds in some areas, dependent on cellular coverage.

3. Satellite Internet

- **Description:** Internet access via satellite signals.
- **Setup:** A satellite dish is installed at the user's location, and signals are sent to and received from a satellite orbiting Earth.
- **Advantages:** Available in remote locations where other options are unavailable.
- **Disadvantages:** High latency, weather conditions can affect performance, expensive.

3. Configuring Internet Access on a Device

Once a network connection (wired or wireless) is established, the device needs to be configured to communicate with the internet. This involves both the network configuration (IP settings, DNS, etc.) and establishing communication with the router and ISP.

a. Network Configuration

1. **Obtain an IP Address:** Devices on a network need an IP address to identify themselves. This can be assigned in two ways:
   - **Dynamic IP (DHCP):** Most home networks use DHCP, which automatically assigns an IP address to each device. This is the most common method for configuring network access.
   - **Static IP:** Some devices may need a fixed IP address (e.g., servers). In this case, the device's IP address, subnet mask, and gateway are manually set.
2. **Configure DNS Servers:** DNS servers resolve domain names (e.g., www.example.com) into IP addresses. The device typically uses the DNS servers provided by the ISP or a third-party service like Google DNS (8.8.8.8, 8.8.4.4) or Cloudflare (1.1.1.1).
3. **Gateway Setup:** The gateway is the device that connects the local network to external networks (including the internet). It's typically the router or modem provided by the ISP.
4. **Wi-Fi Setup (for wireless connections):**
   - Enable Wi-Fi on the device.
   - Scan for available wireless networks (SSIDs).
   - Select the correct network and enter the Wi-Fi password.

b. Network Interface Configuration in Linux

On Linux-based systems, network configuration can be done manually via the command line or through network manager tools. Common methods include:

- **Using NetworkManager:** nmcli command-line tool is used to configure network interfaces.

  nmcli dev wifi connect "SSID_NAME" password "PASSWORD"
- **Static IP Setup:** Modify the /etc/network/interfaces file (for Debian/Ubuntu systems):

  ```
  iface eth0 inet static
    address 192.168.1.100
    netmask 255.255.255.0
    gateway 192.168.1.1
    dns-nameservers 8.8.8.8 8.8.4.4
  ```
- **DHCP Setup:** By default, most systems will be configured to obtain IP addresses dynamically via DHCP. To use DHCP with nmcli:

  nmcli con mod "Ethernet" ipv4.method auto

c. Router Configuration

The router typically handles multiple tasks:

- **Routing:** Forwarding data packets between devices on the local network and external networks (the internet).
- **NAT (Network Address Translation):** A technique to allow multiple devices on a local network to share a single public IP address provided by the ISP.

- **Firewall:** Protecting the network from unauthorized access or threats from external sources.
- **DHCP Server:** Assigning local IP addresses to devices on the network.

To configure the router, users generally access its administrative interface through a web browser using the router's IP address (often 192.168.1.1 or 192.168.0.1).

4. Internet Protocols and Addressing

The internet relies on several key protocols and addressing schemes to ensure that data can be sent and received correctly. Here are some important concepts:

1. **IP Addressing:** Every device on the internet requires a unique IP address, which identifies the source and destination of data packets. IP addresses are either IPv4 (32-bit) or IPv6 (128-bit).
   - IPv4:. 192.168.1.10
   - IPv6: 2001:db8::1
2. **Subnetting:** Subnetting divides an IP network into smaller subnetworks (subnets). Each subnet has its own network address, which helps improve routing efficiency.
3. **TCP/IP:** The suite of protocols that governs internet communication, including:
   - **TCP:** Ensures reliable transmission of data (error checking, sequencing).
   - **UDP:** Provides faster, connectionless transmission (e.g., video streaming).
4. **DNS:** The Domain Name System translates human-readable domain names (e.g., www.example.com) into IP addresses (e.g., 192.168.1.1), allowing devices to locate services on the internet.
5. **HTTP/HTTPS:** Protocols used for web browsing. HTTP is unencrypted, while HTTPS is encrypted for security.

5. Troubleshooting Internet Connectivity

If a device cannot connect to the internet, several steps can help troubleshoot the issue:

1. **Check Physical Connections:** Ensure all cables are securely connected and that the router or modem is powered on.
2. **Verify IP Configuration:**
   - On Linux, use ip addr to check IP addresses.
   - On Windows, use ipconfig.
   - Ensure the device is assigned a valid IP address.
3. **Ping the Router:** Test the connection to the router using ping (e.g., ping 192.168.1.1).
4. **Ping External Addresses:** Test the connection to external sites, such as Google DNS (8.8.8.8), using ping to ensure the device can reach the internet.
5. **Check DNS:** If the device can ping IP addresses but not domain names, the issue might be with the DNS configuration. Try using a different DNS server (e.g., Google's DNS: 8.8.8.8).
6. **Router Reboot:** Reboot the router or modem to reset the connection.

SYSTEM ADMINISTRATION TO BACKUP AND RESTORE PROCEDURES & STRATEGIES FOR KEEPING A SECURE SERVER

System administration involves maintaining the proper operation and health of servers, ensuring they function efficiently and securely. Two critical aspects of system administration are backup and restore procedures and strategies for keeping a secure server. A server is typically a key resource that stores critical data and provides services to users. Thus, ensuring its reliability, integrity, and security is essential. In this in-depth explanation, we will break down both backup and restore procedures as well as server security strategies, explaining how these practices help system administrators safeguard data and protect their infrastructure.

1. Backup and Restore Procedures

Backups are copies of data or system configurations that are made to prevent data loss in case of system failures, disasters, or malicious attacks. A well-planned backup and restore strategy is vital for business continuity. There are different types of backups, various methods for performing them, and ways to restore data when necessary.

A. Types of Backups

1. Full Backup

- **Description:** A full backup involves copying all the files and data from the system or specified directories to the backup medium. This provides a complete snapshot of the system at a particular time.
- **Advantages:** Quick and easy to restore because everything is in one place.
- Disadvantages: Time-consuming and requires significant storage space.

2. Incremental Backup

- **Description:** Only the data that has changed since the last backup (whether full or incremental) is backed up. It keeps track of changes by using timestamps.
- Advantages: Faster than full backups and uses less storage space.
- **Disadvantages:** Restoration is slower, as it requires combining the most recent full backup with all subsequent incremental backups.

3. Differential Backup

- **Description:** Similar to incremental backups, but it saves all data that has changed since the last full backup. For example, if the last full backup was made on Monday, the differential backup on Wednesday will include all changes since Monday.
- **Advantages:** Faster restore times compared to incremental backups, as only the last full backup and the most recent differential backup are needed.
- **Disadvantages:** Requires more storage space than incremental backups, as it includes all changes since the last full backup.

4. Mirror Backup

- **Description:** A mirror backup creates an exact copy of the original data (a mirror image). Any changes made to the source data are reflected immediately in the backup.

- **Advantages:** Always provides the most up-to-date copy of data.
- **Disadvantages:** If data is deleted or corrupted, it will be mirrored in the backup as well.

B. Backup Methods

1. Local Backups

- Backups are stored on physical storage devices connected directly to the server, such as external hard drives, Network Attached Storage (NAS), or tape drives.
- **Advantages:** Fast and easy to manage.
- **Disadvantages:** Vulnerable to physical damage or theft. It can be costly to scale for large amounts of data.

2. Cloud Backups

- Data is backed up to cloud-based storage services, such as AWS S3, Google Cloud Storage, or specialized backup services like Backblaze or Acronis.
- **Advantages:** Off-site storage for disaster recovery, scalability, and easy access from anywhere.
- **Disadvantages:** Dependent on internet connectivity; can be expensive, especially for large volumes of data.

3. Hybrid Backups

- A combination of both local and cloud-based backups. This strategy ensures that the data is both locally available for fast recovery and safely stored off-site for disaster recovery.
- **Advantages:** Provides the best of both worlds with quick local recovery and remote disaster recovery.
- **Disadvantages:** Can be complex to manage and more expensive.

C. Backup Scheduling

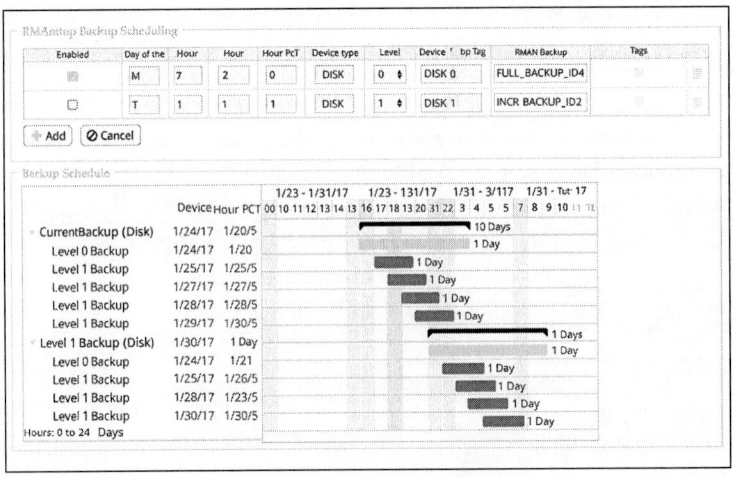

Fig 2.5: Backup Scheduling

A regular backup schedule is critical to ensure data is consistently protected. Typical strategies include:

- Daily incremental backups (to capture only the most recent changes).
- Weekly full backups (to capture everything, ensuring that there's always a comprehensive backup available).
- Monthly off-site backups (for long-term archival storage).

Backup schedules should be adapted based on the criticality of the data, business needs, and the resources available.

D. Restore Procedures

Restore procedures ensure that you can recover your data when disaster strikes or corruption occurs.

1. Restoration Types

- **Full Restoration:** The complete restoration of data from the most recent full backup.
- **Partial Restoration:** Restoring only certain files or directories rather than the entire system.
- **Granular Restoration:** Restoring individual items, like emails, specific files, or application data, from a backup set.

2. Testing Restore Procedures

- Backup systems must be tested periodically to ensure they work as expected. This includes verifying backup integrity, testing restore times, and ensuring data consistency after restoration.
- **Backup Validation:** Check that backups are completed successfully without errors, and ensure that files are not corrupted.
- **Simulate Disaster Recovery:** Regularly simulate recovery scenarios to verify that the restore process is fast and efficient.

3. Disaster Recovery Plan (DRP)

- Having a documented disaster recovery plan is essential. This plan should specify what to do in case of data loss or system failure, the steps for restoring systems from backups, and the roles and responsibilities of the IT team during a disaster.

2. Strategies for Keeping a Secure Server

Securing a server is an ongoing process that requires layers of protection to guard against internal and external threats. Below are several essential strategies for securing servers:

a. Physical Security

1. Server Room Access Control

- Ensure physical security by limiting access to the server room. Use access control mechanisms like biometric scanners, key cards, and security personnel.

2. Environmental Monitoring

- Install environmental monitoring systems to track temperature, humidity, and other factors to prevent hardware failures or damage.

b. Network Security

1. Firewalls

- A firewall is a network security device or software that filters incoming and outgoing traffic based on a set of security rules. It helps block unauthorized access while permitting legitimate traffic.
- **Best Practices:**
  - Use both hardware and software firewalls.
  - Configure the firewall to allow only necessary ports and services.
  - Regularly update firewall rules to adapt to evolving security threats.

2. Intrusion Detection and Prevention Systems (IDS/IPS)

- These systems monitor network traffic for signs of malicious activity, unauthorized access attempts, or potential security breaches.
- IDS alerts administrators of suspicious activity, while IPS can actively block such activities.

3. Network Segmentation

- Divide your network into smaller segments to limit the spread of potential attacks. Use VLANs (Virtual Local Area Networks) or firewalls to separate sensitive systems from other network resources.

4. VPN (Virtual Private Network)

- Use VPNs for secure remote access. This ensures that connections from remote users to the server are encrypted and secure from potential eavesdropping or attacks.

c. Server Hardening

1. Minimize Attack Surface

- Reduce the number of services, applications, and ports running on your server to decrease the chances of exploitation. Disable unnecessary services and ports.

2. Operating System Hardening

- Regularly update the server's operating system (OS) and patch known vulnerabilities.
- Disable unused user accounts and services, and change default passwords for system services.

3. File and Directory Permissions

- Implement the principle of least privilege by setting restrictive file and directory permissions. Ensure that users and processes only have access to the files and resources they need.
- Use tools like SELinux (Security-Enhanced Linux) or AppArmor to enforce security policies on Linux servers.

4. Security Software

- Install and configure anti-virus and anti-malware software to detect and block malicious code.
- Use file integrity monitoring tools to detect unauthorized changes to critical system files and configurations.

d. User Access Management

1. Strong Authentication

- Enforce strong password policies (e.g., using complex passwords with uppercase, lowercase, numbers, and special characters).
- Implement multi-factor authentication (MFA) wherever possible to provide an additional layer of security for critical accounts.

2. SSH Key Authentication

- Use SSH key pairs for secure remote access to Linux servers instead of password-based authentication. Keys are harder to crack, providing better security.

3. Account Auditing

- Implement logging and auditing mechanisms to monitor user activities. Logs should track login attempts, system changes, and suspicious activity.
- Regularly review access logs to identify unusual or unauthorized access patterns.

e. Regular Updates and Patch Management

1. Security Updates

- Keep the operating system and all software up-to-date with the latest security patches. Regularly check for updates from software vendors and apply them promptly.
- Configure your package manager (e.g., apt, yum, dnf) to automatically apply security patches or at least notify you of new updates.

2. Vulnerability Scanning

- Regularly scan your server for known vulnerabilities using tools like Nessus, OpenVAS, or Qualys.
- Perform penetration testing periodically to identify potential weaknesses in the server's security.

f. Backups as Part of Security

Backups not only protect against hardware failure or data corruption but also safeguard against ransomware attacks. Attackers often encrypt or destroy data, but having secure, offline, or cloud-based backups ensures that the server can be restored to a secure state in the event of an attack.

g. Encryption

1. Data-at-Rest

- Encrypt sensitive data stored on the server using encryption technologies like LUKS (Linux Unified Key Setup) or BitLocker (Windows).

2. Data-in-Transit

- Use TLS/SSL (Transport Layer Security/Secure Sockets Layer) for encrypting data being transferred between servers and clients.

♦♦♦

UNIT 3

Open Source Tools and Technologies for Hardware and E-Mail Server

CONFIGURING ADDITIONAL HARDWARE

Configuring additional hardware in a system involves ensuring that various devices are properly installed, recognized, and function as expected by the operating system. This process includes configuring sound cards, displays and display cards, network cards, modems, USB drives, and CD writers. Each piece of hardware serves a different purpose and may require specific steps for installation, driver configuration, and troubleshooting. This guide provides an in-depth explanation of how to configure each of these hardware components.

1. Sound Cards

A sound card (or audio interface) is a hardware component that enables the system to produce sound. It converts digital audio signals to analog signals for output to speakers or headphones, and converts analog signals from microphones into digital signals for recording.

Installation and Configuration Steps

1. Physical Installation

- **PCI/PCIe Sound Card:** For desktop systems, sound cards can be installed into a PCI or PCIe slot on the motherboard.
- **USB Sound Card:** Some sound cards connect via USB ports, offering an easy plug-and-play option.

2. Operating System Detection

- Modern operating systems (like Windows, macOS, and Linux) generally detect sound cards automatically during boot and install the necessary drivers.
- If the sound card is not automatically detected, ensure that the correct drivers are installed from the manufacturer's website or via package managers in Linux.

3. Driver Installation

- **On Linux:** Most sound cards are supported by default with ALSA (Advanced Linux Sound Architecture) drivers. However, for some cards, you may need to install additional drivers and reload the configuration.

```
sudo apt-get install alsa-base alsa-utils
sudo alsa force-reload
```

- **On Windows:** Use the driver installation CD that came with the sound card or download the latest drivers from the manufacturer's website.

4. Testing and Configuration

- **Linux:** After installing the drivers, use tools like alsamixer to adjust volume levels, mute settings, and other sound options.

  alsamixer

- **Windows/macOS:** Sound configuration can be done via the sound settings interface where you can set default output/input devices and adjust system sounds.

5. Troubleshooting

- If the sound card is not working, verify that the audio output device is selected as the default, check the connections (e.g., speakers/headphones), and test with different audio files or applications.

2. Displays and Display Cards (Graphics Cards)

A display card (graphics card, GPU) is responsible for rendering images and video on a computer screen. A display refers to the physical monitor or screen connected to the computer.

Installation and Configuration Steps

1. Physical Installation

- For desktop systems, graphics cards are typically installed into a PCIe x16 slot on the motherboard. For laptops, the graphics chip is often integrated into the motherboard, though some high-end laptops have dedicated GPUs.
- After installing a discrete GPU, connect the monitor using the appropriate video cable (e.g., HDMI, DisplayPort, VGA).

2. Driver Installation

- **Windows:** Most modern Windows operating systems will automatically detect and install basic drivers for the display card. For full functionality (e.g., high resolution, acceleration), install the latest drivers from the manufacturer (NVIDIA, AMD, Intel).
  - For NVIDIA or AMD cards, go to their respective websites and download the latest drivers.
- **Linux:** Linux often supports basic graphics cards, but proprietary drivers might be needed for better performance. Use tools like apt or dnf to install drivers.

  sudo apt install nvidia-driver

  - macOS: For Macs, Apple provides native drivers for the hardware, including graphics cards, ensuring that the system works seamlessly with the display.

3. Configuring Display Settings

- On Windows, access the display settings through Settings > System > Display to adjust screen resolution, orientation, multiple display setups, and primary display.

On Linux, tools like xrandr or graphical tools like Display Settings in GNOME or KDE can be used to configure multi-monitor setups and screen resolution.

```
xrandr --output HDMI-1 --mode 1920x1080 --right-of eDP-1
```

- On macOS, go to System Preferences > Displays to set resolutions, arrange displays, or use additional settings like Night Shift or True Tone.

4. Troubleshooting

- If no display is showing, check cable connections, monitor power, and whether the correct input source is selected on the monitor.
- If resolution or display quality is poor, update graphics drivers or check the system settings for refresh rate and resolution configurations.

3. Network Cards (NICs)

A network interface card (NIC) is used to connect the computer to a network, either via Ethernet (wired) or Wi-Fi (wireless).

Installation and Configuration Steps

1. Physical Installation

- **Ethernet Card:** Typically installed into a PCI/PCIe slot on a desktop system. For laptops, the NIC may be integrated onto the motherboard.
- **Wi-Fi Card:** A wireless network card can either be integrated into the motherboard or plugged into a PCIe slot. Alternatively, USB Wi-Fi adapters can be used.

2. Driver Installation

- **Windows:** Windows should automatically install the required drivers for the network card upon boot. If not, download the drivers from the manufacturer's website.
- **Linux:** Most NICs, including Ethernet and Wi-Fi, are supported by the Linux kernel out of the box. However, some wireless cards may require proprietary drivers (e.g., Broadcom).

  ```
  sudo apt install bcmwl-kernel-source
  ```

- **macOS:** For Apple computers, the network card drivers are typically included in the operating system, and no additional configuration is necessary.

3. Configuring Network Settings

- **Windows:** Use Network and Sharing Center > Change Adapter Settings to configure settings such as static IPs, DNS, and wireless connections.
- **Linux:** Use tools like nmcli (NetworkManager command-line tool) to configure network settings.

  ```
  nmcli dev wifi connect "SSID" password "password"
  ```

- **macOS:** Go to System Preferences > Network, where you can set up Ethernet or Wi-Fi network configurations.

4. Troubleshooting

- Ensure the network cable is properly connected for wired connections or that the Wi-Fi password is correct for wireless networks.
- Use tools like ping and ifconfig (or ip a) to check network connectivity. ping 8.8.8.8

4. Modems

A modem (modulator-demodulator) is a device that allows computers to connect to the internet over a telephone line or cable. It converts digital signals from a computer to analog signals that can travel over communication lines and vice versa.

Installation and Configuration Steps

1. Physical Installation

- **Dial-up Modem:** Connect the modem to the telephone line and the computer using a serial or USB connection.
- **Cable or DSL Modem:** Connect the modem to the phone line (for DSL) or coaxial cable (for cable internet), then connect the modem to the computer via Ethernet.

2. Driver Installation

- Most modern USB modems will be automatically detected by the operating system, but you might need to install specific drivers from the modem's manufacturer.
- **Linux:** Most modems work out of the box, but some require additional configuration or modem drivers (e.g., ppp package for dial-up modems).

  sudo apt install ppp

3. Network Configuration

- **Windows:** Use the Network and Sharing Center to set up dial-up, DSL, or cable connections.
- **Linux:** Use pppconfig to configure a dial-up connection or NetworkManager for DSL/cable connections.

  sudo pppoeconf

4.Troubleshooting

- Verify that the modem is properly connected and powered on.
- For dial-up connections, check that the phone line has a dial tone and that the correct ISP settings are entered.

5. USB Drives

A USB drive is a portable storage device used for data storage, transferring files, and performing backups.

Installation and Configuration Steps

1. Physical Installation

- Simply plug the USB drive into an available USB port on the system.

2. Driver Installation

- **Windows/macOS/Linux:** Most modern operating systems automatically recognize USB drives and install the necessary drivers without requiring user intervention.

3. Configuring USB Storage

- **Windows:** You can manage USB drives via File Explorer by right-clicking and selecting Properties to check the device's health, format, or partition it.
- **Linux:** USB drives are usually mounted automatically. You can check the drive using lsblk or df and mount it manually if necessary.

  sudo mount /dev/sdb1 /mnt/usb

4. Troubleshooting

- If the USB drive is not detected, check if it's formatted with a file system supported by the operating system (e.g., FAT32 or exFAT for cross-platform compatibility).
- Check that the USB port is working by plugging the drive into another port or testing the drive on another computer.

6. CD Writers (Optical Drives)

A CD writer (or DVD/Blu-ray writer) allows the system to write data to optical media such as CDs, DVDs, or Blu-ray discs.

Installation and Configuration Steps

1. Physical Installation

- If using a desktop, install the CD writer into a 5.25-inch bay on the system's case and connect the power and data cables (SATA or IDE).
- Laptops typically come with built-in optical drives, or external USB optical drives can be used.

2. Driver Installation

- Windows/macOS/Linux: Most modern operating systems recognize optical drives and automatically install the necessary drivers.

3. Configuring CD/DVD Burning Software

- Use software such as Windows Media Player, Nero, Brasero (Linux), or Disk Utility (macOS) to burn data to the disc.
- On Linux, use cdrecord or tools like K3b or Brasero for burning.

4. Troubleshooting

- If the optical drive is not detected, check that the cables are properly connected or try using a different disk.
- Ensure the optical drive is not blocked by a software issue by testing it with different applications.

THE OS BOOT-UP PROCESS AND PERFORMING EVERYDAY TASKS USING GNU/LINUX

Understanding the OS boot-up process and how to perform everyday tasks using GNU/Linux is essential for system administrators, developers, and users alike. Below is a detailed breakdown of the boot-up process for GNU/Linux, followed by an explanation of how to perform common everyday tasks using a Linux-based operating system.

1. The OS Boot-Up Process in GNU/Linux

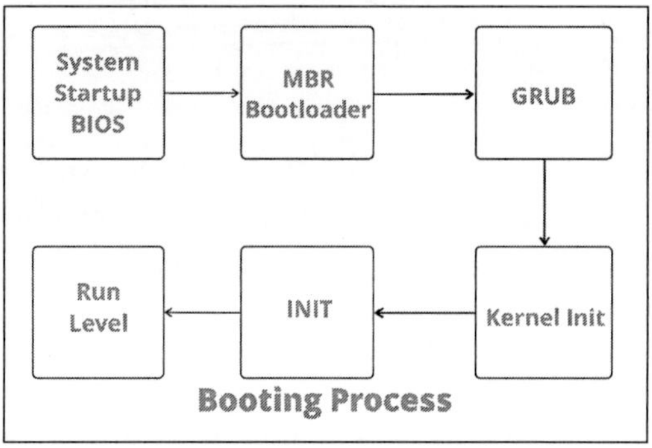

Fig 3.1: *Booting Process*

The boot-up process is a sequence of steps that the operating system follows to load itself into memory and make the system ready for user interaction. The boot process can vary slightly depending on the distribution (e.g., Ubuntu, Fedora, Arch Linux), but the general steps remain consistent across most Linux systems. Here's a detailed breakdown of the boot-up process:

3.1. Power On and BIOS/UEFI Stage

When the computer is powered on, the BIOS (Basic Input/Output System) or UEFI (Unified Extensible Firmware Interface) firmware is initialized. The BIOS/UEFI performs the following tasks:

- **POST (Power-On Self-Test):** It runs diagnostic tests on hardware components (CPU, memory, storage devices, etc.) to ensure they are functioning correctly.
- **Boot Device Selection:** BIOS/UEFI identifies the boot devices (e.g., hard disk, SSD, USB drive, network) and selects the appropriate boot device based on configuration or boot priority.
- **UEFI/BIOS Settings:** For modern systems with UEFI, there's an additional layer for secure boot or booting from GPT partitions.

3.2. Bootloader Stage (GRUB)

Once the BIOS/UEFI identifies the boot device, the bootloader is invoked. On most Linux systems, this is the GRUB (Grand Unified Bootloader), which is responsible for loading the kernel into memory.

- **GRUB Stage 1:** The BIOS/UEFI loads the first stage of GRUB from the boot sector of the disk (MBR or GPT). This stage is minimal but allows for booting the full GRUB menu.

- **GRUB Stage 2:** The second stage of GRUB is loaded, which contains the actual menu and configuration. GRUB presents the user with a menu to choose between multiple boot options (e.g., Linux kernel versions, recovery modes, other operating systems).
- **Kernel Selection:** The user can either select the default kernel or a specific kernel version from the GRUB menu. If no selection is made, GRUB automatically boots the default entry.

3.3. Loading the Linux Kernel

After the kernel is selected, GRUB loads the Linux kernel into memory. The kernel is the core of the operating system and is responsible for interacting with the hardware and managing system resources.

- **Kernel Unpacking:** The kernel is decompressed (if necessary) and initialized.
- **Kernel Initialization:** The kernel configures the system's hardware components (CPU, memory, devices, etc.). The kernel also sets up system resources and mounts the root filesystem (which contains the operating system's essential files).

3.4. Init System (Systemd, Upstart, or SysVinit)

After the kernel has loaded and the system is initialized, the kernel hands over control to the init system. The init system is responsible for starting and managing system services and processes. The most common init system in modern Linux distributions is systemd, but older systems may use Upstart or SysVinit.

Systemd (Most Common)

- Systemd is the default init system for most modern Linux distributions (e.g., Ubuntu, Fedora, CentOS). It is responsible for launching essential services and managing processes.
- **Initialization:** systemd loads a series of predefined configuration files known as "unit files" (service definitions).
- **Parallelization:** systemd initializes services in parallel, which speeds up the boot process.
- **Default Targets:** systemd defines different targets, such as multi-user.target (text mode) or graphical.target (graphical login).

Upstart

- Upstart is an event-driven init system used in older versions of Ubuntu. It listens for events and starts/ends processes based on these events (e.g., networking being enabled, or a user logging in).

SysVinit

- SysVinit is an older init system that uses scripts to start and stop services. It follows a more sequential approach and can be slower than modern systems like systemd.

3.5. User Space Initialization

Once the init system has started the necessary services, the system transitions into user space, where user-level applications and processes run. Common tasks during this phase include:

- **Login Prompt:** The system displays a login prompt for users to authenticate (either through a graphical login manager or a text-based terminal).
- **Launching Services:** Key services like networking, display managers (e.g., GDM, LightDM), and desktop environments are started, allowing the user to interact with the system.

Performing Everyday Tasks Using GNU/Linux

Once the system has booted, the user is ready to interact with the operating system. Below are explanations of how to perform some of the most common everyday tasks in GNU/Linux.

Managing Files and Directories

Linux provides powerful command-line utilities for managing files and directories. Here are some basic tasks:

Viewing Files and Directories

- **List files in a directory:**
  ls
- **View detailed information about files:**
  ls -l
- **Navigate between directories:**
  cd /path/to/directory

Creating, Moving, and Deleting Files

- **Create a new directory:**
  mkdir new_directory
- **Create a new empty file:**
  touch file_name
- **Move or rename a file:**
  mv old_file_name new_file_name
- **Delete a file:**
  rm file_name

Copying Files

- **Copy a file:**
  cp source_file destination

Managing Software Packages

Linux systems allow users to install, update, and remove software packages through package managers.

Package managers vary between distributions, but common ones include APT (Debian-based), YUM/DNF (Red Hat-based), and PacMan (Arch Linux).

Installing Packages

- **Ubuntu/Debian (APT):**
  sudo apt install package_name
- **Fedora/CentOS (DNF/YUM):**
  sudo dnf install package_name

Updating Packages

- **Ubuntu/Debian (APT):**
  sudo apt update
- sudo apt upgrade
- **Fedora/CentOS (DNF/YUM):**
  sudo dnf update

Removing Packages

- **Ubuntu/Debian (APT):**
  sudo apt remove package_name
- **Fedora/CentOS (DNF/YUM):**
  sudo dnf remove package_name

Managing Users and Permissions

Linux allows administrators to manage users and control access permissions.

Creating and Managing Users

- **Create a new user:**
  sudo adduser username
- **Delete a user:**
  Copy
  sudo deluser username

Changing User Passwords

- **Change a user's password:**
  sudo passwd username

Changing File Permissions

- **Change file permissions:**
  chmod 755 file_name
- **Change file ownership:**
  sudo chown user:group file_name

Networking

Linux provides several tools for managing network connections and troubleshooting network issues.

Viewing Network Information

- **Display IP address:**
  ip addr show

- **Display routing table:**
  ip route show

Testing Network Connectivity

- **Ping a remote server:**
  ping example.com
- **Traceroute to a server:**
  traceroute example.com

Configuring Network Interfaces

- **Configure a static IP (temporary):**
  sudo ip addr add 192.168.1.100/24 dev eth0
  sudo ip route add default via 192.168.1.1

Managing System Processes

Linux allows users to manage running processes using the terminal.

Viewing Processes

- **List all processes:**
  ps aux
- **Show processes in real-time:**
  top
- **Find a specific process:**
  ps aux | grep process_name

Killing Processes

- Terminate a process by PID:
  kill pid

System Monitoring and Log Files

Monitoring system health and reviewing log files is crucial for diagnosing issues.

Checking System Resource Usage

- **CPU and memory usage:**
  top
- **Disk usage:**
  df -h

Viewing System Logs

- **View system logs:**
  sudo tail -f /var/log/syslog

Summary

The boot-up process in GNU/Linux involves several key stages starting with the BIOS/UEFI initialization, followed by the bootloader (GRUB), kernel loading, init system (systemd, Upstart, SysVinit), and finally user space initialization. Understanding each stage is essential for troubleshooting and managing the system at a low level. Once the system is up and running, everyday tasks in GNU/Linux are typically performed via the terminal. The command line is central to Linux administration, where tasks like managing files, installing software, managing users, configuring networking, monitoring system resources, and troubleshooting issues can all be done efficiently. Mastering these concepts and tools will allow users to be more effective in navigating and administering a Linux-based operating system.

ACCESSING THE INTERNET AND PERFORMING EVERYDAY TASKS IN GNU/LINUX

GNU/Linux is a versatile and powerful operating system that allows users to perform a wide range of everyday tasks. In this detailed explanation, we will cover key tasks that users frequently perform, such as accessing the internet, playing music, editing documents and spreadsheets, sending and receiving emails, copying files from disks and over the network, playing games, and writing CDs.

Accessing the Internet in GNU/Linux

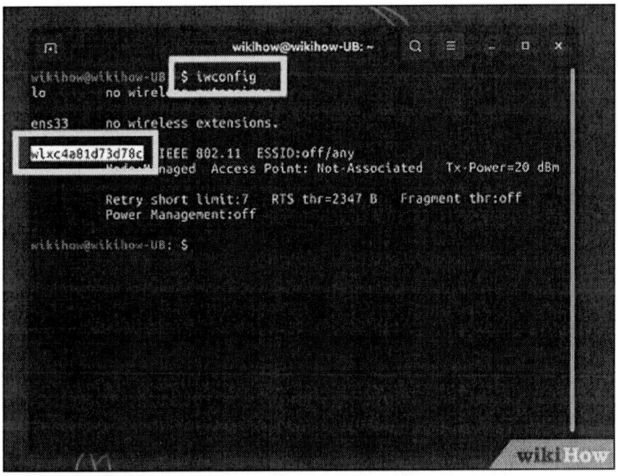

Accessing the internet is a fundamental task for most computer users. GNU/Linux provides several ways to connect to the internet, whether using a wired Ethernet connection, wireless Wi-Fi, or even mobile broadband.

Connecting to the Internet Using Ethernet or Wi-Fi

- **Ethernet (Wired Connection):**
  - For wired connections, most Linux distributions automatically detect Ethernet adapters and configure them for network use.
  - You can check the connection using the ip command or ifconfig to view your network interfaces.

    ip addr show

  - On most systems, the network interface is assigned automatically via DHCP (Dynamic Host Configuration Protocol).

- **Wi-Fi (Wireless Connection)**:
  - NetworkManager is the most common tool for managing wireless connections in modern Linux distributions. It provides graphical and command-line tools to connect to Wi-Fi networks.
- **Using the GUI (Graphical User Interface)**:
  - In desktop environments like GNOME, KDE, or XFCE, you can connect to Wi-Fi by clicking on the network icon in the system tray, selecting your network, and entering the password.
- **Using the Command Line**:
  - If you're using a terminal, you can use nmcli, the command-line client for NetworkManager, to connect to Wi-Fi:

    nmcli dev wifi connect "SSID" password "your_password"
  - Alternatively, for older systems or in the absence of NetworkManager, wpa_supplicant can be used for connecting to Wi-Fi networks.

Troubleshooting Internet Connection

- **Check Network Configuration**: You can verify that your system is receiving an IP address and check the gateway using ip a or ifconfig and ip route. ip route show
- **Test Connectivity**: Use ping to check if the system is able to reach a remote server, such as Google's DNS server:

  ping 8.8.8.8
- **Check DNS**: If you can ping an IP address but not a website, your DNS (Domain Name System) settings might be incorrect. Check /etc/resolv.conf for valid DNS entries. cat /etc/resolv.conf

Playing Music in GNU/Linux

GNU/Linux offers multiple ways to play music, both through graphical media players and command-line tools.

Popular Music Players

- **Rhythmbox**: This is the default music player on GNOME-based distributions. It supports various audio formats, and you can create playlists, stream music, and organize your library.
- Launch it from the applications menu or by running:

  rhythmbox
- **VLC Media Player**: A powerful, cross-platform player that supports a wide range of audio and video formats. Install it via package managers:

  Ubuntu/Debian:

  sudo apt install vlc

  Fedora:

  sudo dnf install vlc
- **Clementine**: A modern music player with an interface inspired by Amarok. It supports music streaming services like Spotify, SoundCloud, and more.

Command-Line Music Players

- **MPD (Music Player Daemon)**: A powerful server-side music player that can be controlled remotely. Install and configure mpd and use a client like ncmpcpp to interact with it.
- **MPlayer**: A command-line tool that plays most audio and video formats. mplayer song.mp3

EDITING DOCUMENTS AND SPREADSHEETS IN GNU/LINUX

- Editing documents and spreadsheets is an essential part of daily computing. On GNU/Linux, there are numerous options for working with office documents.

LibreOffice Suite

- LibreOffice is the most popular office suite on Linux and includes several applications for handling documents, spreadsheets, and presentations.
- **LibreOffice Writer**: For word processing.

  libreoffice –writer
- **LibreOffice Calc**: For spreadsheets.

  libreoffice --calc
- **LibreOffice Impress**: For presentations.

LibreOffice is highly compatible with Microsoft Office file formats (e.g., .docx, .xlsx).

Google Docs (Cloud-based)

If you prefer cloud-based tools, you can use **Google Docs** for word processing and **Google Sheets** for spreadsheets. You can access them via a web browser on Linux:

- Visit docs.google.com to create or edit documents.

Editing Documents via the Command Line

- **vim** or **nano**: For quick editing of text files in the terminal. vim document.txt
- **LibreOffice in Headless Mode**: You can also convert documents without a GUI using LibreOffice in "headless" mode for automation or server environments. libreoffice --headless --convert-to pdf document.odt

Sending and Receiving Email in GNU/Linux

Email management is straightforward on Linux, thanks to various email clients and command-line tools.

GUI Email Clients

- **Thunderbird**: A popular open-source email client that supports POP, IMAP, and SMTP.
- **Install it:**

  sudo apt install thunderbird
- **Evolution**: A robust email client for GNOME that supports email, calendar, and tasks.

Command-Line Email Clients

- **Mutt**: A powerful text-based email client for users comfortable with the command line.
- **Install Mutt:**
  sudo apt install mutt
- **To send an email:**
  mutt -s "Subject" recipient@example.com < message.txt
- **Alpine**: Another popular text-based email client.
  sudo apt install alpine

COPYING FILES FROM DISKS AND OVER THE NETWORK

Copying files is a crucial task, and Linux provides many tools for managing file transfers both locally and over the network.

Copying Files Locally

- **cp**: The basic command to copy files.

  cp source_file destination
- **rsync**: A powerful tool for copying files, supporting remote synchronization over SSH and efficient incremental transfers.

  rsync -av source/ destination/

Copying Files Over the Network

- **SCP (Secure Copy Protocol)**: Copy files between local and remote machines over SSH.

  scp file.txt username@remote_host:/path/to/destination
- **SFTP (Secure File Transfer Protocol)**: A secure alternative to FTP, used for transferring files over SSH.

  sftp username@remote_host
- **NFS (Network File System)**: Set up NFS to mount remote directories and copy files like local files.
- **SAMBA**: Use SAMBA to share files between Linux and Windows systems.

PLAYING GAMES IN GNU/LINUX

GNU/Linux has become increasingly popular as a gaming platform. Many modern games are available for Linux, and tools like **Steam** make it easy to manage a library of games.

Steam

Steam is one of the most popular platforms for gaming, and it has a native Linux client. It supports thousands of Linux-compatible games.

- **Install Steam:**
  sudo apt install steam

Wine and Proton

- **Wine**: A compatibility layer that allows you to run Windows applications on Linux, including many Windows-based games.
  sudo apt install wine
- **Proton**: A tool from Valve integrated into Steam that allows you to play Windows-only games on Linux via Wine.

Emulators

- **DOSBox**: For playing old DOS-based games.
  sudo apt install dosbox
- **RetroArch**: An emulator for a wide range of classic gaming consoles.
  sudo apt install retroarch
- Writing CDs in GNU/Linux
- Although CD/DVD drives are becoming less common, Linux still provides excellent tools for writing CDs and DVDs.
- Using Brasero (Graphical)
- Brasero is the default disc burning application for GNOME-based distributions.
- **Install Brasero:**
  sudo apt install brasero
- To burn a CD/DVD, launch Brasero from the applications menu, select the files to burn, and follow the on-screen prompts.

USING COMMAND LINE TOOLS

- **cdrecord**: A command-line tool for burning CDs and DVDs.
  cdrecord -v speed=4 dev=0,0,0 -data myfiles.iso
- **dd**: A versatile command-line tool used for creating ISO images and writing them to discs.
  sudo dd if=image.iso of=/dev/cdrom

X WINDOW SYSTEM CONFIGURATION

The **X Window System** (or **X11**) is a crucial part of the graphical user interface (GUI) on UNIX-like operating systems, including GNU/Linux. It provides the foundation for displaying graphical elements (windows, buttons, menus, etc.) and handling input from devices like the mouse and keyboard. Understanding how to configure X Windows, detect display devices, and install software is key for both system administrators and users who want to customize their Linux desktop experience.

This detailed explanation will cover the following topics:

1. Introduction to X Window System
2. Configuring X Windows
3. Detecting Display Devices
4. Installing Software for X Windows

1. Introduction to the X Window System

The **X Window System** is the standard windowing system for UNIX-like operating systems. It is designed to provide a framework for building graphical user interfaces (GUIs), but it does not define how applications should look or behave, leaving that to higher-level libraries like **GTK** (GIMP Toolkit) or **Qt**.

Key components of the X Window System

- **X Server**: Manages the display and input devices (mouse, keyboard). It is responsible for rendering the graphics on the screen.
- **X Client**: Applications that communicate with the X Server to display content (e.g., web browsers, file managers).
- **Window Manager**: A program that controls the placement and appearance of windows within the X Server. Examples include **Openbox**, **i3**, **GNOME Shell**, and **KDE Plasma**.
- **X11 Protocol**: The communication protocol used between the X Server and X Clients.

2. Configuring X Windows

Configuring X Windows on GNU/Linux systems requires modifying configuration files and using various utilities. However, modern Linux distributions often auto-configure X11 settings, so manual configuration is typically needed only in specific use cases (e.g., custom setups, multi-monitor configurations, or troubleshooting).

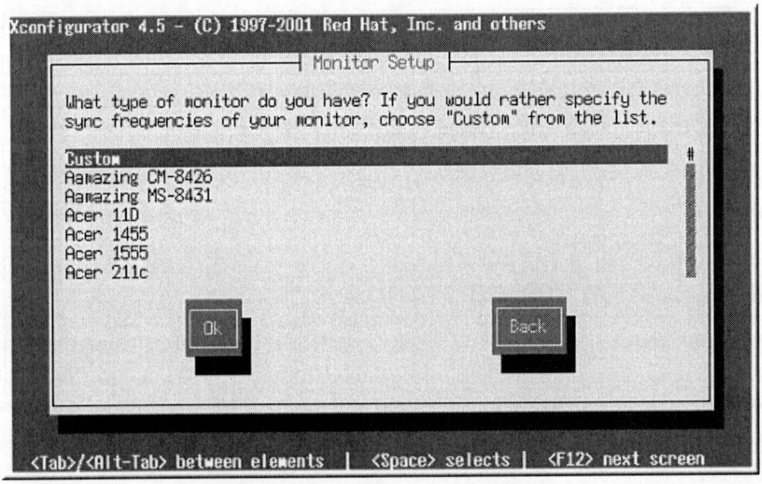

Fig 3.2: *Configuring X Windows*

The xorg.conf File

The main configuration file for X Windows is **xorg.conf**, located at /etc/X11/xorg.conf. This file is used to configure various aspects of the X Server, including display settings, input devices, and more. In many modern Linux distributions, **Xorg** (the X Server implementation) will automatically generate this file during startup, but users can manually edit it for specific configurations.

- To generate a basic xorg.conf file:
  sudo Xorg -configure
  This command generates a file called xorg.conf.new in the current directory. You can then move this file to the correct location:
  sudo mv xorg.conf.new /etc/X11/xorg.conf

Important Sections in xorg.conf

- **Section "Device"**: Defines the graphics card and its settings.
- **Section "Monitor"**: Defines the display monitor settings (e.g., resolution, refresh rate).
- **Section "Screen"**: Specifies the combination of device and monitor for the display.
- **Section "InputDevice"**: Defines keyboard, mouse, or other input devices.

Using xrandr for Dynamic Configuration

While xorg.conf is useful for static configurations, **xrandr** is a dynamic configuration utility that can be used to adjust display settings at runtime, such as changing screen resolution or setting up multiple monitors.

- To see the current state of your displays:
  xrandr
- To set the resolution of a display:
  xrandr --output HDMI-1 --mode 1920x1080
- To detect connected displays:
  xrandr --auto
- To enable multiple monitors:
  xrandr --output HDMI-1 --right-of LVDS-1

The xrandr utility is highly flexible and allows users to adjust their display configurations without restarting X11 or modifying configuration files.

3. Detecting Display Devices

In modern Linux systems, detecting and configuring display devices is often automatic, especially when using a desktop environment like GNOME, KDE, or XFCE. However, for advanced users or troubleshooting, understanding how to detect display devices manually is important.

Using lspci to Detect Graphics Hardware

The **lspci** command lists all PCI devices in your system, including graphics cards (GPUs).

- To list PCI devices and identify the graphics card:
  lspci | grep -i vga

This will show the make and model of your graphics card, e.g., VGA compatible controller: NVIDIA Corporation GP104 [GeForce GTX 1070].

Using xrandr to Detect Displays

As mentioned earlier, xrandr can be used to detect and manage displays dynamically. When you run xrandr without any arguments, it will list all available outputs (displays) and their current resolution settings.

- Example output:
  $ xrandr
- HDMI-1 connected 1920x1080+0+0 256mm x 144mm
- LVDS-1 disconnected (normal left inverted right x axis y axis)
- In the example above:
  - HDMI-1 is an active output with a resolution of 1920x1080.
  - LVDS-1 is a disconnected output (often representing a laptop's built-in display).

Using lshw for Detailed Hardware Information

The **lshw** command provides detailed information about your system's hardware, including display devices and graphics cards.

- To see detailed information about your graphics hardware:
  sudo lshw -C display

This will provide details such as the manufacturer, model, and configuration of the graphics card.

Checking Log Files

You can also check the X server's log files for information about detected display devices. The log file is typically located at /var/log/Xorg.0.log.

- **To examine the log file:**
  less /var/log/Xorg.0.log

Search for lines that indicate detected displays or errors related to the graphics hardware.

4. Installing Software for X Windows

Installing software on GNU/Linux for X Windows typically involves using package managers to install **X11-related** packages or software with GUI components.

Installing X11 Packages

- **Xorg**: The main package providing the X Window Server.

To install the X Server

- **Debian/Ubuntu**:
  sudo apt install xorg
- **Fedora**:
  sudo dnf install xorg-x11-server-Xorg
- **X11 Libraries**: These libraries are required for running X-based applications. Install them as follows:
- **Debian/Ubuntu**:
  sudo apt install libx11-dev
- **Fedora**:
  sudo dnf install libX11-devel

Installing Window Managers and Desktop Environments

- **Window Managers (WM)** are lightweight and provide minimal control over window management. Examples include:
  - **i3**: A tiling window manager.

    sudo apt install i3
- **Openbox**: A highly configurable window manager.

  sudo apt install openbox
- **Desktop Environments (DE)** provide a full suite of tools to manage windows, file management, and system settings. Examples include:
  - **GNOME**:

    sudo apt install gnome-shell
- **KDE Plasma**:

  sudo apt install kde-plasma-desktop

Installing X11-based Applications3

- **Graphical Applications** like web browsers, text editors, and media players are all based on the X Window System. Examples include:
- **Firefox** (web browser):
  sudo apt install firefox
- **LibreOffice** (office suite):
  sudo apt install libreoffice
- **VLC** (media player):
  sudo apt install vlc
- **Applications Using X11 Protocol**: Some software applications use X11 to display graphical content, including remote desktop tools like **VNC** or X11 forwarding with **SSH**. These applications typically require **xorg-x11-server-utils** or similar X11 packages.

SETTING UP EMAIL SERVERS - FROM SOURCE CODE AND USING BINARY PACKAGES, WITH POSTFIX

Setting up an email server is a complex but essential task for organizations, and it involves configuring both **Mail Transfer Agents (MTAs)** and other mail-related components (such as Mail Delivery Agents and Mail User Agents). Among the available MTAs, **Postfix** is a highly popular and flexible MTA used to send and receive email in UNIX-based systems like Linux.

This explanation will walk you through setting up an email server by either compiling from source code or using binary packages, and will specifically focus on **Postfix** as the MTA.

Introduction to Email Servers

An **email server** is a system that handles the sending, receiving, and storing of email. The two primary components involved in email management are:

- **Mail Transfer Agent (MTA)**: Responsible for sending and receiving emails between servers. Examples include **Postfix**, **Sendmail**, **Exim**, and **Qmail**.
- **Mail Delivery Agent (MDA)**: Delivers the email to a user's mailbox. Examples include **Dovecot** and **Procmail**.
- **Mail User Agent (MUA)**: The application used by the end-user to read and manage their emails. Examples include **Thunderbird**, **Mutt**, and web-based MUAs like **Roundcube**.

Postfix is one of the most widely used MTAs, known for its ease of use, security, and flexibility.

Setting Up an Email Server Using Binary Packages

Using **binary packages** for setting up an email server is often the easiest method, as most of the necessary components are pre-compiled, and the installation process is simplified using package management systems.

Installing Postfix via Binary Packages

On modern Linux distributions, Postfix is typically included in the default repositories, and installation is simple using the package manager.

On Debian-based Systems (Ubuntu, Debian, Linux Mint, etc.)

- **Update the package repository**:
  sudo apt update
- **Install Postfix**:
  sudo apt install postfix

  During the installation, you will be prompted to choose the type of mail server configuration. You can select:

  - **Internet Site**: If your server will be sending and receiving emails directly over the internet.
  - **Satellite System**: If your server is only relaying emails via another email server.
  - **Local Only**: For internal mail routing on your local network.
- **Configure Postfix**: After installation, you will need to configure **main.cf** and **master.cf** to fine-tune Postfix behavior. The main configuration file is located in:
  /etc/postfix/main.cf
- Set the **myhostname** (domain name of your email server):
  myhostname = mail.example.com
- Set the **mydomain** (domain part of your email addresses):
  mydomain = example.com
- **Restart Postfix** after making changes:
  sudo systemctl restart postfix
- On Red Hat-based Systems (CentOS, Fedora, RHEL, etc.):
- **Update the package repository**:
  sudo yum update

- **Install Postfix**:
  sudo yum install postfix
- **Start and enable Postfix to start on boot**:
  sudo systemctl start postfix
  sudo systemctl enable postfix
- **Configure Postfix** similarly to the Debian-based system instructions.

Configuring Additional Email Components

Mail Delivery Agent (MDA): To store the email and manage mailbox access, install and configure **Dovecot**, which is commonly used with Postfix.
sudo apt install dovecot-imapd dovecot-pop3d

- **Firewall Configuration**: Ensure your firewall allows the relevant ports for email servers. The typical ports for email are:
  - **SMTP**: Port 25 (for sending emails).
  - **IMAP**: Port 143 (for accessing emails).
  - **IMAPS**: Port 993 (secure IMAP).
  - **POP3**: Port 110 (for accessing emails).
  - **POP3S**: Port 995 (secure POP3).
- Configure your firewall to allow these ports:
  sudo ufw allow 25,143,110,993,995/tcp
  sudo ufw reload
- **DNS Configuration**: To ensure proper email delivery, you must configure DNS records, such as **MX records** (Mail Exchange) for your domain. The MX record points to the server that handles incoming email for your domain.

Setting Up an Email Server From Source Code

Setting up an email server from source code is a more complex and flexible approach. Compiling from source allows you to customize your installation and fine-tune your server setup for specific requirements. It also helps you to install a version of Postfix that is not yet available in the distribution's repositories.

Prerequisites

Before you begin, ensure that you have the necessary build tools installed, such as compilers, libraries, and other dependencies:

- **Debian/Ubuntu**:
  sudo apt install build-essential libssl-dev libsasl2-dev
- **Red Hat/CentOS**:
  sudo yum groupinstall "Development Tools"
  sudo yum install openssl-devel cyrus-sasl-devel

Downloading Postfix Source Code

- **Go to the Postfix website** or the official FTP repository to download the latest source code:

  Official website: Postfix

- **FTP repository:**
  ftp ftp://ftp.porcupine.org/mirrors/postfix-release/
- **Download the Postfix source tarball**:
  wget http://www.postfix.org/ftp/postfix-3.x.x.tar.gz
- **Extract the tarball**:
  tar -xvzf postfix-3.x.x.tar.gz
- **Navigate into the extracted directory**:
  cd postfix-3.x.x

Compiling Postfix from Source

- **Configure the installation**: Postfix uses a configuration script to prepare the build environment.

  make makefiles
- You can pass various flags to customize the installation, such as the installation prefix:

  make makefiles CCARGS="-DUSE_TLS -I/usr/include/openssl" AUXLIBS="-L/usr/lib/openssl"
- **Compile Postfix**:
  make
- **Install Postfix**: After compiling, install Postfix:
  sudo make install
- **Configure Postfix**: Just like the binary installation, you need to configure **main.cf** and **master.cf** for your specific needs.
- **Start Postfix**: After installation, you can start the Postfix service:

  sudo postfix start

Configuring Postfix for Basic Email Sending and Receiving

Basic Postfix Configuration

- **myhostname**: The name of your server (domain or FQDN).

  myhostname = mail.example.com
- **mydomain**: The domain part of email addresses.

  mydomain = example.com
- **mydestination**: Domains that Postfix will handle mail for.

  mydestination = $myhostname, localhost.$mydomain, localhost
- **inet_interfaces**: Define the network interfaces Postfix listens on.

  inet_interfaces = all
- **inet_protocols**: Define which internet protocols (IPv4, IPv6) Postfix should use.

  inet_protocols = ipv4

Testing Postfix

To test if Postfix is configured properly, try sending an email from the command line using sendmail:

```
echo "Subject: Test Email" | sendmail -v recipient@example.com
```

You can also check Postfix logs to verify that the email was successfully processed:

```
tail -f /var/log/mail.log
```

Using Postfix with TLS for Secure Email Sending

For secure email delivery, Postfix supports TLS (Transport Layer Security) to encrypt the email transmission. To configure TLS, make sure the necessary certificates are in place:

1. **Obtain a TLS certificate** from a Certificate Authority (CA), or create a self-signed certificate.

   Configure TLS in Postfix: Edit **main.cf**:
   ```
   smtpd_use_tls = yes
       smtpd_tls_cert_file = /etc/ssl/certs/postfix.crt
       smtpd_tls_key_file = /etc/ssl/private/postfix.key
   ```
2. **Restart Postfix:**
   ```
   sudo systemctl restart postfix
   ```

SETTING UP SMTP SERVICES, IMAP/POP3 SERVICES, WEBMAIL, WEB SERVERS (APACHE), PHP, AND PERL

This explanation covers key aspects of setting up an email and web server environment with different services and tools. Specifically, we will discuss **SMTP services (Postfix or Courier)**, **IMAP and POP3 services (Courier)**, **webmail services (SquirrelMail)**, **web servers (Apache HTTP)**, and **server-side scripting (PHP and Perl)**. These services are integral for enabling web-based email communication, sending and receiving messages, hosting websites, and running dynamic content on websites.

1. SMTP Services - Courier (Postfix)

SMTP (Simple Mail Transfer Protocol) is the protocol used to send email messages from a client to a server or between servers. It's one of the core components for email communication.

- **Courier SMTP**: Courier is a well-known mail server suite that includes an SMTP service, as well as POP3 and IMAP services. It's designed for fast, efficient, and secure email delivery.

Key Features of Courier

- Full support for SMTP (Simple Mail Transfer Protocol) and secure SMTP (SMTPS).
- Integrated with IMAP and POP3 for email retrieval.
- Designed to be fast and efficient, especially for handling high-volume mail traffic.
- Supports both local and remote delivery with flexible routing.
- Configurable to work with SSL/TLS for encrypted email transmission.

Setting up Courier SMTP

- Install Courier with the following command:

- **Debian/Ubuntu**:

  sudo apt install courier-mta

- **CentOS/Red Hat**:

  sudo yum install courier

- Configure **/etc/courier/esmtp.conf** for your SMTP settings:
  - Define parameters like **SMTP port (25)**, **TLS encryption** for secure communication, and the **domain name**.
- Start the Courier SMTP service:

  sudo systemctl start courier

  sudo systemctl enable courier

2. IMAP & POP3 Services - Courier

IMAP (Internet Message Access Protocol) and **POP3** (Post Office Protocol) are two protocols used to retrieve email messages from a mail server.

- **IMAP** is more feature-rich than POP3, allowing users to manage their emails directly on the server, such as organizing emails into folders and reading messages across multiple devices.
- **POP3** is a simpler protocol that typically downloads emails to the local machine and deletes them from the server.

Courier offers both **IMAP** and **POP3** server implementations. The **Courier IMAP** and **Courier POP3** servers are designed to be lightweight and fast.

Setting up Courier IMAP and POP3 Services

- **Install Courier IMAP and POP3**:
  - **Debian/Ubuntu**:

    sudo apt install courier-imap courier-pop

  - **CentOS/Red Hat**:

    sudo yum install courier-imap courier-pop

Configure IMAP and POP3

- Edit **/etc/courier/imapd** for IMAP settings, and **/etc/courier/pop3d** for POP3 settings.
- You can configure encryption, authentication methods, and other important parameters such as which port to use (IMAP uses 143 by default, IMAPS uses 993, and POP3 uses 110 by default).
- **Start the Services**:

  sudo systemctl start courier-imap

  sudo systemctl start courier-pop

- **Enable Services to Start on Boot**:

  sudo systemctl enable courier-imap

  sudo systemctl enable courier-pop

3. Webmail Services - SquirrelMail

SquirrelMail is a widely used **webmail** client that allows users to access their email through a web browser. It is written in PHP and can work with various backends like **IMAP** or **POP3** servers to retrieve messages.

Setting up SquirrelMail

- **Install SquirrelMail**:
  - **Debian/Ubuntu**:
    sudo apt install squirrelmail
  - **CentOS/Red Hat**:
    sudo yum install squirrelmail

Configure SquirrelMail

- After installation, configure SquirrelMail using the built-in configuration utility:
  sudo squirrelmail-configure

1. This utility will guide you through various configuration options, including setting up your IMAP or POP3 server details, user authentication, and email settings.
2. **Access Squirrel Mail**: SquirrelMail typically installs under **/usr/share/squirrelmail**, and you can access it by visiting http://yourdomain.com/squirrelmail in a web browser.

4. Setting up Web Servers - Apache (HTTP Services)

Apache HTTP Server (often simply called Apache) is the most widely used web server software, responsible for serving web pages and web applications.

Setting up Apache Web Server

- **Install Apache**:
  - **Debian/Ubuntu**:
    sudo apt install apache2
  - **CentOS/Red Hat**:
    sudo yum install httpd
- **Start Apache**:
  - **Debian/Ubuntu**:
    sudo systemctl start apache2
  - **CentOS/Red Hat**:
    sudo systemctl start httpd

Enable Apache to Start on Boot

- **Debian/Ubuntu**:
  sudo systemctl enable apache2
- **CentOS/Red Hat**:
  sudo systemctl enable httpd

Configure Apache

- The main configuration file is located at /etc/apache2/apache2.conf (Debian/Ubuntu) or /etc/httpd/conf/httpd.conf (CentOS/Red Hat).
- You can configure things like the document root (default: /var/www/html), virtual hosts, modules, and security settings.

Test Apache

- After installation and configuration, you can test the Apache server by visiting http://yourdomain.com or http://localhost in a web browser. If successful, you should see the default Apache welcome page.

5. PHP (Server-Side Scripting)

PHP (Hypertext Preprocessor) is a popular server-side scripting language used to create dynamic content on web pages. It is widely used with web servers like Apache to serve content based on user interaction or data.

Setting up PHP with Apache

- **Install PHP**:
  - **Debian/Ubuntu**:
    sudo apt install php libapache2-mod-php
  - **CentOS/Red Hat**:
    sudo yum install php php-mysql

Configure Apache to Use PHP

- Apache usually automatically detects PHP if installed with the correct module (libapache2-mod-php), but you can confirm this in **/etc/apache2/mods-enabled/php.conf** or **/etc/httpd/conf.d/php.conf**.

Test PHP Installation

- Create a test PHP file to verify that PHP is working:
  sudo nano /var/www/html/info.php
  Add the following content:
```
<?php
phpinfo();
?>
```
  Visit http://localhost/info.php in a browser. If PHP is correctly installed, you should see a detailed PHP information page.

6. Perl (CGI Support)

Perl is a powerful scripting language often used for CGI (Common Gateway Interface) scripts to generate dynamic web content. It was once widely used for web applications but has since been replaced in many cases by PHP or Python.

Setting up Perl for CGI Support

- **Install Perl**:
  - **Debian/Ubuntu**:

    ```
    sudo apt install perl
    ```
  - **CentOS/Red Hat**:

    ```
    sudo yum install perl
    ```

Configure Apache for CGI

- Apache can be configured to handle Perl scripts using the mod_cgi module. Ensure the module is enabled:

  ```
  sudo a2enmod cgi
  ```
- Create a directory for CGI scripts (e.g., /var/www/cgi-bin), and configure Apache to allow CGI execution: In /etc/apache2/sites-available/000-default.conf (Debian/Ubuntu) or /etc/httpd/conf/httpd.conf (CentOS/Red Hat):

  ```
  ScriptAlias /cgi-bin/ /var/www/cgi-bin/
  <Directory "/var/www/cgi-bin">
     Options +ExecCGI
     AddHandler cgi-script .cgi .pl
  </Directory>
  ```

Test Perl CGI Script

- Create a simple Perl CGI script in /var/www/cgi-bin/:

  ```
  sudo nano /var/www/cgi-bin/test.pl
  ```
- Add the following content:

  ```
  #!/usr/bin/perl
  print "Content-type: text/html\n\n";
  print "<html><body><h1>Hello, Perl CGI!</h1></body></html>\n";
  ```
- Make the script executable:

  ```
  sudo chmod +x /var/www/cgi-bin/test.pl
  ```
- Visit http://localhost/cgi-bin/test.pl to verify that the Perl script is executed.

In this we covered setting up various email and web services for a comprehensive email and web hosting environment:

1. **SMTP Services (Postfix/Courier)**: Configured to handle email sending.
2. **IMAP/POP3 Services (Courier)**: Set up for retrieving emails.
3. **Webmail (SquirrelMail)**: Enabled web-based email access.
4. **Web Servers (Apache HTTP)**: Set up for hosting websites.
5. **PHP**: Installed and configured for server-side scripting to serve dynamic web content.
6. **Perl (CGI Support)**: Enabled for running CGI scripts on Apache.

By following these instructions, you can set up a complete email and web server system capable of sending/receiving emails, hosting websites, and handling dynamic web applications.

SETTING UP FILE SERVICES AND PROXY SERVICES

This guide will explain how to set up file services (using Samba for Windows networks and NFS for GNU/Linux/Unix networks) as well as proxy services (using Squid for HTTP, FTP, and HTTPS proxying). These services are essential for managing file sharing across networks, enhancing security, and controlling internet access.

Setting Up File Services

Using Samba (File and Authentication Services for Windows Networks)

Samba is a free software suite that provides seamless file and print services to SMB/CIFS clients, including Windows systems. It enables Linux/Unix systems to act as file servers for Windows clients, facilitating file sharing and user authentication.

Why Use Samba?

- It allows Linux/Unix machines to share files and printers with Windows machines.
- It supports user authentication via Windows Active Directory or local Linux accounts.
- It works with SMB (Server Message Block) protocol, which is native to Windows.

Installing and Configuring Samba

- **Install Samba:**

  On Debian/Ubuntu:

  sudo apt update

  sudo apt install samba samba-common-bin
- **On CentOS/Red Hat:**

  sudo yum install samba samba-client samba-common
- **Configure Samba:**

  The main Samba configuration file is /etc/samba/smb.conf.
- To set up a **basic file share**, open the configuration file **for editing:**

  sudo nano /etc/samba/smb.conf

Add the following configuration at the end of the file to share a directory, say /srv/samba/shared:

```
[shared]
  path = /srv/samba/shared
  browseable = yes
  writable = yes
  guest ok = yes
  create mask = 0777
  directory mask = 0777
```

Explanation

- **path:** Specifies the directory to share.
- **browseable:** Allows the share to be visible to other network users.

- **writable:** Enables writing to the shared directory.
- **guest ok:** Allows access without authentication (useful for public shares).
- **create mask and directory mask:** Define file and directory permissions.
- **Create the Shared Directory and Set Permissions:**

  ```
  sudo mkdir -p /srv/samba/shared
  sudo chmod -R 0777 /srv/samba/shared
  sudo chown -R nobody:nogroup /srv/samba/shared
  ```

- **Start and Enable Samba Services:**
  - **On Debian/Ubuntu:**

    ```
    sudo systemctl restart smbd
    sudo systemctl enable smbd
    ```

  - **On CentOS/Red Hat:**

    ```
    sudo systemctl start smb
    sudo systemctl enable smb
    ```

- **Access the Shared Directory from Windows:**
  - Open File Explorer on a Windows machine and type the server's IP address in the address bar:

    ```
    \\<Linux_IP_Address>\shared
    ```

  If everything is configured correctly, you will be able to access and modify files in the shared directory.

Samba Authentication (Optional)

For a more secure configuration, you can set up user authentication. To do this, add a Samba user and set a password:

- **Add a user to the Samba password database:**

  ```
  sudo smbpasswd -a <username>
  ```

- **Enable the user:**

  ```
  sudo smbpasswd -e <username>
  ```

Then, modify the Samba share configuration to require authentication by setting guest ok = no and specifying the user:

```
[shared]
  path = /srv/samba/shared
  valid users = <username>
  browseable = yes
  writable = yes
  create mask = 0777
  directory mask = 0777
```

- **Restart Samba:**

  ```
  sudo systemctl restart smbd
  ```

USING NFS (NETWORK FILE SYSTEM) FOR GNU/LINUX/UNIX NETWORKS

NFS is a distributed file system protocol that allows you to share directories and files over a network, making them accessible to other computers. NFS is commonly used in Linux/Unix environments to share files across servers or between systems.

Why Use NFS?

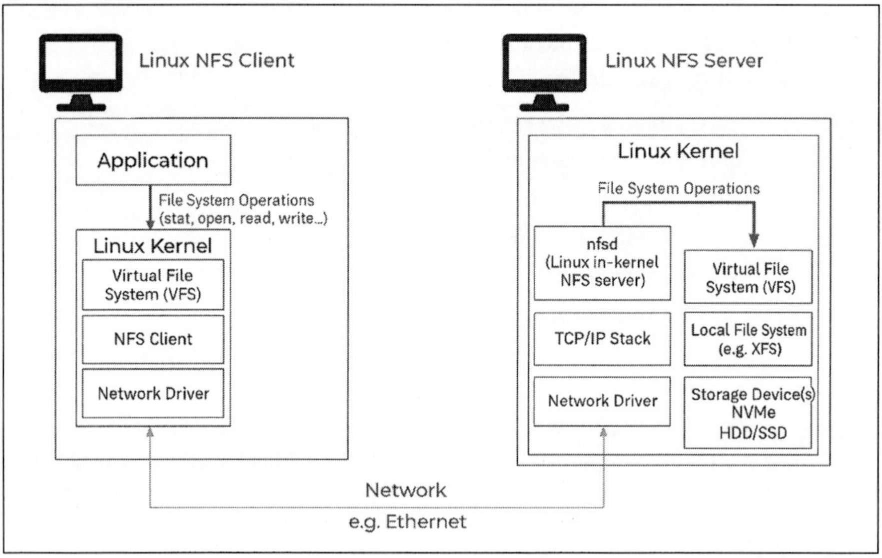

***Fig 3.3:** Network File System*

- NFS is widely supported in Linux/Unix systems, making it ideal for sharing files in these environments.
- It provides robust performance and is relatively simple to configure.
- NFS is used to mount file systems over the network, enabling access to remote directories as if they were local.

Installing and Configuring NFS

- **Install NFS Server and Client:**
  - **On Debian/Ubuntu:**

    sudo apt update

    sudo nano apt install nfs-kernel-server
  - **On CentOS/Red Hat:**

    sudo yum install nfs-utils
- **Configure NFS Export (Share a Directory):**

  Open the /etc/exports file and define which directories you want to share:

  sudo nano /etc/exports

  Example entry to share /srv/nfs/shared with all hosts in the 192.168.1.0/24 subnet:

  /srv/nfs/shared 192.168.1.0/24(rw,sync,no_subtree_check)

Explanation

- **rw:** Read-write access.
- **sync:** Ensures that changes are written to disk before a response is sent.
- **no_subtree_check:** Improves performance by disabling subtree checking.
- **Create and Set Permissions for the Shared Directory:**

  sudo mkdir -p /srv/nfs/shared

  sudo chmod -R 777 /srv/nfs/shared
- **Export the Shared Directory:** After editing the /etc/exports file, run the following command to export the shared directory:

  sudo exportfs -a
- **Start and Enable NFS Server:**
  - **On Debian/Ubuntu:**

    sudo systemctl restart nfs-kernel-server

    sudo systemctl enable nfs-kernel-server
  - **On CentOS/Red Hat:**

    sudo systemctl start nfs-server

    sudo systemctl enable nfs-server
- **Allow NFS in Firewall (if applicable):**
  - **On Debian/Ubuntu:**

    sudo ufw allow from 192.168.1.0/24 to any port nfs
  - **On CentOS/Red Hat:**

    sudo firewall-cmd --permanent --add-service=nfs

    sudo firewall-cmd --reload
- **Mount NFS Share on the Client:**
  - On a client machine (another Linux system), mount the shared directory using the following command:

    sudo mount <server_ip>:/srv/nfs/shared /mnt
- **Ensure NFS Mount is Persistent:** To ensure the NFS share is mounted automatically on boot, add the following line to /etc/fstab:

  <server_ip>:/srv/nfs/shared /mnt nfs defaults 0 0

Setting Up Proxy Services

Using Squid (HTTP/FTP/HTTPS Proxy Services)

Squid is a highly flexible and powerful proxy server that supports HTTP, HTTPS, and FTP protocols. It can be used to cache content, improve browsing speeds, and provide secure internet access control.

Why Use Squid Proxy?

- Squid caches web content to reduce network traffic and speed up access to frequently requested resources.

- It can be used for access control, allowing or blocking specific websites or services.
- Squid is used in environments to monitor and filter web traffic for security and productivity purposes.

Installing Squid Proxy

- **Install Squid:**
  - **On Debian/Ubuntu:**

    sudo apt update

    sudo apt install squid
  - **On CentOS/Red Hat:**

    sudo yum install squid
- **Configure Squid:**
  - The main configuration file for Squid is /etc/squid/squid.conf. Open it for editing:

    sudo nano /etc/squid/squid.conf

Key configuration options

- **HTTP Port:** By default, Squid listens on port 3128. You can modify it in the http_port directive:

  http_port 3128
- **Access Control Lists (ACLs):** You can configure ACLs to allow or deny traffic based on IP addresses, domains, etc. For example, to allow access only from the local network:

  acl localnet src 192.168.1.0/24

  http_access allow localnet

  http_access deny all
- **Cache Configuration:** Squid can cache content to speed up response times for frequently accessed resources. You can configure cache settings in the cache_dir section:

  cache_dir ufs /var/spool/squid 100 16 256
- **Start Squid:**
  - **On Debian/Ubuntu:**

    sudo systemctl start squid

    sudo systemctl enable squid
  - **On CentOS/Red Hat:**

    sudo systemctl start squid

    sudo systemctl enable squid

Configure Clients to Use Squid Proxy: On the client machines, configure the browser or operating system to use the Squid proxy server. In most browsers, you can enter the proxy server's IP address and port (default is 3128).

PRINTER INSTALLATION IN GNU/LINUX SYSTEMS

Printer installation on Linux systems can vary depending on the printer model and the distribution in use, but the general steps are similar across different environments. Printers can be installed either through **CUPS (Common Unix Printing System)**, **IPP (Internet Printing Protocol)**, or other tools like **System-config-printer** or third-party utilities.

In this guide, we'll cover:

1. CUPS Installation and Configuration
2. Installing Printers using CUPS
3. Network Printer Configuration
4. Troubleshooting Printer Issues

1. CUPS Installation and Configuration

CUPS is the standard printing system used on Unix-like operating systems, including Linux. It provides a printing service that supports a wide variety of printers, including local, network, and USB printers. It is compatible with various printer models from different manufacturers.

Installing CUPS

CUPS is typically installed by default on most Linux distributions. However, in case it is missing, you can manually install it.

- **On Debian/Ubuntu:**

  sudo apt update

  sudo apt install cups
- **On CentOS/RHEL/Fedora:**

  sudo yum install cups

Starting and Enabling the CUPS Service

Once CUPS is installed, you need to start and enable the CUPS service to ensure it runs on boot.

- **On Debian/Ubuntu:**

  sudo systemctl start cups

  sudo systemctl enable cups
- **On CentOS/RHEL/Fedora:**

  sudo systemctl start cups

  sudo systemctl enable cups
- **Configuring CUPS**

  After installing and starting CUPS, you can access the **CUPS web interface** to manage your printers.
- **Open a web browser and go to:**

  http://localhost:631

This will bring up the **CUPS Administration Interface**. You can use this interface to:

- Add printers

- Configure printer settings
- Manage print jobs
- Modify CUPS settings

Allow remote administration (optional): If you want to manage CUPS remotely, you may need to edit the CUPS configuration file **/etc/cups/cupsd.conf**. Open it with a text editor:

```
sudo nano /etc/cups/cupsd.conf
```

- Change the following lines to allow remote access:
  ```
  # Listen on all interfaces
  Listen 0.0.0.0:631
  ```
- Restart CUPS:
  ```
  sudo systemctl restart cups
  ```

2. Installing Printers using CUPS

CUPS provides a simple way to add printers, either local or networked, through its web interface or using command-line tools.

Step 1: Add Printer via CUPS Web Interface

- **Access the CUPS web interface** by navigating to http://localhost:631 in your web browser.
- Click on the **Administration** tab.
- Select **Add Printer** under the "Printers" section.
- You may be prompted to log in with your **root** or **sudo** credentials to proceed.

Choose the Printer Type

- **Local Printers**: If your printer is connected via USB or directly to the computer, it should appear here. Choose the correct printer and click **Continue**.
- **Network Printers**: If you are adding a network printer, choose the relevant protocol (e.g., IPP, LPD, or AppSocket/JetDirect for TCP/IP printing). Enter the printer's IP address or hostname.

1. **Select Printer Driver**: CUPS will attempt to detect the correct driver for the printer. You may be prompted to choose a manufacturer and model. If the driver isn't automatically detected, you can download the correct driver from the printer manufacturer's website or search for it in the **"OpenPrinting"** database for Linux-compatible drivers.
2. **Set Printer Options**: Configure printer settings like default printer, paper size, print quality, etc.
3. **Test the Printer**: Once configured, CUPS may prompt you to print a test page to ensure everything is set up correctly.
4. Click **Add Printer** to complete the process.

Step 2: Add Printer via Command Line (LP and LPR Tools)

If you prefer using the command line, you can use lpadmin to add a printer.

- **Example command to add a local printer:**

  sudo lpadmin -p printer_name -v usb://HP/DeskJet_2600?serial=XYZ123 -m everywhere -E

- **Example command to add a network printer:**

  sudo lpadmin -p printer_name -v ipp://printer_ip_address/ipp/print -m everywhere -E

  - -p printer_name: Specifies the printer name.
  - -v usb://...: The URI for the printer, either USB or network.
  - -m everywhere: Automatically detects the driver.
  - -E: Enables the printer after installation.

- **To check the printer status:**

  lpstat -p

- **To print a test page:**

  lp -d printer_name /path/to/test_page.txt

3. Network Printer Configuration

Network printers are printers that are shared over a network. These printers can either use protocols like **IPP**, **LPD**, **JetDirect (Socket)**, or **SMB**.

Add a Network Printer via CUPS

Follow the same steps as before using the CUPS web interface. When adding a printer, instead of selecting a **local printer**, choose a network printer.

CUPS supports several types of network printing protocols:

- **IPP (Internet Printing Protocol)**: A common protocol used by many printers.
- **LPD (Line Printer Daemon)**: An older protocol used by some printers.
- **JetDirect/Socket (AppSocket)**: Used by HP and many other brands for direct TCP/IP printing.

To add a printer over the network, select the appropriate protocol and input the printer's IP address or hostname.

- **Example: Adding an IPP Printer**

  If your printer supports IPP, you can manually add it by specifying the printer's URI, which might look like:

  ipp://192.168.1.100/ipp/print

  You can add it using the CUPS web interface or command line:

  sudo lpadmin p printer_name -v ipp://192.168.1.100/ipp/print -m everywhere -E

Troubleshooting Network Printers

- Ensure the printer is powered on and connected to the network.
- Verify the printer's IP address (either through its display or the router's admin interface).
- Use **ping** to verify network connectivity:

  ping 192.168.1.100

If the printer is still not accessible, check the firewall settings on both the Linux machine and the printer.

4. Troubleshooting Printer Issues

Common Printer Issues

- **Printer Not Detected**:
  - **Check cables or network connectivity**: Ensure the printer is connected to the network or system.
  - **Check printer drivers**: Make sure the appropriate driver is installed for the printer model.
- **Permissions Issues**:
  - Ensure that the user has the necessary permissions to access the printer. The user might need to be added to the lp group:

    ```
    sudo usermod -aG lp <username>
    ```
- **CUPS Services Not Running**:
  - Make sure the CUPS service is running. If it is not, start it:

    ```
    sudo systemctl start cups
    sudo systemctl enable cups
    ```
- **Test Page Not Printing**:
  - Check for errors in CUPS logs:

    ```
    tail -f /var/log/cups/error_log
    ```
  - Verify that the correct printer driver is selected.
- **Paper Jams/Other Hardware Issues**:
  - These issues are more physical than software-related, so consult the printer's manual or check for any visible blockages.
- **Incorrect Print Quality**:
  - Check the print settings in CUPS or your printer's configuration page. You can adjust print quality, paper type, and other settings for different print jobs.

Conclusion

Installing and configuring a printer on a GNU/Linux system is generally straightforward using **CUPS** (Common Unix Printing System), which supports a wide range of printers. The process involves:

1. Installing CUPS and configuring the CUPS service.
2. Using the CUPS web interface or command-line tools to add local or network printers.
3. Managing printer queues and jobs through CUPS.
4. Troubleshooting common printer issues like connection problems, print errors, and driver issues.

♦♦♦

UNIT 4

Understanding GNU LIBC Libraries, Compilers and Linker

GNU COMPILER TOOLS

A collection of open-source compilers and associated tools for linking and compiling programs written in languages such as C and C++ is known as the GNU Compiler Collection (GCC). When it comes to Linux and Unix software development, these tools are essential.

1. Components of the GNU Compiler Toolchain

The main elements that convert source code into executable programs make up the GNU Compiler Toolchain. C and C++ code can be compiled into machine code using GCC (GNU Compiler Collection), and assembly language can be converted into object files using GNU Assembler (as).

To generate executables, the GNU Linker (ld) joins object files and libraries, while Binutils (which includes programs like objdump, nm, and are) aid in the management, analysis, and optimization of binaries. A potent open-source compilation and debugging environment is created by combining these tools.

Tool	Purpose
Gcc	The GNU C Compiler (compiles .c files into executable).
g++	The GNU C++ Compiler (compiles .cpp files).
Cpp	The C preprocessor (handles macros and header files).
as	The assembler (translates assembly code into machine code).
ld	The linker (Combines object files into an executable).
nm	List symbols in an object file or executable
objdump	Display detailed information about object files.
ar	Creates and manage static libraries (.a files)
ranllb	Index static libraries for faster linking
strip	Removes debugging symbols from binaries to reduce size

Fig 4.1: Components of the GNU Compiler Toolchain

2. Compilation Process

Preprocessing, Compilation, Assembly, and Linking are the four primary steps in the GNU

Compiler Toolchain compilation process. The source code is converted into a representation more like to machine code at each step.

1. Preprocessing (cpp)

- Expands macros (#define), processes
- **#include** directives, and removes comments.
- Generates an intermediate source file (.i). Command:

  cc -E main.c -o main.i

  Example:

  #include <stdio.h> #define PI 3.14

  int main () {print("PI = %f\n, PI"); return o;}

  After preprocessing:

  int main() {printf("PI = %f\n, 3.14"); return 0;}

2. Compilation (cc1)

- Converts preprocessed C code into assembly code (.s).
- Optimizations (-O2, -O3) and warnings (-Wall, -Wextra) can be applied.
- Command:

  gcc -S main.i -o main.s

GCC (GNU C Compiler) vs. G++ (GNU C++ Compiler)

Although they are both a component of the GNU Compiler Collection (GCC), G++ (g++) and GCC (gcc) are used for different languages and behave differently.

GCC (GNU C Compiler)

The GNU C Compiler (GCC) is a robust open-source compiler for the C programming language that is frequently used to create embedded systems, applications, and system software. It creates executable programs by putting C source code through a number of steps, such as preprocessing, compilation, assembly, and linking.

- Compiles C source files (.c → .o → executable).
- Requires explicit linking with libstdc++ when using C++ libraries.
- Default file extension: .c

  // main.c

  #include <studio.h> Int main () {

  Printf("Hello, c!\n");

  }

G++ (GNU C++ Compiler)

One essential part of the GNU Compiler Collection (GCC), which was created especially for producing C++ programs, is the GNU C++ Compiler (G++). It automatically links the C++ Standard Library (libstdc++) after processing C++ source files (.cpp,.cc,.cxx) via preprocessing, compilation, assembly, and linking steps.

- Compiles C++ source files (.cpp → .o → executable).
- Automatically links libstdc++ (C++ Standard Library).
- Default file extension: .cpp
- Allows cout, cin, and object-oriented programming features.

```
// main.cpp
#include <iostream> Using namespace std; Int main () {
Cout<< "Hello, C++"<< endl; Return 0;
}
```

Key Differences Between GCC and G++

Feature	gcc (C Compiler)	g++(C++ Compiler)
Language Support	C	C++
File Extensions	.c	.cpp, .cc, .cxx
Standard Libraries	Requires -lstdc++ for C++ libararies	Automatically links C++ Standard Library
Default Linking	Links only the C standard library (libc)	Links Both libc and libstdc++
Object oriented programming	Not Supported	Fully supports classes, inheritance, and polymorphism
Compilation Command	Gcc main.c -o main	g++ main.cpp -o main

LINKING AGAINST OBJECT ARCHIVES (.A LIBRARIES)

Static libraries, often known as archive libraries or.a files, are used in C and C++ programming to hold precompiled object files that may be linked into an executable. By linking previously compiled functions rather of recompiling them, this permits code reuse and cuts down on compilation time.

Creating and Linking Against a Static Library (.a file)

A collection of precompiled object files that may be linked into an executable at build time is known as a static library (.a file) in C or C++. This decreases compilation time and enhances modularity and code reuse.

1. Compile Source Files into Object Files (.o)
2. Create a Static Library (.a) using ar (Archiver)
3. Link the Static Library to a Program
4. Run the Executable.

1. Compile Source Files into Object Files (.o)

Building C and C++ programs requires that source files be compiled into object files (.o). Human-readable source code (.c or.cpp files) is converted into machine-readable object files (.o) using the GCC compiler (gcc for C or g++ for C++). The -c option, which compiles the source files but does not link them, is used for this.

Example:

gcc -c file1.c file2.c

This generates file1.o and file2.o, which contain compiled code.

Advantages of Separate Compilation

- **Faster Build Process:** Only modified files need to be recompiled.
- **Modular Code Management:** Helps in organizing large projects.
- **Easier Debugging:** Errors are easier to track in individual files.

2. Create a Static Library (.a) using ar (Archiver)

The ar (archiver) tool is used to bundle several object files (.o) into a static library (.a file). In C and C++ projects, this enables code modularity and reuse.

Example:

ar rcs libmylib.a file1.o file2.o

This creates libmylib.a, which stores the compiled object files.

Advantages of Static Libraries (.a Files)

- **Encapsulation:** Hides implementation details from users.
- **No Runtime Dependencies:** Unlike shared libraries, all code is included in the final executable.
- **Faster Execution:** No dynamic linking at runtime.

3. Link the Static Library to a Program

A static library (.a file) must be linked to a program once it has been created in order for the executable to utilize its features. The GCC compiler is used for this, and the library and its location are specified.

Example:

gcc main.c -L. -lymlib -o myprogram

L. tells the compiler to look for libraries in the current directory.

lmylib links libmylib.a (without the lib prefix).

Advantages of Static Linking

- No need to distribute extra library files.
- Faster execution (no runtime dependency resolution).
- Code encapsulation and security.

4. Run the Executable

The program must be successfully compiled and linked with a static library (.a) before the resultant binary file may be run.

Example:

./myprogram

Advantages of Using .a Libraries

- **Faster Compilation:** No need to recompile shared code.
- **Portability:** Easy to distribute and use without source files.
- **Encapsulation:** Hides implementation details from the end-user.

DYNAMIC SHARED OBJECT LIBRARIES (.SO LIBRARIES)

Dynamic Shared Object (.so) libraries are Linux shared libraries that let several programs utilize the same code without having to integrate it in the executable itself. Shared libraries are loaded at runtime, minimizing executable size and facilitating effective memory management, in contrast to static libraries (.a files), which are linked at compile time. Gcc -fPIC -c file.c is used to compile source files into position- independent object files, which are then merged into a.so file using gcc -shared -o libmylib.so file.o to produce a shared library.

Programs must guarantee that the library is available at runtime (export LD_LIBRARY_PATH=.:$LD_LIBRARY_PATH) and link to the.so library during compilation (gcc main.c -L. -lmylib -o myprogram). Updates are made easier with this method since changes made to the.so file automatically affect all dependant programs without the need for recompilation.

Creating and Using a Shared Library (.so File)

Multiple programs can share common code dynamically at runtime by creating and utilizing a shared library (.so file). First, gcc -fPIC -c file1.c file2.c is used to compile source files into position-independent object files.

The command gcc -shared -o libmylib.so file1.o file2.o is then used to merge these object files into a shared library. Lastly, the shared library must be available at runtime using export LD_LIBRARY_PATH=.:$LD_LIBRARY_PATH. Programs can link to it during compilation with gcc main.c -L. -lmylib -o myprogram.

Compile Source Files into Object Files (.o)

One of the most important steps in creating C and C++ applications is compiling source files into object files (.o). Human-readable source code (.c or.cpp) is converted into machine-readable object files (.o) by the GCC compiler (gcc for C and g++ for C++). The -c flag is used to accomplish this, compiling the source files without linking them.

For instance, file1.o and file2.o are produced when gcc -c file1.c file2.c is performed. Compilated code found in these object files can subsequently be linked with other object files or libraries to produce an executable. This approach facilitates modular programming, speeds up development because only updated files require recompilation, and facilitates debugging.

```
gcc -Fpic -c file1.c file2.c
```

- fPIC → Generates Position-Independent Code (PIC) required for shared libraries.

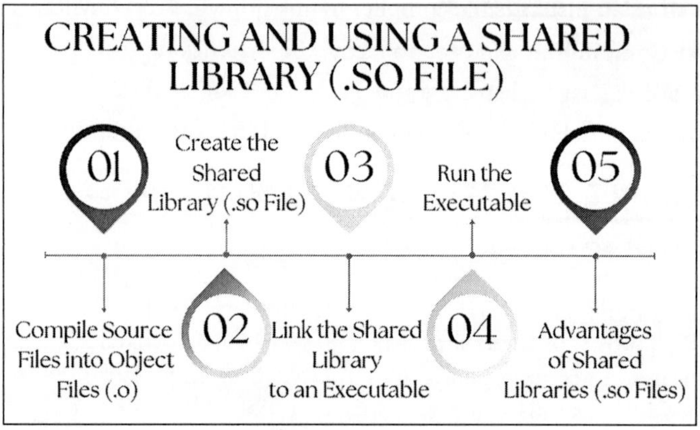

Create the Shared Library (.so File)

Multiple programs can access common functions dynamically at runtime in C/C++ by creating a shared library (.so file), which reduces executable size and increases efficiency. Using gcc -fPIC -c file1.c file2.c, source files are first compiled into position- independent object files (.o), where -fPIC guarantees that the code can be loaded at any memory address. gcc -shared -o libmylib.so file1.o file2.o is then used to construct the shared library, where -shared creates the.so file.

Then, using gcc main.c -L. -lmylib -o myprogram, this library can be linked to other programs. To make sure it is available at runtime, use export **LD_LIBRARY_PATH=.:$LD_LIBRARY_PATH.**

Example:

gcc -shared -o libmylib.so file.o file2.o

- shared → Creates a shared library.

Link the Shared Library to an Executable

An executable can use external functions without embedding the library's code by linking a shared library (.so file) to it. The application is compiled with the location of the shared library specified in order to accomplish this. The command gcc main is used with GCC.c -L. -lmylib -o Myprogram instructs the compiler to link libmylib.so (- lmylib, removing the lib prefix) and search for it in the current directory (-L.).

Setting export **LD_LIBRARY_PATH=.:$LD_LIBRARY_PATH** will guarantee that the system finds the shared library when the program is executed. This method allows the library to be updated independently and makes executables smaller.

Example:

gcc -shared -o libmylib.so file1.o file2.o

- shared → Creates a shared library.

Link the Shared Library to an Executable

An executable can use external functions without embedding the library's code by linking a shared library (.so file) to it. The application is compiled with the location of the shared library specified in order to accomplish this. The command gcc main is used with GCC.c -L.

-lmylib -o Myprogram instructs the compiler to link libmylib.so (- lmylib, removing the lib prefix) and search for it in the current directory (-L.).

Setting export **LD_LIBRARY_PATH=.:$LD_LIBRARY_PATH** will guarantee that the system finds the shared library when the program is executed. This method allows the library to be updated independently and makes executables smaller.

Example:

gcc main.c -L. -lmylib -o myprogram

- L. → Looks for libmylib.so in the current directory.
- lmylib → Links the shared library (libmylib.so, omit lib prefix).

Run the Executable

Make that the program is appropriately generated and that the system can find the library at runtime before launching an executable linked to a shared library (.so file). Use./myprogram to run the program after compilation (gcc main.c -L. -lmylib -o myprogram). The library might not be found by the system if an error message appears, such as "cannot open shared object file". To fix this, use export **LD_LIBRARY_PATH=.:$LD_LIBRARY_PATH** to set the library path, instructing the system to search the current directory for shared libraries. Rerunning./myprogram after it has been set should allow it to use the functions from the. so file.

Example:

./myprogram

If you get a "cannot open shared object file" error, set the library path: export LD_LIBRARY_PATH=.:$LD_LIBRARY_PATH

./myprogram

Advantages of Shared Libraries (.so Files)

- **Smaller Executable Size:** Code is stored separately, reducing program size.
- **Memory Efficiency:** Multiple programs can share the same .so file.
- **Easy Updates:** Updating the .so file updates all dependent programs without recompiling them.

GENERATING STATICALLY LINKED BINARIES AND LIBRARIES

The executable is self-contained and independent of external shared libraries since all necessary code is immediately embedded within it thanks to the generation of statically linked binaries and libraries. First, gcc -c file1.c file2.c is used to compile source files into object files. The object files are then archived using ar rcs libmylib.a file1.o file2.o to generate a static library (.a file). The software is compiled using gcc main to produce a completely statically linked binary.c -L. where -static forces static linking and -lmylib -static -o myprogram.

Generating Statically Linked Binaries

Statically linked binaries are self-sufficient and can execute on any system without the need for external dependencies because they contain all the required libraries within the executable itself. They are typically bigger than dynamically linked binaries, though.

Steps to Generate a Statically Linked Binary

1. Compile the Source Code into Object Files (.o)
2. Link the Object Files Statically
3. Verify Static Linking

1. Compile the Source Code into Object Files (.o)

An essential step in creating a software is compiling the source code into object files (.o) before assembling it into an executable. The GCC compiler converts each source file (.c or.cpp) into machine code separately, keeping external references for linking at a later time. The -c flag is used for this, compiling the source files but not linking them. For instance, the built code for each source file is contained in main.o and utils.o, which are produced when gcc -c main.c utils.c is invoked. To enable modular development and effective recompilation of only updated files, these object files are subsequently coupled with additional object files or libraries to produce a whole executable.

Example:

```
Gcc -c main.c utils.c
```

- This step generates main.o and utils.o.

Example: Compile Source Code into Object Files (.o):

In C or C++, compiling source files into object files is an essential step in creating executable programs. Below is a simple example demonstrating how to compile a C program into object files before linking.

Step 1: Create a Source File (example.c)

```
#include <studio.h> Void hello () {
Printf ("Hello, world\n");
}
int main () { hello ();
return 0;
}
```

Step 2: Compile the Source Code into an Object File (.o)

Use the gcc compiler with the -c flag to generate an object file: gcc -c example.c -o example.0

Step 3: Link the Object File to Create an Executable

To generate an executable from the object file, run: gcc example.o -o example

Now, the executable example can be run using:

```
./example
```

This method allows modular compilation, making it efficient for managing large projects with multiple source files.

2. Link the Object Files Statically

Statically linking object files removes the need for external shared libraries by producing a self-contained executable with all required code. The GCC compiler connects source files with the -static parameter after turning them into object files (.o). To embed all necessary libraries, for instance, gcc -static main.o utils.o -o my program merges the object files into my program. As a result, the executable is highly portable and may operate on any system without the need for shared libraries. Unlike dynamic linking, which loads shared libraries at runtime, static linking includes all library code, which results in larger files.

Example:

```
gcc -static main.o utils.o -o myprogram
```

- The -static flag forces static linking, embedding all required libraries into my program.

Static linking combines object files and libraries into a single executable, ensuring it does not rely on external shared libraries at runtime.

Step 1: Create Source Files

We will create two source files: hello.c and main.c.

hello.c (contains a function definition):

```
#include <studio.h> Void hello (){
Printf ("Hello, world! (Static Linking Example)\n");
}
```

main.c (calls the hello function)

```
#include <stdio.h>
Void hello (); // Function Prototype int main () {
hello (); // call the funcation return 0;
}
```

Step 2: Compile Source Files into Object Files

Compile each source file separately into object files (.o files):

```
gcc-c hello.c -o hello.o
gcc-c main.c -o main.o
```

Step 3: Link Object Files Statically

Now, link both object files into a single statically linked executable:

```
gcc -static
hello.o -o static_example
```

Step 4: Run the Statically Linked Executable

Execute the generated binary:

```
./static_example
```

Expected Output

Hello,World! (static Linking Example)

This demonstrates static linking, where all required code is embedded within the final executable, making it self-contained and independent of external shared libraries.

3. Verify Static Linking

The ldd program, which examines an executable's dependency on shared libraries, is frequently used to confirm static linking. Running ldd my program will return "not a dynamic executable" if an executable is fully statically linked, indicating that the binary contains all necessary libraries.

As an alternative, the binary type can be found with the file my program command, and the nm my program lists contained symbols can be used to confirm that there are no external dynamic references. In contrast to dynamically linked executables, static linking results in a greater file size but guarantees portability and independence from system libraries.

Run the following command:

```
ldd myprogram
```

- If it returns "not a dynamic executable", the binary is fully statically linked.

Although statically linked binaries remove dependency problems, they make files larger. They are helpful in secure settings where shared library versions may differ, embedded systems, and portable applications.

Example: Verify Static Linking

After statically linking object files, we can verify that the executable does not depend on shared libraries by using the ldd command.

Step 1: Create Source Files

We'll use the same example as before, with hello.c and main.c.

hello.c (Function Definition)

```
#include <stdio.h> Void hello () {;
Print ("Hello, world! (Static Linking Verification)\n");
}
```

main.c

(Main Function)

```
#include <studio.h>
Void hello(); //Funcation Prototype Int main () {
Hello (); // call the funcation Return 0;
}
```

Step 2: Compile Source Files into Object Files

```
gcc -c
hello.c -o
hello.o gcc
-c main.c
-o main.o
```

Step 3: Link Object Files Statically

```
gcc -static hello.o main.o -o static_example
```

Step 4: Verify Static Linking

To check whether the binary is statically linked, use the ldd command:

ldd static_example

Expected Output

Not a dynamic executable

This confirms that the binary is statically linked and does not rely on shared libraries.

LIBRARIES

Libraries are sets of precompiled code that developers use to reuse functionality without having to write it from scratch, making programming easier. There are two primary categories of them: shared libraries (.so files) and static libraries (.a files). In order to integrate their code into the final executable and make it self-contained but larger, static libraries are linked at compile time. On the other hand, shared libraries are linked during runtime, which improves efficiency by lowering the executable size and enabling numerous programs to use the same library. Libraries include necessary features that improve program modularity and maintainability, including file processing, mathematical operations, and GUI elements.

Generating dynamically linked libraries

Creating dynamically linked libraries (.so files) reduces executable size and increases memory efficiency by enabling numerous programs to share code. Using gcc -fPIC -c file1.c file2.c, source files are first compiled into position-independent object files. - fPIC guarantees that the code can be loaded at any memory address. The shared library is then made with gcc -shared -o libmylib.so file1.o file2.o, which generates the.so file with the -shared flag. Programs use gcc main.c -L. -lmylib -o myprogram to link to the shared library, where -L. indicates the location of the library.

Ensuring that export **LD_LIBRARY_PATH=.:$LD_LIBRARY_PATH** is set will help the system find the.so file, which is necessary for the executable to run. Code reuse across various programs, quicker updates, and economical memory utilization are all made possible by this strategy.

Steps to Create a Dynamically Linked Library

1. Compile Source Files into Object Files (.o)
2. Create the Shared Library (.so File)
3. Link the Shared Library to a Program
4. Run the Program with the Shared Library

1. Compile Source Files into Object Files (.o)

In order to create executables and libraries, source files must be compiled into object files (.o). Each source file (.c or.cpp) is converted into machine-readable object code by the GCC compiler, which leaves external references unresolved for linking at a later time. The -c flag is used to accomplish this, compiling the files without producing an executable.

For Example, file1.o and file2.o are produced when gcc -c file1.c file2.c is performed. The -fPIC (Position-Independent Code) flag is used when producing shared libraries (.so files): gcc -fPIC -c file1.c file2.c. This ensures that the produced code can be loaded at any memory address. The final executable or shared library is then created by linking these object files together.

gcc -FPIC -c file1.c file2.c

- fPIC (Position-Independent Code) is required for shared libraries.

2. Create the Shared Library (.so File)

Compiling source files into position-independent object files using gcc -fPIC -c file1.c file2.c is the first step in creating a shared library (.so file). The -fPIC flag guarantees that the code can be loaded at any memory address. Then, link these object files with gcc -shared -o libmylib.so file1.o file2.o to create the shared library. The -shared flag creates a dynamically linked.so file.

Multiple programs can use the resulting shared library, which lowers executable size and memory utilization. Set the LD_LIBRARY_PATH environment variable with export LD_LIBRARY_PATH=.:$LD_LIBRARY_PATH to guarantee the system locates the library at runtime.

Example:

gcc -shared -o libmylib.so file1.o file2.o

- shared generates the .so file.

3. Link the Shared Library

Compile the main source file and include the library's location when linking a shared library (.so file) to a program. Make use of gcc main.The code c -L. -lmylib -o myprogram instructs the compiler to search the current directory for the library, while - lmylib links against libmylib.so (omitting the lib prefix and.so suffix).

If the system is unable to find the shared library at runtime, use export LD_LIBRARY_PATH=.:$LD_LIBRARY_PATH to set the LD_LIBRARY_PATH.

This makes sure the shared library loads dynamically in the program, which minimizes executable size and makes it simple to update without recompiling the program.

Example:

gcc main.c -L. -lmylib -o myprogram

- L. tells the compiler to look for the library in the current directory.

4. Run the Program with the Shared Library

The system must be able to find the shared library (.so file) during runtime in order for a program to execute. An error such as "cannot open shared object file" could appear if the library is not in a standard place.

To fix this, use export **LD_LIBRARY_PATH=.:$LD_LIBRARY_PATH** to set the environment variable **LD_LIBRARY_PATH**. This instructs the system to search the current directory for shared libraries. Next, use./myprogram to run the program. Using ldconfig to update the dynamic linker cache might also be beneficial if the shared library is installed in a shared directory, such as /usr/lib. This method guarantees effective memory use and makes it simple to update the shared library without having to recompile the application.

If the system cannot find the .so file, set the library path:

export LD_LIBRARY_PATH=.:$LD_LIBRARY_PATH

./myprogram

Libraries that are dynamically linked minimize redundancy, facilitate updates, and maximize memory utilization across several applications.

Using the GNU debugging tools

Strong features for debugging C and C++ programs are offered by the GNU debugging tools, particularly GDB (GNU Debugger). To find mistakes and improve efficiency, they let developers go through code, check variables, establish breakpoints, and examine the call stack.

To use GDB, execute the program inside GDB (gdb./myprogram) after compiling it with debugging symbols (gcc -g). To track execution and identify problems, use commands like break, run, next, step, print, and backtrace. These technologies are crucial for resolving logical flaws, diagnosing failures, and enhancing program dependability. To effectively identify flaws, GDB enables variable inspection, breakpoints, step-by-step execution, and backtracing.

Basic Steps to Debug a Program Using GDB

1. Compile with Debugging Information
2. Start GDB
3. Set Breakpoints
4. Run the Program
5. Step Through Execution
6. Inspect Variables
7. View the Call Stack
8. Exit GDB

1. Compile with Debugging Information

The -g switch must be used during compilation in order to compile a program with debugging information using the GNU debugging tools (GDB). In order for GDB to map machine instructions back to the source code for effective debugging, this setting makes sure that symbolic debugging information is present in the binary.

Steps to Compile with Debugging Information

a. Compile the program with -g
b. Start debugging with GDB
c. Verify debugging symbols inside GDB

a. Compile the Program with -g

The -g switch needs to be added during compilation in order to compile a program with debugging information using the GNU debugging tool (GDB). By ensuring that symbolic debugging information is present in the executable, this flag enables GDB to effectively debug by mapping machine instructions back to the original source code. An executable (myprogram) with embedded debugging symbols is produced, for instance, when gcc -g -o myprogram myprogram.c is used for compilation.

This lets developers move through code, check variables while it's running, and set breakpoints. The program can be debugged via gdb./myprogram after it has been compiled. Compiling with -g greatly improves debugging capabilities, which facilitate error detection and correction.

Example:

gcc -g -o myprogram

myprogram.c

- g: Includes debugging symbols.
- o myprogram: Specifies the output executable.

b. Start debugging with GDB

First, use the -g flag to compile the program with debugging symbols (gcc -g -o myprogram myprogram.c) before beginning to debug using GDB. Run gdb./myprogram to load the program into the debugger after it has been compiled. Developers can run the program (run), step through execution (next or step), create breakpoints (break main), and inspect variables (print variable_name) within GDB. In the event that the program crashes, the backtrace command aids in call stack analysis. GDB makes it possible to analyse program execution step-by-step, which facilitates the detection of flaws, error correction, and performance optimization. Use the quit command to get out of GDB.

Example:

Gdb ./myprogram

c. Verify debugging symbols

inside GDB

Make that the program was compiled with the -g flag (gcc -g -o myprogram myprogram.c) before attempting to validate debugging symbols inside GDB. Next, use

gdb./myprogram to launch GDB. To verify whether the source file is loaded and contains debugging information, use the info source command once you're within GDB. Running info functions also provides a list of all accessible functions along with the symbols that correspond to them.

If the symbols are missing, it may indicate that the program was compiled without -g, or the binary was stripped of debugging information. When debugging, proper verification guarantees that step-through execution, variable inspection, and breakpoints function as intended.

Run the following command in GDB to check debugging information:

Info source

Using the -g flag ensures that developers can use GDB effectively for breakpoints, variable inspection, and step-by-step execution, making debugging easier.

2. Start GDB

Make that the program has been compiled with debugging symbols by using the -g flag (gcc -g -o myprogram myprogram.c) before starting GDB. In the terminal, type gdb./ myprogram to start GDB after it has been compiled. Developers can then examine the program's execution, create breakpoints, step through code, and examine variables by loading it into the GNU Debugger (GDB).

Debugging may be done efficiently inside GDB by using commands like run (to run the program), break main (to set a breakpoint at the main function), and print variable_name

gdb ./myprogram

(to investigate variable values). The program may require a -g recompile if the debugging symbols are absent. The quit command is used to exit GDB.

Setting breakpoints, stepping through execution, inspecting variables, and analyzing program behavior are all made possible by loading the program into GDB (GNU Debugger). Debugging effectively within GDB is possible with commands like break main, run, next, and print variable_name. The quit command is used to exit GDB.

3. Set Breakpoints

To set breakpoints in GDB, first, start the debugger by running gdb ./myprogram after compiling the program with the -g flag. Inside GDB, use the break command to set a breakpoint at a specific function or line number. For example, break main sets a breakpoint at the main function, while break 10 sets a breakpoint at line 10 of the source code. When the program is executed with run, it will pause at the breakpoint, allowing developers to inspect variables and step through execution. To remove a breakpoint, use delete <breakpoint_number>. Setting breakpoints helps isolate and debug problematic code sections efficiently.

Inside GDB, set a breakpoint at main() or a specific function:

break main

4. Run the Program

To run the program in GDB, first, ensure it is compiled with debugging symbols using gcc -g -o myprogram myprogram.c. Start GDB by running gdb ./myprogram, then use the run command to execute the program. If breakpoints are set (e.g., break main), the execution will pause at those points, allowing you to inspect variables or step through the code. If no breakpoints are set, the program runs normally until completion or crashes. Command-line arguments can also be passed using run arg1 arg2. Running the program inside GDB helps in diagnosing errors, tracking execution flow, and debugging crashes effectively.

run

5. Step Through Execution

To step through execution in GDB, first ensure the program is compiled with debugging symbols using gcc -g -o myprogram myprogram.c. Start GDB with gdb ./myprogram, set a breakpoint (break main), and then run the program using run. Once the breakpoint is hit, use next to execute the next line while staying in the current function or step to enter function calls for deeper inspection. The continue command resumes execution until the next breakpoint, while finish exits the current function. Stepping through execution helps trace program flow, inspect variable values, and debug logic errors efficiently.

- next → Executes the next line.
- step → Steps into function calls.
- continue → Resumes execution until the next breakpoint.

6. Inspect Variables

To inspect variables in GDB, first compile the program with debugging symbols using gcc -g -o myprogram myprogram.c, then start GDB with gdb ./myprogram. Set a breakpoint (break main) and run the program (run). Once execution pauses, use the print command to check variable values, such as print variable_name. For more detailed inspection, display variable_name continuously shows the variable's value after each step.

To examine memory addresses, use x (e.g., x/10x &variable_name for hexadecimal output). The info locals command lists all local variables, while info variables shows global variables. Inspecting variables helps identify incorrect values, memory issues, and logic errors in debugging.

Print variable_name

7. View the Call Stack

To view the call stack in GDB, first compile the program with debugging symbols using gcc -g -o myprogram myprogram.c, then start GDB with gdb./myprogram. Set a breakpoint (break main) and run the program (run). When execution pauses, use the backtrace (or bt) command to display the call stack, which shows the sequence of function calls leading to the current execution point. Each frame in the stack includes the function name, source file, and line number. To inspect a specific frame, use frame <n>. Viewing the call stack helps trace program flow, diagnose crashes, and debug function calls effectively.

backtrace

8. Exit GDB

To exit GDB, simply type the quit or q command and press Enter. If a program is running, GDB will ask for confirmation before terminating it. You can also force exit by using quit followed by y. Alternatively, pressing Ctrl + D will also exit GDB. If you need to restart debugging later, just reopen GDB with gdb ./myprogram. Exiting GDB properly ensures that resources are released and prevents unintended debugging sessions from lingering.

quit

With the use of GDB's robust debugging features, developers can effectively investigate crashes, track down mistakes, and improve performance.

Gdb to debug programs

The GNU Debugger (GDB) is a powerful tool for debugging C and C++ programs, allowing developers to analyze program execution, identify bugs, and diagnose crashes. To use GDB, the program must be compiled with debugging symbols using the -g flag (gcc -g -o myprogram myprogram.c). Once compiled, GDB is started with gdb

./myprogram, where users can set breakpoints (break main), run the program (run), and step through execution using next (move to the next line) or step (enter functions).

Variables can be inspected using print variable_name, and the call stack can be analyzed with backtrace. If an issue is found, developers can modify the code, recompile, and continue debugging. GDB provides an interactive way to troubleshoot logic errors, memory access violations, and program crashes, making it an essential tool for software development. To exit GDB, use the quit command.

Example C Program (buggy_code.c):

This program calculates the sum of an array, but contains a bug (accessing an out-of-bounds index).

```
#include <stdio.h>
void compute_sum(int arr[], int size) { int sum = 0;
for (int i = 0; i <= size; i++) { // Bug: Accessing out-of-bounds index sum += arr[i];
}
printf("Sum: %d\n", sum);
}
int main() {
int numbers[] = {1, 2, 3, 4, 5}; int size = 5; // Size of the array compute_sum(numbers, size); return 0;
}
```

Steps to Debug Using GDB

1. Compile with Debug Symbols
2. Start GDB
3. Set Breakpoints
4. Run the Program
5. Step Through Execution
6. Inspect Variables
7. View the Call Stack
8. Continue Execution
9. Exit GDB

1. Compile with Debug Symbols

When using GCC or G++ to compile a program, use the -g flag to include debugging symbols. By including debugging information in the executable, this flag enables efficient program analysis and debugging by tools like GDB.

Example: Compiling a C Program with Debug Symbols:

```
gcc -g -o myprogram myprogram.c
```

Example: Compiling a C++ Program with Debug Symbols:

```
g++ -g -o myprogram myprogram.cpp
```

The -g option does not affect optimization but adds extra debugging metadata, enabling breakpoints, variable inspection, and step-through execution in GDB. After compilation, you can start debugging using:

```
gdb./myprogram
```

Using debugging symbols makes it easier to identify **memory issues, logical errors, and crashes** in a program.

To start GDB, first ensure that your program is compiled with debugging symbols using the -g flag. Then, launch GDB with the following command:

Compile with Debug Symbols

gcc -g -o myprogram myprogram.c # For C

programs g++ -g -o myprogram myprogram.cpp # For C++ programs

2. Start GDB

gdb ./myprogram

This will load the program into GDB, allowing you to debug it interactively.

Basic GDB Commands After Starting:

- Run the program: run
- Set a breakpoint: break main (or any function/line number)
- Step through execution: next (line by line) or step (enter function)
- Inspect variables: print variable_name
- View call stack: backtrace
- Exit GDB: quit or q

Starting GDB this way allows detailed program analysis, helping identify bugs, crashes, and logic errors effectively.

3. Set Breakpoints

In GDB, a breakpoint halts program execution at a designated moment, enabling variable inspection and step-by-step debugging. Breakpoints can be placed at memory addresses, functions, or particular line numbers.

Start GDB:

Set Breakpoints:

At a function:

gdb ./myprogram

break main

(Pauses execution at the beginning of main().)

At a specific line number:

break 10

(Breaks at line 10 of the current source file.)

In a specific file:

break file.c:20

(Breaks at line 20 in file.c.)

Conditional breakpoint (only stops if a condition is met):

break myfunction if x > 5 (Breaks inside myfunction() only if x > 5.)

View Breakpoints:

Remove Breakpoints:

Delete a specific breakpoint.

Delete all breakpoints:

info breakpoints

delete 1 Delete

Breakpoints help analyze execution flow, inspect variables, and debug efficiently.

4. Running the Program in GDB

Once GDB is started and breakpoints are set, you can run the program to begin execution.

1. **Start GDB:**

   gdb ./myprogram

2. **Run the Program:**

   To **start execution** from the beginning.

   Run

   (Runs the program until a breakpoint is hit or it finishes execution.)

   To run the program with command-line arguments:

   run arg1 arg2

   (Passes arg1 and arg2 as arguments to the program.)

   If the program crashes or stops at a breakpoint, you can:

   - Inspect variables (print var_name)
   - Step through code (next, step)
   - View the call stack (backtrace)

3. **Restarting the Program:**

   After making changes, restart execution with:

   Run

   (GDB will ask if you want to restart if the program has already run.)

   To force restart without confirmation:

   run -restart

4. **Continue Execution After a Breakpoint:**

   If execution stops at a breakpoint, resume with:

   Continue

   (Runs until the next breakpoint or program termination.)

   Using run in GDB helps analyze execution, detect crashes, and debug issues efficiently.

5. Step Through Execution

You can examine variables, debug line-by-line, and examine the program's flow by stepping through execution with GDB.

1. **Start GDB and Run the Program:**

   gdb ./myprogram

   Then, set a breakpoint to pause execution:

   Break main run

2. **Step Through Execution:**

   Once the program stops at a breakpoint, use the following commands.

- Step into a function (step)

Step

Moves to the next line, entering function calls.

- Move to the next line (next)

Next

Moves to the next line **without entering functions.**

- Step out of a function (finish)

Finish

Executes the rest of the current function and returns to the caller.

- Continue execution until the next breakpoint (continue).

Continue

6. Inspect Variables While Stepping

Use these commands to examine variables at each step:

- Print variable value:

  print var_name
- Display variable on every step:

  display var_name
- Show all local variables:

  info locals

Stepping through execution helps you identify logical errors, track variable changes, and debug efficiently.

Inspect Variables

Inspecting variables in GDB allows you to monitor their values during execution, track changes, and debug errors effectively.

1. **Start GDB and Run the Program:**

   gdb ./myprogram

   Set a breakpoint to pause execution at a specific function or line:

   break main run
2. **Print Variable Values:**
   - Print a single variable:

     print var_name

     (Displays the current value of var_name.)
   - Print a pointer's value:

     print *ptr

     (Dereferences a pointer to see the stored value.)
   - Print an array or structure:
   - print my_array print my_struct

3. **Watch Variable Changes:**
   - Automatically display a variable on each step:
   - display var_name
   - List all displayed variables:

   info display
   - Stop displaying a variable:

     undisplay 1

     (Removes the first displayed variable.)
4. **Inspect All Variables:**
   - Show all local variables in the current function:

     info locals
   - Show function arguments:

     info args
5. **Monitor Variable Changes Dynamically:**
   - Set a watchpoint to track a variable's value in memory:

     watch var_name

     (Breaks execution whenever var_name changes.)
   - List all watchpoints:

     info watchpoints

These commands help you examine, track, and debug variables efficiently while analyzing program execution.

7. View the Call Stack

Debugging crashes, infinite loops, and improper function calls is made easier by the call stack, which displays the order of function calls that led to the present execution point.

1. **Start GDB and Run the Program:**

   gdb ./myprogram

   Set a breakpoint to pause execution:
2. **View the Call Stack:**

   break main run

   Show the call stack (backtrace):

   Backtrace

   (Displays all active function calls in the order they were invoked.)
   - Show a full backtrace (with local variables):

     backtrace full

     (Includes function arguments and variable values for each stack frame.)
3. **Navigate the Call Stack:**
   - Move to a specific stack frame:

     frame 2

(Switches to the second function in the stack.)

- Move up one level in the stack:

  up
- Move down one level in the stack:

  down

4. **Inspect Variables in a Stack Frame**

   After switching to a specific frame:

   info locals

   (Shows local variables in the current stack frame.)

   print var_name

   (Prints a specific variable value.)
5. **Exit the Call Stack View:**

   Simply continue execution or quit GDB:

   continue quit

By analyzing the call stack, you can trace function calls, debug crashes, and understand program execution flow.

8. Continue Execution

The continue command in GDB resumes program execution after it has been paused at a breakpoint or watchpoint.

1. **Start GDB and Run the Program**

   gdb ./myprogram

   Set a breakpoint to pause execution:
2. **Continue Execution:**

   break main run

   - Resume execution after hitting a breakpoint:

     continue

     (The program runs until it hits the next breakpoint or finishes.)
   - Shortcut for continue:

     c
   - Continue execution until a specific line:

     until 42

     (Continues execution until it reaches line 42.)
3. **Handling Signals:**
   - Ignore signals and continue execution:

     handle SIGINT nostop

     continue

     (Prevents GDB from stopping when receiving SIGINT.)
4. **Restart Execution After Modification:**

- If changes are made, restart execution:

  run

Using **continue** in GDB allows seamless debugging while maintaining control over program execution.

Continue Execution in GDB

The continue command (c) in GDB resumes program execution after it has been paused at a breakpoint, watchpoint, or signal interruption.

1. **Start GDB and Run the Program:**

   gdb ./myprogram

   Set a breakpoint to pause execution:

2. **Resume Execution:**

   break main run

   Continue execution after hitting a breakpoint:

   continue

   (Resumes execution until the next breakpoint, watchpoint, or program termination.) Shortcut for continue:

   c

3. **Continue Until a Specific Line:**
   - Run the program until it reaches line 50:

     until 50

     (Useful in loops or to skip over function calls.)

4. **Handle Signals and Continue Execution:**
   - Ignore a signal and continue execution:

     handle SIGINT nostop

     continue

     (Prevents GDB from stopping when SIGINT is received.)

5. **Restart Execution if Needed:**

   Restart the program from the beginning:

   run

Using the continue command in GDB helps you efficiently control execution flow while debugging.

9. Exit GDB

Exiting GDB properly ensures that debugging sessions are closed safely.

1. **Quit GDB:**
   - Use the quit command:

     quit

     (This immediately exits GDB.)
   - Shortcut for quit:

q

2. **Confirm Exit if Running a Program:**

   If the program is still running, GDB may ask for

   confirmation: A debugging session is active. Quit anyway?

   (y or n)

   Press **y** to confirm and exit.

3. **Exit GDB and Kill the Debugged Process:**

   Force quit without confirmation:

   kill quit

   (Terminates the running program before exiting GDB.)

4. **Exit GDB After a Command Execution:**

   Run a command and exit immediately:

   gdb -ex "run" -ex "quit" ./myprogram

   (Executes run, then exits GDB.)

By using these commands, you can **exit GDB safely and efficiently.**

GRAPHICAL DEBUGGERS LIKE DDD

Comparing graphical debuggers like DDD (Data Display Debugger) to command-line tools like GDB, the former offer a more user-friendly visual interface for debugging applications, which facilitates the analysis of execution flow. DDD serves as a front- end for debuggers like GDB, DBX, JDB, and others, enabling users to step through code, set breakpoints, examine variables, and graphically depict memory structures. Both novice and seasoned developers can find debugging easier with DDD's capabilities, which include graphical breakpoints, hover-based variable inspection, and an integrated command console. It is especially helpful for debugging complicated programs since it provides a visual representation of data structures and function calls.

Debugging becomes more efficient when users interact with their application using buttons rather than manually inputting commands. DDD is compatible with Linux and UNIX-based systems and supports a number of languages, including C, C++, Java, Python, and more. For developers who want a more interactive debugging experience, this makes it a useful tool.

Here is a simple C program that you can debug using DDD (Data Display Debugger). This program calculates the sum of an array but contains a small bug that you can identify using DDD.

Example C Program (sum_array.c):

```
#include <stdio.h>
int sum_array(int arr[], int size) { int sum = 0;
for (int i = 0; i <= size; i++) { // Bug: Should be i < size, not i <= size sum += arr[i];
}
return sum;
}
```

```
int main() {
int numbers[] = {1, 2, 3, 4, 5};
int size = sizeof(numbers) / sizeof(numbers[0]); int result = sum_array(numbers, size);
printf("Sum: %d\n", result);
return 0;
}
```

Graphical Debuggers Like DDD (Data Display Debugger)

DDD (Data Display Debugger) is a graphical front-end for command-line debuggers like GDB, DBX, JDB, and others. It provides an intuitive GUI for debugging programs visually, making it easier to analyze program execution, inspect variables, and control breakpoints.

- Installing DDD
- Running DDD
- Key Features of DDD
- Basic Debugging in DDD
- Advantages of DDD Over GDB

1. Installing DDD

Installing DDD (Data Display Debugger) is straightforward and depends on your operating system. On Debian-based Linux distributions like Ubuntu, you can install it using the package manager with the command: sudo apt install ddd. For Fedora, use sudo dnf install ddd, and for Arch Linux, install it with sudo pacman -S ddd. If you are using macOS, you can install DDD through Homebrew with brew install ddd, though additional dependencies like XQuartz may be required for graphical support.

After installation, you can launch DDD by running ddd in the terminal. If you encounter any missing dependencies, ensure that GDB and the necessary X11 libraries are installed. Once installed, DDD provides a graphical interface to help debug programs visually, making it easier to inspect variables, set breakpoints, and step through execution.

Installing DDD:

On Debian/Ubuntu: sudo

apt install add sudo

apt install add

On Fedora:

On Arch Linux:

sudo

dnf

install

ddd

Sudo

pacom -S

ddd

2. Running DDD

- To start debugging a program:

  ddd ./myprogram

  This opens a GUI where you can interact with GDB using buttons and visual elements.

3. Key Features of DDD

- **Graphical Breakpoints:** Set breakpoints with a click.
- **Variable Inspection:** Hover over variables to see their values.
- **Data Visualization:** View memory structures graphically.
- **Step Execution:** Run the program step by step.
- **Integrated GDB Console:** Use GDB commands within the GUI.

4. Basic Debugging in DDD

- **Set a breakpoint:** Click on a line or run:

  break main
- Run the program:

  Click

  Run or type:

  run
- **Step through execution:** Click *Step* or type
- **Inspect variables:** Hover over them or use:
- Continue execution:
- **Exit DDD:**

  Click *File* → *Exit* or type Print var_name
- Next Quit

5. Advantages of DDD Over GDB

- Easier to visualize program execution
- Graphical variable tracking
- User-friendly interface for complex debugging tasks

DDD is a powerful **graphical alternative** to command-line debugging, making it a great tool for both beginners and experienced developers.

MEMORY DEBUGGING/PROFILING LIBRARIES MPATROL AND VALGRIND: MEMORY DEBUGGING

The process of finding and resolving memory-related problems, including as buffer overflows, memory leaks, uninitialized memory access, and unauthorized memory use in programs, is known as memory debugging. These problems may result in crashes, erratic behavior, and wasteful use of resources. Developers can examine memory use and find faults with the aid of tools like Electric Fence, mpatrol, AddressSanitizer, and Valgrind.

While mpatrol intercepts memory functions to log consumption and find leaks, Valgrind's Memcheck utility monitors memory allocations and reports invalid accesses.

Address Sanitizer offers real-time memory fault detection with little overhead when it is integrated into GCC and Clang. By guaranteeing appropriate memory management, avoiding security flaws, and enhancing performance, debugging tools help developers create more reliable and safe apps.

Example C Program (memory_leak.c):

This program allocates memory dynamically but forgets to free it, causing a memory leak.

```
#include <stdio.h> #include <stdlib.h>
void memory_leak_example()
{
int *ptr = (int *)malloc(5 * sizeof(int)); // Allocating memory for 5 integers
if (ptr == NULL) {
printf("Memory allocation
failed\n"); return;
}
for (int i = 0;
i < 5; i++) {
ptr[i] = i * 10;
printf("ptr[%d] = %d\n", i, ptr[i]);
}
// Bug: Memory is not freed (causing a memory leak)
}
int main() {
memory_leak_example();
return 0;
}
```

Detecting the Memory Leak with Valgrind

1. Compile with Debug
   Symbols (-g flag) gcc -g
   memory_leak.c -o memory_leak
2. Run the Program with
   Valgrind: valgrid –leak-check=full –show-leak -Kinds=all ./memory _leak
3. Expected Output from Valgrind (Leak Detected): LEKE SUMMAY
   Definitely lost: 20 byte in 1 blocks Possibly
   lost: 0 byte in 0 blocks Still reachable: 0
   byte in 0 blocks
   This shows that **20 bytes (5 integers)** were allocated but never freed.

Fixing the Memory Leak

Modify the function to **free the allocated memory**: void memory_leak_example()

```
{
int *ptr = (int *)malloc(5 * sizeof(int)); if (ptr == NULL) {
printf("Memory allocation failed\n"); return;
}
for (int i = 0; i < 5; i++) { ptr[i] = i * 10;
printf("ptr[%d] = %d\n", i, ptr[i]);
}
free(ptr);  // Fix: Free allocated memory
}
```

Re-run Valgrind to Confirm Fix

After recompiling and running the program again:

valgrind – leak-check=full ./memory

Expected output:

All heap blocks were freed – no leaks are possible This confirms the memory leak is fixed.

This approach helps detect and fix memory-related bugs in C/C++ programs efficiently.

Profiling Libraries: mpatrol and Valgrind

mpatrol is a powerful memory debugging and profiling library for C and C++ programs, designed to detect memory leaks, buffer overflows, and uninitialized memory usage. It works by replacing standard memory management functions like malloc, free, new, and delete, allowing it to track and log memory allocations and deallocations. Unlike runtime tools such as Valgrind, mpatrol operates at compile time, making it lightweight with minimal performance overhead.

Developers can use it to generate detailed logs, identify inefficient memory usage patterns, and improve overall program stability. By linking applications with mpatrol, it becomes easier to pinpoint memory-related bugs and optimize resource utilization, making it a useful tool for software development and debugging.

1. mpatrol

mpatrol is a library-based memory debugging and profiling tool that tracks memory allocations, deallocations, and leaks in C/C++ programs. It replaces standard memory functions (malloc, free, new, delete) and logs detailed reports.

Key Features

- Detects memory leaks and corruption
- Tracks memory allocations and deallocations
- Generates detailed profiling logs

Usage

- Install Valgrind

To install **mpatrol**, you need to ensure your system has the necessary development tools. On **Debian-based** Linux distributions like **Ubuntu**, you can install it using the package manager with the command: sudo apt install maptrol # Debian/Ubuntu

- Install mpatrol:

  sudo apt install maptrol # Debian/Ubuntu

- Compile with mpatrol:

  Run the program and analyze logs:

  Gcc -g -o myprogram.c -lmpatrol

  ./myprogram # Generates a memory usage report

2. Valgrind

Valgrind is a runtime instrumentation framework used for profiling, memory debugging, and performance analysis. It includes tools like Memcheck (for memory errors) and Callgrind (for CPU profiling).

Key Features

- Detects memory leaks and uninitialized memory reads
- Tracks CPU time and function calls
- Analyzes cache usage and branch prediction

Usage

- Install Valgrind

  sudo apt install valgrind # Debian/ubuntu

- Run memory profiling with Memcheck
- valgrind –tool=memcheck –leak-check=full ./program
- Run CPU profiling with Callgrind
- valgrind –tool=callgrind ./myprogram
- **Analyze results with KCacheGrind** (GUI for Callgrind) kcachegrind callgrind out.*

mpatrol vs. Valgrind: A Comparison

Feature	Mpatrol	Valgrind
Type	Yes	Yes
CPU Profiling	No	Yes (Callgrind)
Performance Overhead	Low	High
Ease of Use	Requires Linking at compile time	High

Conclusion

- Use mpatrol if you want low-overhead memory profiling during development.
- Use Valgrind for in-depth memory debugging and performance analysis atruntime.

Both tools are valuable for optimizing and debugging C/C++ applications.

INTRODUCTION TO BASH, SED & AWK SCRIPTING

Bash, **sed**, and **awk** are powerful scripting tools commonly used in Linux and Unix environments for automation, text processing, and system administration.

Introduction to Bash

Bash (Bourne Again Shell) is a robust scripting language and command-line shell that is frequently used in Unix and Linux systems for task execution, automation, and system administration. It adds features like command-line editing, enhanced scripting capabilities, and support for functions and arrays to the original Bourne Shell (sh). With the use of bash scripts, users may effectively manage files, automate tedious jobs, alter text, and regulate system operations. Complex processes and system interactions are made possible by Bash's built-in support for variables, conditionals, and loops. Bash is still a vital tool for developers, administrators, and power users in the Linux ecosystem, regardless of whether it is being used for simple command execution or complex scripting.

sed (Stream Editor)

sed is a powerful command-line tool used for text processing and manipulation in Unix and Linux environments. It operates on input streams, allowing users to perform search, replace, insert, delete, and transform operations on text without opening a text editor. **sed** works line-by-line and can handle large files efficiently. One of its most common uses is text substitution using the **s** command, such as:

sedd's/old_text/new_text/g' filetxt

his replaces all occurrences of "old_text" with "new_text" in file.txt.

Additionally, sed can delete lines, modify patterns, and apply complex transformations using regular expressions. Its ability to process data in pipelines makes it an essential tool for shell scripting, log analysis, and text automation tasks.

awk (Pattern Scanning & Processing Language)

Awk is a robust text processing and pattern scanning language that is used in Unix and Linux systems to extract, analyze, and work with structured text data. For working with column-based files like CSV, logs, and reports, it is perfect since it scans data line by line, looks for patterns, and executes predetermined actions. Effective data processing and text transformation are made possible by awk's integrated support for variables, arithmetic operations, string functions, and loops. Users can filter particular entries, establish custom field separators, and dynamically format output. An indispensable tool for shell scripting and data manipulation, awk can be used for automation, log analysis, or report preparation.

A simple example extracts the second column from a space-separated file:

awk '{print $2}' file.txt

awk supports arithmetic operations, string manipulation, conditional statements, and loops, making it highly flexible for data analysis. It also allows users to define field separators for structured data processing. For example, processing a CSV file with , as a delimiter:

With its built-in functions and pattern-matching capabilities, **awk** is widely used for automating reports, analyzing logs, and formatting text data efficiently.

Awk -F "," '{print $1, $3}' data.csv

UNIT 5

Open-Source Programming Techniques

OPEN-SOURCE PROGRAMMING TECHNIQUES

The main goals of open-source programming approaches are code reuse, transparency, and cooperative software development. Git and other version control systems are used by developers to effectively manage contributions and track changes. Because code is frequently developed using reusable and modular design principles, it is simpler to maintain and expand. Code stability and quality are guaranteed by continuous integration (CI/CD) and automated testing.

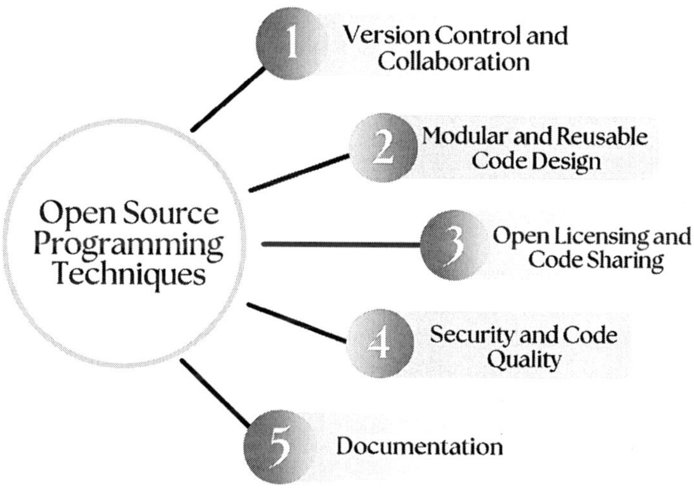

Peer reviews, issue tracking, and documentation enhancements are encouraged in open-source projects, which adhere to community-driven development. To specify usage rights, developers employ copyleft (GPL) or permissive (MIT, Apache) licenses. These methods promote creativity and international cooperation while making software scalable, safe, and of excellent quality.

1. Version Control and Collaboration

In order for teams to effectively track, manage, and merge code changes, version control and collaboration are essential components of contemporary software development. Developers may easily build branches, make changes, and merge code with Git, the most popular version control system. Platforms that provide pull requests, issue tracking, and code review tools, such as GitHub, GitLab, and Bitbucket, improve teamwork. Teams frequently use organized processes like Git Flow, in which feature branches are generated and then reviewed before being merged into the main branch.

2. Modular and Reusable Code Design

Software maintainability, scalability, and efficiency are improved by modular and reusable code design, which divides programs into separate, self-contained modules. Because each module serves a distinct purpose and can be used to many projects, it reduces redundancy and speeds up development. Code is written by developers using concepts like SOLID and DRY (Don't Repeat Yourself). Microservices architecture and MVC (Model-View-Controller) are two design paradigms that further encourage modularity. Using package managers, such as npm, pip, and cargo, facilitates effective dependency management. Reusable, well-structured code makes it easier to collaborate, test, and debug software, maintaining its flexibility and scalability over time.

3. Open Licensing and Code Sharing

Open-source software development is based on the fundamental ideas of open licensing and code sharing, which foster cooperation, openness, and creativity. Open-source licenses, including the GPL, MIT, and Apache, specify how software may be distributed, altered, and utilized. While copyleft licenses like the GPL mandate that derivative works remain open-source, permissive licenses like MIT permit unlimited use. Code sharing is made easier by platforms like GitHub, GitLab, and Bitbucket, which let developers from all over the world contribute, evaluate, and enhance projects. Compliance with licensing terms is ensured via clear documentation, such as a **LICENSE.md file**. Developers promote an international ecosystem of reusable, superior software by adopting open licenses and exchanging code.

4. Security and Code Quality

Code quality is maintained through clean architecture, adherence to coding standards, and automated testing (unit, integration, and regression tests); regular security audits, dependency management, and continuous monitoring further enhance software resilience; secure coding practices, such as input validation, encryption, and access control, help prevent security threats like SQL injection and buffer overflows; and tools like static code analysis (SonarQube, ESLint) and dynamic testing (fuzzing, penetration testing) identify potential weaknesses early.

5. Documentation

Software development requires documentation to make sure that code is comprehensible, maintained, and available to contributors, users, and developers. It facilitates productive teamwork by providing code comments, API references, user manuals, and contribution guidelines. To create organized documentation, programs like JSDoc, Doxygen, Sphinx, and Markdown are frequently utilized. Debugging and future changes are made easier by well-documented code, which adheres to unambiguous naming standards and explains intricate reasoning. **A README.md file** provides an overview, installation instructions, and usage guidelines for open-source projects. Developers can improve software usability, shorten onboarding times, and increase long-term project sustainability by keeping thorough and current documentation.

APPLICATION PROGRAMMING

The process of creating software applications with programming languages, frameworks, and tools to carry out particular functions or offer services is known as application programming. To construct useful applications, it entails programming code that communicates with databases, operating systems, APIs, and user interfaces. Python, Java, C++, and JavaScript are among the languages used by developers to create desktop, mobile, online, and embedded applications.

Scalability and maintainability are made possible by fundamental ideas like object-oriented design, modular programming, and API integration. To guarantee effective and user-friendly software solutions, modern application development also integrates security protocols, performance optimization, and user experience (UX) design.

BASICS OF THE X WINDOWS SERVER ARCHITECTURE

A graphical user interface (GUI) for UNIX-like operating systems is offered by the client-server X Window System (X11). By separating the programs (X Clients) from the display server (X Server), it enables them to operate on separate computers connected to a network. Applications that request display and input services from the X Server are known as X Clients.

The X Server is in charge of handling user interactions, managing input/output devices, and generating graphics. The X Protocol is how they communicate with one other. Window placement, scaling, and decoration are managed by a Window Manager (like Mutter in GNOME or KWin in KDE). The Display Server, such as Xorg or Wayland, is in charge of controlling user input and displaying visuals on the screen.

X is very adaptable due to its modular design, which supports many desktops, remote apps, and different UI designs. In contemporary Linux settings, Wayland and other more recent alternatives seek to replace X11 in order to increase security and performance.

X Windows Server Architecture

A client-server architecture called the X Window System (X11) was created for operating systems that resemble UNIX and allows for graphical user interfaces (GUIs). It divides the X Clients—applications that ask for graphical services—from the X Server, which controls user input and display rendering. Applications can be executed locally or remotely thanks to communication between them via the X Protocol. Window placement, decorations, and user interactions are managed by a window manager (such as Mutter, KWin, or Openbox).

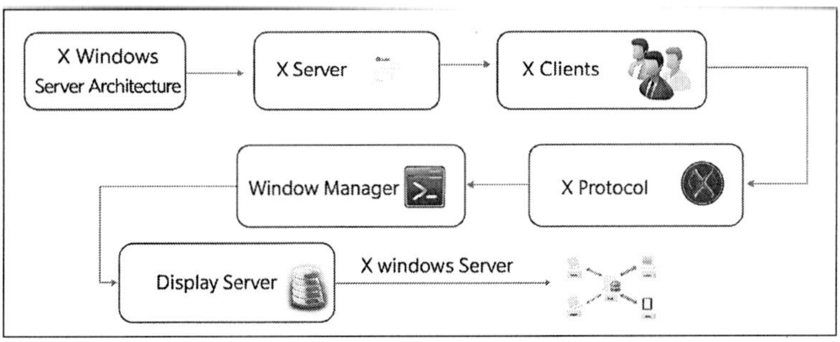

Fig 5.1:: X Windows Server Architecture

Graphical rendering and input device management, including keyboards and mice, are handled by the display server, like Xorg. The creation of alternatives like Wayland, which seeks to replace X11 in contemporary Linux systems in order to increase security and efficiency, is a result of the performance restrictions caused by this modular structure, which offers flexibility.

X Server

The central part of the X Window System (X11), which controls the graphical user interface and display, is the X Server. It serves as a bridge between the computer's hardware and the X Clients (applications), controlling screen output, processing user inputs (keyboard, mouse, and touch), and generating graphics. The X Protocol is used by the X Server to connect with clients, enabling graphical user interfaces to be displayed by both local and distant applications.

It does not control window behaviour or decorations; a Window Manager such as Mutter, KWin, or Open box does this. With its support for hardware acceleration, network transparency, and high flexibility, Xorg is the most used X Server implementation. However, contemporary Linux versions are progressively switching to Wayland, a more straightforward and effective substitute for X11, because to security and performance issues.

Limitations of X Server

- **High Latency:** X Server's client-server model introduces delays in rendering, especially in networked environments, affecting real-time performance.
- **Security Vulnerabilities:** X Server allows applications to monitor and manipulate each other's windows and input events, posing security risks.
- **Resource Overhead:** Requires additional components like Window Managers and Compositing Managers, increasing system complexity and resource consumption.
- **Outdated Graphics Model:** Lacks efficient support for modern GPU acceleration and high-performance rendering, leading to inefficiencies compared to Wayland.

X Clients

Applications known as "X Clients" communicate with the X Server to show graphical user interfaces in the X Window System (X11). In order to render windows, draw graphics, and handle user input, these clients submit requests to the X Server, which handles these requests and controls hardware interactions. Network-transparent GUI applications are made possible by X Clients, which can operate remotely over a network or on the same computer as the X Server. Web browsers (Firefox), terminal emulators (xterm), text editors (Gedit), and file managers (Nautilus) are a few examples of X Clients. A Window Manager (such as Metacity or KWin) is necessary to manage user interactions, scaling, and decorations because the X Server does not control window location or appearance.

Despite the flexibility and remote execution provided by X Clients, Wayland and other contemporary display protocols are displacing X11 because of their enhanced security and performance.

Limitations of X Clients in X11

- Latency Issues: Network transparency can introduce lag in remote applications.

- **Security Concerns:** X11 has weak security mechanisms, making remote execution risky.
- **Performance Overhead:** X11's design leads to inefficiencies in graphics rendering.

Wayland clients, which interact directly with the display compositor for enhanced performance, security, and decreased latency, are replacing X clients as a result of Wayland's growth.

X Protocol

In the X Window System (X11), X Clients (applications) can communicate with the X Server thanks to the X Protocol. It outlines how clients ask the server to perform tasks like launching windows, creating images, and managing user input. The server then responds to these requests and relays back events like mouse clicks and keystrokes. Applications can execute remotely while displaying locally thanks to the protocol's support for network transparency. It works asynchronously, which increases responsiveness but can occasionally cause latency problems. The protocol's event-driven architecture aids in managing dynamic interactions, and its binary format guarantees effective communication.

However, because to its antiquated design, X Protocol has performance overhead and security flaws. Because Wayland integrates rendering and input handling directly into the display server, it does away with the need for a separate communication protocol, which is why current Linux systems are switching to it.

Limitations of X Protocol

- **Security Risks:** X11 lacks built-in encryption and authentication, making remote execution vulnerable without SSH tunneling.
- **High Latency:** Network transparency, while flexible, introduces performance bottlenecks in modern high-speed graphics rendering.
- **Complexity:** The protocol has many legacy features, leading to inefficiencies in modern GUI environments.

Modern Linux systems are moving toward Wayland, which improves simplicity, security, and performance by doing away with the X Protocol and enabling direct client-display server communication.

Window Manager

One essential part of the X Window System (X11) that regulates the positioning, look, and operation of application windows is a window manager. The Window Manager is in charge of duties like window decorating (title bars, borders, and buttons), resizing, reducing, maximizing, and controlling window focus because the X Server only offers rudimentary windowing functions. Additionally, it manages user interfaces like as virtual desktops and keyboard shortcuts.

There are various kinds of window managers, including:

Overlapping windows are permitted by stacking (floating) window managers (like Metacity and Openbox). Compositing Window Managers (like Compiz, KWin) offer sophisticated visual effects, while Tiling Window Managers (like i3, AwesomeWM) arrange windows in a non-overlapping grid. For a smooth user experience, certain desktop environments, such as GNOME and KDE, include their own Window Managers. Wayland replaces X11, which depends on a Window Manager for proper operation, by including window management straight into the display server.

Limitations of Window Manager

- **Lack of Standardization:** Different Window Managers have unique features and configurations, leading to inconsistencies across Linux distributions.
- **Performance Overhead:** Compositing Window Managers consume more system resources, which can slow down performance on low-end hardware.
- **Complex Configuration:** Many advanced Window Managers require manual setup and scripting, making them difficult for beginners to use.
- **Security Concerns:** Since X11 separates the Window Manager from the display server, it can be vulnerable to security issues like window snooping or unauthorized access.

Display Server

An essential part of a graphical user interface (GUI) system that controls communication between programs and the hardware display is a display server. Input from keyboards and mice is processed, and graphical output is sent to the screen. The X Server serves as the display server in the X Window System (X11), responding to requests from X Clients (applications) using the X Protocol. X11 does, however, have drawbacks, such as significant latency and security flaws.

Wayland, which improves security and efficiency by directly integrating display server functionality with window management, is replacing other Linux systems in modern contexts. In comparison to X11, Wayland offers a more seamless and effective experience by removing the requirement for an external Window Manager and lowering graphical overhead.

Limitations of Display Server

- **High Latency in X11:** The X Window System (X11) has a client-server architecture that introduces delays, especially over network connections.
- **Security Vulnerabilities:** X11 allows applications to access each other's windows and input events, creating potential security risks.
- **Complex Configuration:** Display Servers, especially X11, require external Window Managers and Compositing Managers to function properly, increasing system complexity.
- **Inefficient Graphics Handling:** X11 relies on outdated graphics rendering techniques, leading to performance bottlenecks compared to newer systems like Wayland.

QT PROGRAMMING

Qt is a robust, cross-platform C++ framework for creating embedded systems and Graphical User Interface (GUI) applications. It offers a vast array of frameworks and tools for creating cutting-edge, responsive apps that work natively on several operating systems, including Windows, Linux, macOS, Android, and iOS.

Key features of Qt include

- Qt Widgets
- Qt Quick (QML)
- Cross-platform development
- Support for OpenGL and hardware acceleration
- Built-in localization, networking, and database handling

Qt Widgets

The Qt framework's Qt Widgets module offers a comprehensive collection of user interface components for creating desktop programs with a conventional windowed interface. It comes with a number of pre-made widgets that may be altered to construct intricate user interfaces, including buttons, labels, text fields, tables, and dialog boxes. With Qt Widgets' event-driven design, user input (such as keyboard strokes or mouse clicks) initiates pre-programmed signals and event-handling slots.

Qt Widgets is best suited for traditional, high-performance desktop programs that need a native appearance and feel, as opposed to Qt Quick (QML), which concentrates on contemporary, animated user interfaces. Applications that require a reliable and conventional GUI environment are best suited for Qt Widgets since they are effective, lightweight, and cross-platform.

Qt Quick (QML)

The declarative Qt Quick (QML) framework is used to create contemporary, fluid, and animated graphical user interfaces (GUIs). It makes use of a language similar to JavaScript called QML (Qt Modeling Language) to design user interface elements in a comprehensible, dynamic, and structured way. Because it allows developers to create responsive designs, touch-friendly interfaces, and fluid animations, Qt Quick is perfect for modern desktop, embedded, and mobile apps.

Its smooth integration with C++ is made possible by the Qt C++ backend, which enables sophisticated logic handling and performance optimization. Applications needing dynamic layouts, interactive animations, and sophisticated visual effects like media players, mobile apps, and automobile interfaces are more suited for Qt Quick than Qt Widgets.

Cross-Platform Development

Cross-platform development refers to the practice of creating software applications that can run on multiple operating systems (Windows, macOS, Linux, Android, iOS, etc.) with minimal modifications. Frameworks like Qt, Flutter, React Native, and Electron enable developers to write code once and deploy it across various platforms, reducing development time and maintenance efforts. Qt, for example, offers Qt Widgets for traditional desktop applications and Qt Quick (QML) for modern, touch-friendly interfaces, both of which are cross-platform. It abstracts platform-specific details, allowing developers to focus on application logic rather than OS compatibility.

Support for OpenGL in Qt

Qt provides comprehensive support for OpenGL, enabling developers to create high-performance graphics applications with hardware-accelerated rendering. OpenGL integration in Qt is available through classes like QOpenGLWidget, QOpenGLWindow, and QOpenGLFunctions, allowing applications to render 2D and 3D graphics efficiently.

For modern UI development, Qt Quick (QML) leverages OpenGL via the Qt Scene Graph, enabling smooth animations, complex visual effects, and real-time rendering. Qt also supports OpenGL ES, making it suitable for embedded systems and mobile devices.

Hardware Acceleration in Qt

Applications can use the GPU (Graphics Processing Unit) for calculations, animations, and graphics rendering thanks to hardware acceleration in Qt, which greatly increases efficiency and performance. Hardware acceleration via OpenGL, OpenGL ES, Vulkan, and Direct3D is supported by Qt. The Qt Scene Graph, which is used by Qt Quick (QML) for 2D and 3D graphics, employs OpenGL or Vulkan to speed up UI rendering, improving the responsiveness and smoothness of apps.

QOpenGLWidget in Qt Widgets enables high-performance rendering by directly utilizing OpenGL. Additionally, OpenGL-based apps can run on Direct3D in Windows environments thanks to Qt's support for ANGLE (Almost Native Graphics Layer Engine). Furthermore, effective media processing is guaranteed by Qt's hardware-accelerated video playback (via Qt Multimedia).

Built-in localization, networking, and database handling

Qt is an effective framework for creating global, networked, and data-driven applications because it has extensive built-in support for localization, networking, and database management.

- Localization
- Networking
- Database Handling

Localization

Localization in Qt enables applications to support multiple languages and regional settings, making them accessible to a global audience. Qt provides built-in internationalization (i18n) and localization (l10n) support using **QTranslator**, **translation files (.ts, .qm)**, and the **Qt Linguist tool**. Developers mark text for translation using tr () in C++ or qsTr () in QML. The lupdate tool extracts translatable strings, which can be edited in Qt Linguist and compiled into.qm files using lrelease. At runtime, translations are loaded dynamically using QTranslator or Qt.locale(). Qt also supports **right-to-left (RTL) text, date/number formatting, and Unicode**, ensuring smooth adaptation for different languages and cultures.

Networking

Qt provides a powerful networking module (Qt Network) that enables seamless communication over TCP/IP, UDP, HTTP, WebSockets, and SSL/TLS. Using classes like QNetworkAccessManager, applications can send and receive HTTP requests, making it easy to interact with REST APIs. For low-level socket programming, QTcp Socket and QUdp Socket facilitate real-time data exchange. Secure communication is ensured with built-in SSL/TLS support.

Qt also supports asynchronous operations, allowing non-blocking network requests for improved performance. With cross-platform compatibility, Qt's networking capabilities are widely used in applications requiring data synchronization, cloud connectivity, and real-time messaging.

Database Handling in Qt

Qt provides built-in database handling through the Qt SQL module, allowing applications to interact with various databases like SQLite, MySQL, PostgreSQL, Oracle, and ODBC-compatible databases. The QSql Database class manages database connections, while QSqlQuery enables executing SQL commands for data retrieval, insertion, updating, and deletion.

Qt also supports QSql TableModel and QSql QueryModel for seamless integration with UI components like QTableView. It offers both synchronous and asynchronous database operations, ensuring efficient performance. With its cross-platform support, Qt simplifies database integration, making it ideal for data-driven applications, enterprise software, and embedded systems.

Explanation

QApplication initializes the Qt application.

QPushButton creates a button widget.

button.show() displays the button.

app.exec() starts the event loop to keep the application running.

Example

```
int main(int argc, char *argv[]){
    QApplication app(argc, argv);
    QpushButton button("Click Me!");
    button.resize(200,50);
    button.show();
    return app.exec();
}
```

GTK+ PROGRAMMING

A cross-platform, open-source toolkit for creating graphical user interfaces (GUIs) is called GTK+ (GIMP Toolkit). It is extensively utilized in cross-platform GUI development, Linux applications, and the GNOME desktop environment. Because GTK+ supports languages like Python, JavaScript, C, and C++, it may be used for a variety of programming tasks.

GTK+ follows an object-oriented approach using the GObject system and provides a rich set of widgets such as buttons, labels, menus, and text inputs. It also supports CSS-based styling, internationalization (i18n), accessibility (a11y), and themes for modern UI design. With built-in support for event-driven programming, 2D graphics (via Cairo), and window management, GTK+ allows developers to create responsive and visually appealing applications. It is widely used in desktop applications, embedded systems, and mobile development.

Features of GTK+ Programming

- Cross-Platform Support
- Rich Widget Set
- Theming and CSS Styling
- Event-Driven Programming
- Language Bindings

Cross-Platform Support in GTK+

GTK+ is designed to be cross-platform, meaning applications built with it can run on Linux, Windows, and macOS without significant modifications. This makes GTK+ a preferred choice for developers who want to create portable and consistent graphical user interfaces. It provides a unified API, ensuring that applications maintain the same look and functionality across different operating systems. Additionally, GTK+ supports Wayland, X11, and Windows GDI as backend rendering engines. With its compatibility across platforms, GTK+ enables developers to build desktop, embedded, and even mobile applications, making it highly flexible for various use cases.

Rich Widget Set

GTK+ provides a comprehensive set of widgets for building modern graphical user interfaces. These widgets include buttons, labels, text entries, menus, dialogs, tree views, progress bars, and sliders, among many others. The GtkWidget class serves as the base for all UI elements, ensuring flexibility and consistency.

GTK+ also includes container widgets like boxes, grids, and notebooks, which help organize UI components efficiently. Developers can customize these widgets using CSS-based styling to create visually appealing applications. Additionally, GTK+ supports dynamic UI building through GtkBuilder, allowing developers to define interfaces in XML files without writing extensive code.

Theming and CSS Styling in GTK+

With GTK+'s support for theming and CSS-based styling, developers may design cutting-edge, aesthetically pleasing user interfaces. Developers can use Cascading Style Sheets (CSS) to edit widgets with the GTK CSS engine, just like they would with web design. Fine control over background pictures, margins, padding, colors, fonts, and borders is made possible by this.

Because GTK+ themes can be used system-wide or per-application, it's simple to keep several apps looking the same. Custom widget styling, animations, and dark mode are also supported. While enabling customisation according to user preferences, GTK themes (such as Adwaita, Breeze, and Arc) enable applications to mimic the native appearance of the operating system.

Event-Driven Programming

GTK+ follows an event-driven programming model, where the application waits for user interactions and responds accordingly. Instead of executing code sequentially, GTK+ listens for events such as button clicks, mouse movements, keyboard input, and window resizing.

GTK+ uses GLib and GSignal for event handling. Signals are emitted when a specific action occurs, and developers can connect callback functions to these signals using functions like g_signal_connect(). This architecture ensures that applications remain responsive and efficient, processing only the necessary actions when an event is triggered.

By using this event-driven model, GTK+ applications can handle **real-time user interactions** while efficiently managing system resources, making it ideal for building **interactive and dynamic GUI applications**.

Language Bindings in GTK+

GTK+ is primarily written in C, but it supports multiple programming languages through language bindings. This allows developers to use GTK+ with Python, C++, JavaScript, Rust, Ruby, and more, making it accessible to a wider range of developers.

For example:

- PyGObject provides GTK+ support for Python.
- gtkmm is the official C++ binding for GTK+.
- GJS enables GTK+ development using JavaScript.
- Rust bindings like gtk-rs allow GTK+ applications in Rust.

These bindings ensure that developers can leverage GTK+'s powerful UI toolkit while working in their preferred programming language, making GTK+ highly flexible and adaptable.

Basic GTK+ Application (C Program)

```
#include <gtk/gtk.h>
static void on_button_clicked(GtkWidget *widget, gpointer data) {
    g_print("Button Clicked!\n");
}
int main (int argc, char *argv[]) {
    gtk_init(&argc, &argv);
    GtkWidget *window = gtk_window_new(GTK_WINDOW_TOPLEVEL);
    gtk_window_set_title(GTK_WINDOW(window), "GTK+ Example");
    gtk_window_set_default_size(GTK_WINDOW(window), 300, 200);
    GtkWidget *button = gtk_button_new_with_label("Click Me!");
    g_signal_connect(button, "clicked", G_CALLBACK(on_button_clicked), NULL);
    gtk_container_add(GTK_CONTAINER(window), button);
    g_signal_connect(window, "destroy", G_CALLBACK(gtk_main_quit), NULL);
    gtk_widget_show_all(window);
    gtk_main();
  return 0;
}
```

Explanation:

gtk_init() initializes GTK.

gtk_window_new() creates a window.

gtk_button_new_with_label() creates a button.

g_signal_connect() handles button clicks and window close events.

gtk_main() starts the event loop.

Advanced GTK+ Features

- **GTK4 & GDK:** Modern rendering with OpenGL/Vulkan.
- **Threading:** Uses GTask and GThread for async operations.
- **Networking:** GIO library supports HTTP and file handling.
- **Databases:** Works with SQLite, PostgreSQL, and MySQL via GDA.
- **CSS Styling:** Customize UI using CSS-like stylesheets.

GTK+ vs. Qt

Feature	GTK+	Qt
Language	C(GObject)	C++
UI Design	Declarative (CSS-like)	Qt Weidgets/QML
Cross-platform	Yes	Yes
Performance	Lightweight	Feature-rich but heavier
Community	GNOME Foundation	Qt Company + Open Source

GTK+ is ideal for **lightweight, native Linux applications**, while **Qt** is better for **cross-platform commercial apps**.

PYTHON PROGRAMMING

Python is a high-level, interpreted, and dynamically typed programming language known for its simplicity, readability, and versatility. It supports multiple programming paradigms, including object-oriented, procedural, and functional programming. Python is widely used in web development, data science, artificial intelligence, automation, and GUI applications.

With its vast ecosystem of libraries and frameworks, such as Django for web development, NumPy for scientific computing, and TensorFlow for machine learning, Python enables developers to build a wide range of applications efficiently. Additionally, tools like PyGTK and PyQt allow for easy GUI development. Python's large community, extensive documentation, and strong standard library make it one of the most popular programming languages today.

Key Features of Python

- Easy to Learn & Readable
- Dynamically Typed
- Extensive Libraries
- Cross-Platform
- Multi-Paradigm
- Strong Community Support

Easy to Learn & Readable

Python is designed to be beginner-friendly with a simple and readable syntax that resembles natural language. Unlike other languages that require complex syntax, Python emphasizes code clarity by using indentation instead of braces or semicolons. This makes it easier to write, read, and maintain code.

For example, printing a message in Python is as simple as:

Print ("Hello, World")

Python's high-level nature allows developers to focus on problem-solving rather than low-level details like memory management. With minimal syntax and powerful built-in functions, Python is an excellent choice for beginners and experienced programmers alike.

Dynamically Typed in Python

Python is a **dynamically typed language**, meaning that **variable types are determined at runtime** rather than needing explicit declarations. This makes coding **faster and more flexible**, as developers don't need to specify data types when defining variables.

For example:

X=10 #Integer

X="Hello" # Now it's a string

Since Python automatically detects the data type, it reduces **boilerplate code** and makes development more **efficient**. However, dynamic typing can also lead to **runtime errors** if the expected data type changes unexpectedly. To address this, Python introduced **type hints** for better code readability and debugging.

Extensive Libraries

Python has a **vast standard library** and a rich ecosystem of third-party libraries, making development faster and easier. These libraries cover a wide range of applications, including:

- **Web Development**: Django, Flask
- **Data Science & Machine Learning**: NumPy, Pandas, TensorFlow, Scikit-learn
- **Automation & Scripting**: Selenium, BeautifulSoup, PyAutoGUI
- **GUI Development**: PyQt, Tkinter, Kivy
- **Networking & Security**: Requests, Paramiko, Scapy

With these pre-built libraries, developers can **avoid reinventing the wheel** and focus on solving problems efficiently. Python's **package manager (pip)** makes installing and managing libraries seamless.

Cross-Platform in Python

Python is a cross-platform language, meaning that code written in Python can run on Windows, macOS, Linux, and even mobile operating systems with little to no modification. This is possible because Python is an interpreted language and has implementations for different platforms, such as CPython, PyPy, and Jython.

Many Python libraries, such as Tkinter, PyQt, and Kivy, allow developers to create cross-platform GUI applications. Additionally, frameworks like Flask and Django enable the development of web applications that run on any OS with a web browser. Python's cross-platform nature makes it a preferred choice for software development, automation, and scripting, ensuring that developers can write code once and deploy it anywhere.

Multi-Paradigm in Python

Python supports **multiple programming paradigms**, allowing developers to choose the best approach for their projects. The three main paradigms supported are:

Procedural Programming: Writing step-by-step instructions using functions.

```
Def greet(name):
    Print (f"Hello, {name}!")
greet("Alice")
```

Object-Oriented Programming (OOP): Using classes and objects to structure code.

```
class Person:
   def __init__(self, name):
      self.name = name
  def greet(self):
      print(f"Hello, {self.name}!")
p = Person("Bob")
p.greet()
```

Functional Programming: Using functions as first-class objects and applying concepts like **map, filter, and lambda functions.**

```
numbers = [1, 2, 3, 4]
squared = list(map(lambda x: x**2, numbers))
print(squared)
```

Python's **flexibility** makes it ideal for different types of applications, from small scripts to large-scale enterprise solutions.

Object-Oriented Programming (OOP) in Python

```
class car:
    def _init_(self, brand, year):
        self.brand = brand
      self.year = year
   def display(self):
     print(f"{self.brand}-{self.year}")
car1 = car("Tesla",2003)
car1.display()
```

Python Libraries & Applications

Field	Libraries/Frameworks
Data Science	Numpy, pands, Matplotlib, Seaborn
Machine Learning	Scikit-learn, TensorFlow, PyTorch

Field	Libraries/Frameworks
Web Development	Flas, Django, FastAPI
Automation	Selenium, OpenCV, PuAutoGUI
Cybersecurity	Scapy, Requests, PyCryptodome

EXECUTION ENVIRONMENT IN PYTHON

An execution environment in open-source development controls dependencies, runtime settings, and system resources to guarantee that software operates uniformly across various systems. Tools like Docker for containerized environments, virtual environments (Conda, Venv) for dependency isolation, and CI/CD pipelines for testing and deployment automation are all used in open-source development methodologies. Linux-based systems, which offer versatility and compatibility with a wide range of programming languages, are frequently used in open-source execution environments.

The **execution environment** in Python refers to the setup in which Python code runs. This includes the **interpreter, system libraries, dependencies, and runtime settings**. Python can be executed in various environments, such as:

- Local Development Environment
- Virtual Environments
- Cloud-Based Environments
- Embedded Systems & IoT
- Production Servers

Local Development Environment

A **local development environment** is the setup on a developer's computer used to write, test, and run Python programs. It includes

- **Python Interpreter**: Installed from python.org or managed via version managers like pyenv.
- **Text Editors & IDEs**: Popular choices include VS Code, PyCharm, Jupyter Notebook, and Sublime Text.
- **Virtual Environments**: Tools like venv and conda help isolate dependencies for different projects.
- **Package Management**: pip (Python's package manager) allows installation of libraries from PyPI (Python Package Index).
- **Debugging Tools**: Python provides built-in debugging with pdb and IDE-integrated debuggers.

Setting up a well-configured local development environment improves efficiency, maintains code consistency, and helps in collaboration on Python projects.

Virtual Environments

A **virtual environment** in Python is an isolated workspace that allows developers to manage dependencies for different projects without conflicts. This ensures that each project has its own set of libraries, independent of the system-wide Python installation.

Why Use Virtual Environments?

- Prevents conflicts between dependencies of different projects.
- Allows using different Python versions for different projects.
- Keeps the system Python environment clean.

Creating and Using a Virtual Environment

- Create a virtual environment:
  Python -m venv myenv
- Activate the virtual environment:
  - On Windows:
    myenv\Script\activate
  - On Mac/Linux:
    Source myenv/bin/activate
- Install dependencies inside the environment
  pip install requests numpy
- Deactivate the virtual environment:
  deactivate

Using virtual environments ensures better dependency management and makes Python projects more portable and reproducible.

Cloud-Based Environments for Python

A **cloud-based environment** allows developers to write, run, and deploy Python applications on remote servers without needing local setup. These environments provide **scalability, flexibility, and collaboration**.

Common Cloud-Based Python Environments

- Google Colab
- AWS Lambda
- Microsoft Azure Functions
- Google Cloud Functions
- Heroku & Render
- JupyterHub

Google Colab

Google Colab (Colaboratory) is a free, cloud-based Jupyter Notebook environment provided by Google that allows users to write and execute Python code directly in a web browser. It is widely used for **machine learning, data science, and deep learning** due to its seamless integration with **Google Drive** and support for **GPU/TPU acceleration**.

Key Features of Google Colab

- **Free Access to GPUs & TPUs:** Ideal for deep learning and AI applications.
- **Pre-Installed Libraries:** Comes with popular libraries like TensorFlow, PyTorch, NumPy, and Pandas.

- **Easy Collaboration:** Allows multiple users to work on the same notebook in real time.
- **Seamless Google Drive Integration:** Directly save and access files from Google Drive.
- **No Setup Required:** Runs entirely in the cloud, eliminating the need for local installation.

Google Colab is an excellent tool for researchers, students, and developers looking to experiment with Python-based machine learning models without the need for powerful local hardware.

AWS Lambda

AWS Lambda is a **serverless computing service** by Amazon Web Services (AWS) that lets developers run code without provisioning or managing servers. It automatically scales based on demand, executing functions in response to events from **AWS services, HTTP requests, or scheduled triggers**.

Key Features of AWS Lambda

- **Serverless Execution:** No need to manage infrastructure; AWS handles everything.
- **Auto-Scaling:** Scales dynamically based on the number of requests.
- **Supports Multiple Languages:** Runs Python, Java, Node.js, Go, C#, Ruby, and more.
- **Event-Driven:** Triggers from AWS services like S3, DynamoDB, API Gateway, and CloudWatch.
- **Cost-Effective:** Pay only for the execution time, not idle compute resources.

AWS Lambda is widely used for **microservices, automation, real-time data processing, and API backends**, providing a highly efficient and scalable solution for cloud-based application development.

Microsoft Azure Functions

Azure Functions is a **serverless computing service** provided by Microsoft Azure, allowing developers to run event-driven code without managing infrastructure. It automatically scales based on demand, making it ideal for microservices, automation, and cloud-based applications.

Key Features of Azure Functions

- **Serverless Execution:** Eliminates the need for server management.
- **Event-Driven Triggers:** Supports events from Azure services (Blob Storage, Cosmos DB, Event Grid, etc.), HTTP requests, and scheduled tasks.
- **Supports Multiple Languages:** Works with Python, C#, Java, JavaScript, PowerShell, and more.
- **Auto-Scaling:** Adjusts resources dynamically based on workload.
- **Integration with Azure Services:** Seamlessly connects with Azure Storage, Azure SQL, and AI/ML services.
- **Consumption-Based Pricing:** Pay only for the compute time used, reducing costs.

Azure Functions is widely used for **webhooks, API backends, automation, and IoT applications**, providing a scalable and cost-effective cloud computing solution.

Google Cloud Functions

Google Cloud Functions is a **serverless execution environment** that allows developers to run event-driven code in the cloud without managing infrastructure. It integrates seamlessly with **Google Cloud services** and scales automatically based on demand.

Key Features of Google Cloud Functions

- **Event-Driven Execution:** Triggers from Cloud Storage, Pub/Sub, Firebase, HTTP requests, and scheduled events.
- **Multiple Language Support:** Supports Python, Node.js, Go, Java, .NET, and Ruby.
- **Auto-Scaling:** Dynamically adjusts resources based on incoming traffic.
- **Seamless Integration:** Works well with Google Cloud services like Firestore, BigQuery, and Cloud Run.
- **Cost-Effective:** Pay only for the function execution time, making it budget-friendly.

Google Cloud Functions is widely used for **real-time data processing, IoT automation, chatbots, webhooks, and cloud automation**, providing a scalable and flexible solution for modern cloud applications.

Heroku & Render

Heroku

Heroku is a **Platform-as-a-Service (PaaS)** that enables developers to deploy, manage, and scale applications effortlessly. It supports multiple languages like **Python, Node.js, Ruby, Java, Go, and PHP**.

Key Features of Heroku

- **Fully Managed Platform:** Handles infrastructure, so developers can focus on coding.
- **Supports Various Languages:** Works with multiple programming languages.
- **Dynos for Scaling:** Uses isolated containers (dynos) for auto-scaling.
- **Integrated Add-ons:** Offers databases, logging, caching, and monitoring tools.
- **Free Tier Available:** Provides a basic plan for small applications.

Render

Render is a modern **cloud hosting platform** that provides an alternative to Heroku, offering **automatic scaling, built-in CI/CD, and free SSL**. It supports **web services, static sites, cron jobs, and databases**.

Key Features of Render

- **Simple Deployment:** Supports Git-based deployment for easy updates.
- **Scalable Infrastructure:** Auto-scales based on traffic needs.

- **Built-in Database Support:** Provides managed PostgreSQL, Redis, and object storage.
- **Competitive Pricing:** More cost-effective than Heroku with a generous free tier.

Heroku is ideal for **quick prototyping and small applications**, while Render is gaining popularity for its **performance, affordability, and flexibility** in cloud deployments.

JupyterHub: Multi-User Jupyter Notebooks

JupyterHub is a multi-user version of Jupyter Notebook, designed for teams, classrooms, and research groups. It allows multiple users to access and run Jupyter notebooks on shared infrastructure while maintaining separate environments for each user.

Key Features of JupyterHub

- **Multi-User Support:** Each user gets an isolated Jupyter environment.
- **Authentication & Security:** Supports OAuth, LDAP, and other authentication systems.
- **Scalability:** Can be deployed on local servers, Kubernetes, or cloud platforms.
- **Flexible Deployment:** Works with Docker, Kubernetes, and traditional servers.
- **Supports Various Kernels:** Runs Python, R, Julia, and more.

JupyterHub is widely used in **education, data science teams, and research labs**, providing a **centralized, scalable, and collaborative environment** for interactive computing.

For Example:

The Python interpreter (e.g., CPython, PyPy), virtual environments (venv, Conda) for isolation of dependencies, and technologies such as Docker for containerized execution are examples of execution environments for Python. To launch programs, developers use cloud platforms like Google Colab and AWS Lambda, or they use integrated development environments (IDEs) like PyCharm and VS Code.

Tools like Docker, Kubernetes, and CI/CD pipelines are used in open-source development to standardize execution environments and guarantee consistent software behavior across systems. Software execution efficiency, portability, and dependability are all enhanced by a properly set execution environment.

PROGRAMMING GUI APPLICATIONS WITH LOCALISATION SUPPORT

Localization (l10n) is essential for making Graphical User Interface (GUI) applications accessible to users in different languages and regions. It involves translating UI text, adapting layouts, and supporting local date, time, and currency formats.

Key Techniques for Localization in GUI Development

- Use Translation Files
- Internationalization (i18n) Support
- Resource Bundles
- Unicode and Encoding
- Date, Number, and Currency Formatting

Use Translation Files

Translation files store text separately from the source code, making it easy to translate GUI applications into multiple languages without modifying the code. These files contain key-value pairs where each key represents a phrase, and each value is its translated version.

Common Translation File Formats

- **.po / .mo Files (Gettext format):** Used in GTK, Python (gettext), and other frameworks.
- **.ts Files (Qt Linguist format):** Used for Qt-based applications.
- **.json / .xml Files:** Common for JavaScript, web apps, and Android applications.
- **.strings Files:** Used in Apple iOS/macOS applications.

Example of a .po File (Gettext Format)

```
msgid "Hello, World!"
  msgstr "Hola, Mundo!"
```

In this example, "Hello, World!" is the source text, and "Hola, Mundo!" is the translated text.

Using Translation Files in Code (Python Example with Gettext)

```
import gettext
# Load the translation file
gettext.bindtextdomain('messages', 'locales/')
gettext.textdomain('messages')
_ = gettext.gettext
# Use translated text in the application
print(_("Hello, World!"))  # Output: "Hola, Mundo!" (if Spanish locale is set)
```

Translation files help **separate text from code**, allowing **easy updates and multi-language support** in GUI applications.

Internationalization (i18n) Support

Internationalization (i18n) is the process of designing software applications to support multiple languages, regions, and cultural preferences without requiring significant changes to the source code. It prepares the application for **localization (l10n)**, allowing easy adaptation for different languages.

Key Aspects of i18n in GUI Development

1. **Text Extraction & Translation:** Store translatable text separately using gettext (.po/.mo), Qt Linguist (.ts), JSON, or XML.
2. **Right-to-Left (RTL) Language Support:** Adjust UI layouts dynamically for Arabic, Hebrew, and Persian languages.
3. **Unicode (UTF-8) Encoding:** Ensure the application correctly handles multilingual characters.
4. **Locale-Specific Formatting:** Adapt date, time, currency, and number formats using locale-aware libraries.

5. **Font & Input Method Support:** Provide proper fonts and keyboard layouts for different languages.

Example: Python i18n with Gettext

```
import gettext
# Set up translation
gettext.bindtextdomain('messages', 'locales/')
gettext.textdomain('messages')
_ = gettext.gettext
# Translatable UI text
print(_("Welcome to our application!"))
```

With i18n, applications become **globally accessible**, providing a seamless experience for users across different regions.

Resource Bundles in Internationalization (i18n)

Resource Bundles are files used to store localized text, messages, and other UI elements separately from the application logic. This allows developers to support multiple languages without modifying the core code.

Key Features of Resource Bundles

1. **Language-Specific Storage:** Different resource files for each language (e.g., messages_en.properties, messages_es.properties).
2. **Key-Value Structure:** Text is stored in key-value pairs, making it easy to retrieve based on the user's locale.
3. **Dynamic Locale Loading:** The application loads the appropriate bundle based on user settings or system locale.
4. Used in Java, JavaScript, Python, and Qt for GUI localization.

Example: Java Resource Bundle (.properties file format)

```
messages_en.properties (English):
welcome=Welcome to our application!
exit=Exit
messages_es.properties (Spanish):
welcome=¡Bienvenido a nuestra aplicación!
exit=Salir
```

Loading Resource Bundles in Java

```
import java.util.Locale;
import java.util.ResourceBundle;
public class Main {
  public static void main(String[] args) {
    Locale locale = new Locale("es", "ES"); // Spanish
    ResourceBundle bundle = ResourceBundle.getBundle("messages", locale);
```

System.out.println(bundle.getString("welcome")); // Output: ¡Bienvenido a nuestra aplicación!

}

}

Benefits of Using Resource Bundles

- **Easy Maintenance:** Separate translation files make updates simple.
- **Scalability:** Supports multiple languages without changing code.
- **User-Friendly:** Automatically adapts to the user's locale settings.

Resource Bundles are an essential part of localization (l10n) and internationalization (i18n), making applications more accessible worldwide.

Unicode and Encoding

Unicode is a universal character encoding standard that assigns a unique number (code point) to every character across different languages and scripts. It ensures consistent text representation across platforms and devices.

Encoding is the process of converting Unicode code points into a specific format (bytes) for storage or transmission. Different encoding schemes represent Unicode characters in different ways.

Common Unicode Encodings

1. **UTF-8:** Variable-length encoding (1 to 4 bytes per character). Most common and backward-compatible with ASCII.
2. **UTF-16:** Uses 2 or 4 bytes per character. Common in Windows systems.
3. **UTF-32:** Uses 4 bytes per character. Simple but memory-intensive.

Example: Unicode Representation

- haracter: **A** → Unicode Code Point: **U+0041**
- Character: 你 **(Chinese 'you')** → Unicode Code Point: **U+4F60**

Python Example: Encoding & Decoding

```
text = "Hello, 世界" # "Hello, World" in Chinese
encoded_text = text.encode("utf-8") # Encode to UTF-8
print(encoded_text) # Output: b'Hello, \xe4\xb8\x96\xe7\x95\x8c'
decoded_text = encoded_text.decode("utf-8") # Decode back to string
print(decoded_text) # Output: Hello,
```

Why Unicode Matters?

- Supports multiple languages
- Prevents encoding mismatches (e.g., mojibake)
- Essential for web and database applications

Using UTF-8 is the best practice for most modern applications as it efficiently stores and processes text in different languages.

Date, Number, and Currency Formatting

International applications must format **dates, numbers, and currencies** correctly based on the user's locale. This ensures clarity and improves user experience across different regions.

1. Date and Time Formatting

Different countries use different date formats. For example:

- **US:** MM/DD/YYYY → 02/22/2025
- **UK:** DD/MM/YYYY → 22/02/2025
- **ISO Standard:** YYYY-MM-DD → 2025 02 22

In **Python**, the locale and datetime modules help format dates according to the user's locale.

```
import locale
from datetime import datetime
locale.setlocale(locale.LC_TIME, 'fr_FR')  # Set locale to French
date = datetime.now()
print(date.strftime("%x"))  # Output: '22/02/2025' (French format)
```

2. Number Formatting

Numbers are written differently in various locales:

- **English (US):** 1,234.56 (comma as thousands separator, dot as decimal)
- **German (DE):** 1.234,56 (dot as thousands separator, comma as decimal)

Python example using locale:

```
locale.setlocale(locale.LC_NUMERIC, 'de_DE')  # German format
number = 1234.56
print(locale.format_string("%n", number))  # Output: '1.234,56'
```

3. Currency Formatting

Currencies vary in **symbols, placement, and decimal usage**.

- **US Dollar:** $1,234.56
- **Euro:** 1.234,56 €
- **Japanese Yen:** ¥1,234 (No decimal)

Python example using locale:

```
locale.setlocale(locale.LC_ALL, 'en_US.UTF-8')  # US format
amount = 1234.56
print(locale.currency(amount, grouping=True))  # Output: '$1,234.56'
```

Why is Formatting Important?

- Ensures clarity in international applications
- Prevents misunderstandings (e.g., 1,000 vs. 1.000)
- Enhances user experience

Using localization-aware libraries ensures that applications adapt seamlessly to different regions and user preferences.

Key Localization Techniques in GUI Development

In GUI programs, localization (L10n) makes sure that the program can adjust to various languages, cultural contexts, and regional tastes. The following are crucial methods for incorporating localization into GUI development:

- **Using Translation Files (gettext, Qt Linguist, etc.):** Store translations in .po, .mo, or .ts files.
- **Dynamic Locale Switching:** Update UI text and formatting dynamically based on user settings.
- **Unicode Support:** Ensure UTF-8 encoding to support multiple languages.
- **Automatic Right-to-Left (RTL) Layouts:** Adjust UI for languages like Arabic and Hebrew.
- **Localizing Images & Icons:** Change images/icons based on cultural relevance.

Why Localization Matters?

- Expands the application's global reach.
- Enhances user experience by making content accessible.
- Meets regional compliance requirements.

OPEN SOURCE EQUIVALENT OF EXISTING COMMERCIAL SOFTWARE

Many commercial software applications have open-source alternatives that provide similar functionality without licensing fees. Open-source software is community-driven, customizable, and often just as powerful as proprietary solutions. Below are some key open-source alternatives to popular commercial software:

- Operating Systems
- Office Suites
- Graphic Design & Video Editing
- Web Browsers & Email Clients
- Programming & Development Tools
- Database Management
- Virtualization & Cloud Services
- Video Conferencing & Communication
- Cybersecurity & Networking

Operating Systems

An **Operating System (OS)** is system software that manages computer hardware, software resources, and provides common services for programs. It acts as an interface between users and the computer hardware. Operating systems come in different types, including proprietary (commercial) and open-source alternatives.

- **Proprietary Operating Systems** (Commercial)
- **Open-Source Operating Systems** (Free & Customizable)
- **Server and Cloud**-Based Operating Systems

Proprietary Operating Systems (Commercial)

Proprietary operating systems are closed-source software developed and maintained by companies that restrict modification, redistribution, and access to their source code. These operating systems are typically licensed, requiring users to purchase or subscribe to use them legally.

Examples of Proprietary Operating Systems

1. **Windows (Microsoft)**
   - One of the most widely used OS for desktops and laptops.
   - Comes in different editions like Windows 10, Windows 11, and Windows Server.
   - Offers a user-friendly interface, extensive software support, and enterprise features.
2. **macOS (Apple)**
   - Exclusive to Apple's Mac computers.
   - Known for stability, security, and seamless integration with Apple devices.
   - Features a Unix-based core and a polished graphical user interface (GUI).

Windows → Linux (Ubuntu, Fedora, Debian, etc.)

macOS → FreeBSD

Open-Source Operating Systems (Free & Customizable)

Open-source operating systems are freely available and allow users to modify, distribute, and customize the source code according to their needs. They are widely used in personal computing, servers, embedded systems, and enterprise environments due to their flexibility, security, and cost-effectiveness.

Examples of Open-Source Operating Systems

Linux Distributions (Various)

Based on the Linux kernel, with different distributions tailored for various use cases.

Examples:

- **Ubuntu:** User-friendly and widely used in desktops and servers.
- **Debian:** Stable and secure, often used for servers.
- **Fedora:** Cutting-edge technologies, used by developers.
- **Arch Linux:** Lightweight and customizable, for advanced users.
- **Kali Linux:** Security-focused distribution for penetration testing.
- **CentOS (Now AlmaLinux/Rocky Linux):** Enterprise-grade, derived from Red Hat Enterprise Linux (RHEL).
- **BSD:** Based Operating Systems (Berkeley Software Distribution)
- **Unix:** like OS known for security, performance, and stability.

Examples:

- **FreeBSD:** Used in servers, networking, and embedded systems.
- **OpenBSD:** Security-focused OS with strong cryptographic features.
- **NetBSD:** Designed for portability across different hardware architectures.

Server and Cloud-Based Open-Source Operating Systems

Server and cloud-based operating systems are designed to handle large-scale computing, data centers, and cloud infrastructure. These operating systems are optimized for performance, security, and scalability to support enterprise applications, virtualization, and cloud computing environments.

Linux-Based Server Operating Systems

Most cloud and server environments rely on Linux due to its stability, security, and open-source nature. Examples include:

- **Ubuntu Server:** A widely used server OS with strong cloud and enterprise support.
- **Debian Server:** Known for its stability and security, often used in enterprise environments.
- **CentOS Stream/Alma Linux/Rocky Linux:** Enterprise-grade alternatives to Red Hat Enterprise Linux (RHEL).

Open-Source Office Suites

Open-source office suites provide free and customizable alternatives to proprietary software like Microsoft Office. They offer word processing, spreadsheets, presentations, and other productivity tools while maintaining compatibility with widely used file formats.

LibreOffice

- One of the most popular open-source office suites, derived from OpenOffice.
- Includes **Writer (Word Processor), Calc (Spreadsheet), Impress (Presentation), Draw (Graphics), Base (Database), and Math (Formula Editor).**
- Supports Microsoft Office file formats (DOCX, XLSX, PPTX).
- Available on Windows, macOS, and Linux.

Microsoft Office (Word, Excel, PowerPoint) → FREE LibreOffice, OnlyOffice, Apache OpenOffice

Google Docs, Sheets, Slides → FREE Collabora Online, CryptPad

These open-source office suites offer powerful features for document creation, editing, and collaboration, making them viable alternatives to proprietary software for individuals and businesses.

Open-Source Alternatives for Graphic Design & Video Editing

Open-source software provides powerful and free alternatives to commercial graphic design and video editing tools, offering flexibility, customization, and community support.

Graphic Design Software

1. **GIMP (GNU Image Manipulation Program)**
   - Alternative to Adobe Photoshop.
   - Supports layers, masks, filters, and plugins.
   - Available for Windows, macOS, and Linux.
2. **Inkscape**
   - Alternative to Adobe Illustrator.

- Vector-based drawing tool for logos, illustrations, and icons.
- Supports SVG, PDF, EPS, and AI formats.

3. **Krita**
   - Alternative to Corel Painter and Photoshop for digital painting.
   - Optimized for concept art, illustrations, and comics.
   - Offers a variety of brushes, stabilizers, and animation tools.
4. **Blender (For 2D & 3D Design)**
   - Alternative to Autodesk Maya and 3ds Max.
   - Full 3D modeling, rendering, and animation suite.
   - Features Grease Pencil for 2D animation.

Video Editing Software

1. **Kdenlive**
   - Alternative to Adobe Premiere Pro and Final Cut Pro.
   - Non-linear video editor with multi-track support.
   - Supports real-time preview, effects, and transitions.
2. **OpenShot**
   - Beginner-friendly alternative to iMovie.
   - Simple drag-and-drop interface with keyframe animation.
   - Supports multiple formats and resolutions.
3. **DaVinci Resolve (Free Version)**
   - Alternative to Adobe Premiere Pro and Final Cut Pro.
   - Professional-grade editing, color correction, and VFX tools.
   - Free version includes powerful editing features but has some limitations.
4. **Shotcut**
   - Lightweight alternative to Sony Vegas.
   - Supports various video formats with hardware acceleration.
   - Includes effects, transitions, and timeline editing.

These open-source tools offer professional-grade features without licensing costs, making them ideal for individuals, businesses, and creative professionals.

Open-Source Alternatives for Web Browsers & Email Clients

Open-source software provides free, customizable, and privacy-focused alternatives to proprietary web browsers and email clients.

Web Browsers

1. **Mozilla Firefox**
   - Alternative to Google Chrome, Microsoft Edge, and Safari.
   - Emphasizes privacy with built-in tracking protection and enhanced security.

- Supports extensive add-ons, themes, and developer tools.
- Available on Windows, macOS, Linux, and mobile devices.

2. **Brave**
   - Privacy-focused alternative with built-in ad and tracker blocking.
   - Offers a cryptocurrency-based rewards system for viewing ads.
   - Based on Chromium but with enhanced privacy features.
3. **Chromium**
   - Open-source version of Google Chrome, without proprietary Google services.
   - Used as the base for other browsers like Microsoft Edge, Brave, and Opera.
4. **Tor Browser**
   - Focused on anonymous browsing using the Tor network.
   - Blocks trackers, prevents fingerprinting, and hides user IP addresses.
   - Ideal for secure and private web surfing.

Email Clients

1. **Mozilla Thunderbird**
   - Alternative to Microsoft Outlook and Apple Mail.
   - Supports multiple email accounts, calendar integration, and encryption.
   - Open-source with extensive add-ons and customization options.
2. **Evolution**
   - Linux-based alternative for Outlook, developed by GNOME.
   - Includes email, calendar, contacts, and task management features.
   - Supports Microsoft Exchange and other mail protocols.
3. **KMail (Kontact Suite)**
   - Part of KDE's Kontact suite for Linux users.
   - Supports PGP encryption, filters, and advanced email management.
4. **Claws Mail**
   - Lightweight alternative with fast performance.
   - Offers powerful filtering and customization but lacks HTML email support.

These open-source browsers and email clients provide a secure, privacy-friendly, and customizable experience without reliance on proprietary software.

Open-Source Alternatives for Programming & Development Tools

Open-source software provides powerful alternatives to proprietary development tools, offering flexibility, transparency, and community-driven improvements.

Integrated Development Environments (IDEs) & Code Editors

1. **VS Code (VSCodium)**
   - Alternative to Microsoft Visual Studio.
   - Lightweight, feature-rich, and extensible with plugins.
   - VSCodium is a telemetry-free open-source build of VS Code.

2. **Eclipse**
   - Alternative to IntelliJ IDEA and Microsoft Visual Studio.
   - Ideal for Java development but supports multiple languages through plugins.
3. **JetBrains Fleet (Community Edition)**
   - Alternative to JetBrains paid tools like PyCharm and WebStorm.
   - A smart and lightweight IDE with collaborative features.
4. **Geany**
   - Lightweight alternative to Notepad++ and Sublime Text.
   - Fast, simple, and supports many programming languages.
5. **Vim & Emacs**
   - Highly customizable text editors for programming.
   - Vim is efficient for keyboard-driven editing, while Emacs is highly extensible.

These open-source tools empower developers with cost-effective, customizable, and community-supported alternatives to proprietary software, ensuring flexibility and control over development workflows.

Open-Source Alternatives for Database Management

Open-source database management systems (DBMS) provide robust, scalable, and cost-effective solutions for handling structured and unstructured data. These alternatives offer high flexibility, strong community support, and security compared to proprietary commercial databases.

Relational Database Management Systems (RDBMS)

MySQL (MariaDB & Percona Server)

- Alternative to **Microsoft SQL Server and Oracle MySQL Enterprise**.
- MariaDB is a drop-in replacement with additional features and better performance.
- Percona Server provides optimized performance for large-scale applications.

Open-source database solutions offer powerful, flexible, and cost-efficient alternatives to proprietary databases. Whether for enterprise applications, web development, or cloud computing, these databases provide scalability, performance, and strong community support.

Open-Source Alternatives for Virtualization & Cloud Services

Open-source virtualization and cloud platforms provide cost-effective, scalable, and customizable solutions for businesses and developers. These alternatives rival proprietary platforms like VMware vSphere, Microsoft Hyper-V, and Amazon Web Services (AWS), offering flexibility, security, and strong community support.

Virtualization Platforms (Hypervisors)

1. **KVM (Kernel-based Virtual Machine)**

- Alternative to **VMware ESXi and Microsoft Hyper-V**.
- Built into Linux, provides enterprise-grade virtualization with performance close to bare-metal.

2. **Xen**
   - Alternative to **VMware vSphere and Citrix Hypervisor**.
   - Used in large-scale cloud platforms (AWS, Oracle Cloud). Supports paravirtualization and hardware-assisted virtualization.
3. **VirtualBox**
   - Alternative to **VMware Workstation and Parallels**.
   - Cross-platform, lightweight virtualization software for desktops and development.
4. **Proxmox Virtual Environment (Proxmox VE)**
   - Alternative to **VMware vSphere**.
   - Combines KVM and LXC containers with a web-based management interface.
5. **oVirt**
   - Alternative to **Red Hat Virtualization (RHV) and VMware vCenter**.
   - Enterprise-grade open-source virtualization for managing large VM infrastructures.

Open-source virtualization and cloud solutions empower businesses with scalable and cost-efficient alternatives to proprietary platforms. These tools support on-premise and hybrid cloud deployments while providing flexibility, security, and automation capabilities.

Open-Source Alternatives for Video Conferencing, Communication

Open-source software provides powerful and secure alternatives to proprietary communication and cybersecurity tools. These solutions offer cost-effective, customizable, and privacy-focused platforms for businesses, developers, and individuals.

Video Conferencing & Communication

1. **Jitsi Meet**
   - Alternative to Zoom, Microsoft Teams, and Google Meet.
   - Secure, web-based video conferencing with end-to-end encryption and no account requirement.
2. **BigBlueButton**
   - Alternative to Cisco Webex and Adobe Connect.
   - Designed for online learning, featuring whiteboards, recording, and breakout rooms.
3. **Mattermost**
   - Alternative to Slack and Microsoft Teams.
   - Secure, self-hosted messaging for team collaboration and DevOps workflows.
4. **Rocket.Chat**
   - Alternative to Slack and Discord.
   - Open-source team communication with video calls, file sharing, and self-hosted deployment.
5. **Nextcloud Talk**
   - Alternative to Google Meet and Skype.

- Private, end-to-end encrypted video calling integrated with file storage.

6. **Element (Matrix Protocol)**
   - Alternative to Microsoft Teams and WhatsApp.
   - Decentralized, encrypted messaging with secure VoIP and video calling.

Open-Source Alternatives for Cybersecurity & Networking

Open-source cybersecurity and networking tools offer powerful and flexible alternatives to proprietary solutions. These tools help protect systems, monitor network activity, and secure communications without high licensing costs.

1. Firewalls & Network Security

1. **pfSense**
   - Alternative to Cisco ASA, Fortinet FortiGate
   - Advanced firewall and router solution with VPN, intrusion detection, and web filtering.
2. **OPNsense**
   - Alternative to Sophos XG Firewall
   - Secure, user-friendly firewall with real-time threat monitoring and traffic shaping.
3. **Suricata**
   - Alternative to Snort (Intrusion Detection System - IDS/IPS)
   - Network monitoring tool with deep packet inspection and anomaly detection.
4. **iptables & nftables**
   - Alternative to Windows Firewall, Cisco Firepower
   - Linux-based firewall solutions for controlling traffic at the packet level.

2. VPN & Secure Remote Access

1. **OpenVPN**
   - Alternative to Cisco AnyConnect, NordVPN
   - Secure and encrypted VPN service for remote access and privacy.
2. **WireGuard**
   - Alternative to IPsec, ExpressVPN
   - Fast, lightweight VPN protocol with strong cryptographic security.
3. **SoftEther VPN**
   - Alternative to Pulse Secure, FortiClient VPN
   - Multi-protocol VPN with cross-platform support and high-speed connectivity.

3. Network Monitoring & Traffic Analysis

1. **Wireshark**
   - to Microsoft Network Monitor, SolarWinds Deep Packet Inspection
   - Packet analyzer that captures and inspects network traffic in real-time.

2. **Nagios**
   - Alternative to Zabbix, PRTG Network Monitor
   - Network and system monitoring tool that detects failures and security threats.
3. **Prometheus + Grafana**
   - Alternative to Datadog, Splunk
   - Real-time metrics collection and visualization for network and system performance.
4. **Nmap (Network Mapper)**
   - Alternative to Nessus (Basic Scanning Features)
   - Network scanning and security auditing tool for detecting open ports and vulnerabilities.
5. **Zeek (Bro IDS)**
   - Alternative to Cisco Stealthwatch
   - Network security monitoring tool for traffic analysis and anomaly detection.

4. Encryption & Secure Communication

1. **GnuPG (GPG)**
   - Alternative to PGP (Pretty Good Privacy)
   - Open-source encryption for emails, files, and secure data exchange.
2. **Let's Encrypt**
   - Alternative to DigiCert, GoDaddy SSL
   - Free SSL/TLS certificates for securing websites.
3. **Tor (The Onion Router)**
   - Alternative to Proprietary VPNs, Private Internet Access (PIA)
   - Encrypted, anonymous browsing over a decentralized network.
4. **Signal (Self-Hosted Option Available)**
   - Alternative to WhatsApp, Telegram (without encryption)
   - End-to-end encrypted messaging and voice calls.

5. Identity & Access Management

1. **FreeIPA**
   - Alternative to Microsoft Active Directory
   - Centralized authentication and identity management for Linux environments.
2. **Keycloak**
   - Alternative to Okta, Microsoft Azure AD
   - Open-source identity and access management with single sign-on (SSO) and multi-factor authentication (MFA).
3. **Authentik**
   - Alternative to Duo Security, Google OAuth
   - Self-hosted identity provider for user authentication and authorization.

Exercise

1. What is Free/Open Source Software (FOSS)?
2. How does FOSS differ from proprietary software?
3. What are the core principles of Free Software as defined by Richard Stallman?
4. What is the GNU Project, and what are its primary objectives?
5. What were the key milestones in the development of GNU/Linux?
6. How did the free software movement begin, and what were its major achievements?
7. What are the main advantages of using Free Software?
8. How does GNU/Linux compare to proprietary operating systems in terms of security and cost?
9. What is the purpose of software licensing in general?
10. How do open source licenses differ from commercial licenses?
11. What are some common types of open source licenses?
12. How do permissive licenses like the MIT License differ from copyleft licenses like the GPL?
13. What is the role of copyright in software development?
14. How do patents affect the open source software community?
15. What are the key characteristics of a commercial software license?
16. What are the benefits and drawbacks of using open source licenses for businesses?
17. What are the basic principles of copyright law as they apply to software?
18. How do contracts influence software licensing agreements?
19. What are some common issues related to copyrights and patents in the context of open source software?
20. What is the typical warranty status of open source software?
21. How do disclaimers of warranty impact the use of open source software?
22. What are the core values of the Free and Open Source Software philosophy?
23. How does the FOSS philosophy influence software development and distribution?
24. What are the current global trends in the adoption of FOSS?
25. How is FOSS being utilized in India, and what are the trends in that region?
26. What is the General Public License (GPL), and what are its key features?
27. How does the Affero General Public License (AGPL) differ from the GPL?

28. What is the Lesser General Public License (LGPL), and in what scenarios is it used?
29. What does the Free Documentation License (FDL) cover, and how does it apply to documentation?
30. What are the implications of choosing a specific FOSS license for a project?
31. How do different FOSS licenses affect the distribution and modification of software?
32. Can you provide examples of popular FOSS projects and their impact on their respective domains?
33. What are some widely-used FOSS tools and applications in various industries?
34. What are some common programming practices recommended for developing FOSS?
35. What guidelines should developers follow when contributing to GNU/Linux projects?
36. A company is considering transitioning from proprietary software to open source solutions for its business operations. What are the potential benefits and challenges of making this transition, and how might it impact the company's overall strategy?
37. A new developer is joining an open source project and is unfamiliar with the concepts of FOSS and GNU. How would you explain the fundamental principles of FOSS and the goals of the GNU Project to help them understand the project's philosophy and their role?
38. You are giving a presentation on the history of GNU/Linux and the free software movement to a group of students. How would you highlight the key milestones and figures that shaped the development of GNU/Linux and the impact of the free software movement on modern technology?
39. An organization is evaluating whether to adopt GNU/Linux for its server infrastructure. What are the key advantages of GNU/Linux over proprietary alternatives in terms of cost, security, and flexibility, and how might these advantages influence the decision-making process?
40. A startup is developing a new software product and is unsure about which licensing model to choose. How would you advise them on selecting an appropriate license, considering their goals for intellectual property, collaboration, and commercialization?
41. A developer is working on a project and needs to incorporate third-party libraries with different licenses. How should they navigate the complexities of integrating libraries with various licenses to ensure compliance and avoid legal issues?
42. A software company is facing a legal challenge over a patent claim related to its open source product. How should the company address the patent claim, and what strategies can be employed to protect its intellectual property while maintaining open source principles?
43. A business is considering offering its software under a dual licensing model, where users can choose between a commercial license and an open source license. What are the potential benefits and drawbacks of this approach, and how might it affect the company's revenue and community engagement?
44. A non-profit organization wants to release its software project under an open source license but is concerned about potential legal issues. How should the organization approach open source licensing, and what considerations should they keep in mind regarding copyright and contract law?

45. A customer is using an open source software package and encounters a critical issue. How should the lack of warranty in open source software impact their expectations for support and resolution, and what steps can they take to address the issue?
46. A new tech company is adopting the FOSS philosophy in its development practices. How should the company integrate the values of transparency, collaboration, and user freedom into its software development processes and corporate culture?
47. A technology analyst is preparing a report on global trends in FOSS adoption and its future potential. What are the key trends to highlight, and how might they influence the technology landscape in different regions, including emerging markets like India?
48. A development team is considering which open source license to apply to their new project. How would the choice between GPL, AGPL, LGPL, and FDL impact the project's distribution, modification, and integration with other software?
49. A company is planning to contribute to an open source project but is concerned about the implications of different open source licenses on their proprietary code. What are the potential risks and benefits of contributing to an open source project under various licenses?
50. An educational institution wants to incorporate FOSS into its curriculum and research projects. What are some notable examples of FOSS projects that could be included, and how can these examples be leveraged to demonstrate the practical applications and benefits of open source software?
51. An organization is onboarding new developers for a GNU/Linux-based project. What programming practices and guidelines should they follow to ensure high-quality code and effective collaboration within the open source community?
52. What are the key steps involved in installing a GNU/Linux distribution on a new machine?
53. How do you configure disk partitions and file systems during the installation of a GNU/Linux distribution?
54. What considerations should be made when selecting partitions and file systems for a Linux installation?
55. What are the basic shell commands for logging into a GNU/Linux system?
56. How can you list files and directories using shell commands?
57. What commands are used to edit files from the command line in GNU/Linux?
58. How can you copy and move files using shell commands?
59. Which commands are used to view the contents of files in GNU/Linux?
60. How do you change file modes and permissions using shell commands?
61. What are the common shell commands for managing processes in GNU/Linux?
62. How can you view and manage active processes using command-line tools?
63. What commands are used to create and manage users and groups in GNU/Linux?
64. How can you modify user accounts and group memberships from the command line?
65. How does file ownership work in GNU/Linux, and how can it be changed?
66. What are the different file permissions in GNU/Linux, and how can you modify them?
67. What is PAM (Pluggable Authentication Modules), and how does it relate to authentication in GNU/Linux?

68. How can PAM be configured to enhance security on a GNU/Linux system?
69. What are some common system configuration files in GNU/Linux, and what do they control?
70. How can you locate and interpret log files on a GNU/Linux system?
71. What are the basic steps for configuring networking on a GNU/Linux system?
72. How do you set up TCP/IP networking and routing on a Linux machine?
73. What are the common methods for connecting a GNU/Linux system to the Internet?
74. How do you troubleshoot connectivity issues in GNU/Linux?
75. System Administration – Backup and Restore Procedures
76. What are some common strategies for backing up and restoring data on a GNU/Linux system?
77. How can you automate backup procedures in GNU/Linux?
78. What are the best practices for maintaining security on a GNU/Linux server?
79. How can you implement and manage firewall rules in GNU/Linux?
80. What tools and techniques can be used to monitor and secure a GNU/Linux server?
81. You have a new server and need to install a GNU/Linux distribution to set up a web server. What are the key steps you should follow to complete the installation successfully?
82. During the installation of GNU/Linux on a server with multiple drives, you need to configure disk partitions and file systems. How would you decide on the partitioning scheme and file systems to use?
83. You are installing GNU/Linux on a system with both SSD and HDD. What considerations should you take into account when selecting partitions and file systems to optimize performance and storage?
84. You have just logged into a new GNU/Linux system via SSH. What are the basic shell commands you would use to start working with the system?
85. You need to check the contents of a directory and find specific files on a GNU/Linux system. Which commands would you use to list the files and directories effectively?
86. You need to edit a configuration file on a GNU/Linux server. What commands would you use to open and edit the file from the command line?
87. You need to move a log file from one directory to another and create a backup copy. How would you achieve this using shell commands?
88. You need to change the permissions of a script file so that only the owner can execute it. Which command would you use to modify the file permissions?
89. Your server is running slowly, and you suspect a process is using too many resources. What commands would you use to identify and manage the processes consuming the most resources?
90. You need to stop a background process that is no longer needed. How would you find and terminate this process using command-line tools?
91. A new employee is joining your team, and you need to create a user account for them with specific group memberships. What commands would you use to set up the user and manage their group memberships?

92. An employee has left the company, and you need to remove their user account and associated groups. How would you accomplish this using command-line tools?
93. You are setting up a shared directory where multiple users need read and write access, but no one else should be able to access it. How would you configure file ownership and permissions to achieve this?
94. A script that you wrote is not executing as expected due to permission issues. How can you modify the file permissions to ensure the script runs properly?
95. Your organization wants to enhance security by integrating multi-factor authentication (MFA) into the login process. How would you configure PAM to support MFA on a GNU/Linux system?
96. You need to set up PAM to restrict access to certain system services based on user groups. How would you configure PAM to achieve this?
97. You need to troubleshoot a network issue on your GNU/Linux server. What configuration files and log files would you review to diagnose and resolve the problem?
98. You need to modify the system's network configuration to use a static IP address. What configuration files would you need to edit, and how would you interpret and apply the changes?
99. Your company is expanding, and you need to configure a new GNU/Linux server with a static IP address and set up routing for internal network traffic. What are the basic steps you should follow?
100. You need to set up a new VPN connection on a GNU/Linux server to securely connect to a remote network. What steps are involved in configuring TCP/IP networking and routing for this setup?
101. A GNU/Linux system in your office is unable to connect to the Internet. What steps would you take to diagnose and resolve the connectivity issue?
102. You need to configure a GNU/Linux system to connect to a public Wi-Fi network. What are the common methods for achieving this, and what troubleshooting steps should you consider?
103. Your company's data is crucial, and you need to implement a backup strategy for your GNU/Linux server. What are some common strategies for backing up and restoring data?
104. You need to automate daily backups of critical system files on a GNU/Linux server. How would you set up an automated backup procedure, and which tools couldyou use?
105. You are responsible for maintaining the security of a GNU/Linux server. What are the best practices you should follow to ensure the server remains secure?
106. You need to implement a firewall on your GNU/Linux server to restrict access to certain services. How would you configure and manage firewall rules to secure the server?
107. You need to monitor the security of a GNU/Linux server to detect and respond to potential threats. What tools and techniques can you use to monitor and secure the server effectively?
108. You've installed a new sound card on a GNU/Linux machine, but the system does not recognize it. What steps would you take to configure the sound card and ensure it works correctly?

109. You've connected a new high-resolution display to your GNU/Linux system, but the display isn't using its full resolution. How would you configure the display settings to utilize the full resolution?
110. After installing a new network card on a GNU/Linux server, it fails to connect to the network. What steps would you follow to configure and troubleshoot the network card?
111. You need to set up a dial-up modem on a GNU/Linux system for occasional Internet access. What configuration steps are necessary to get the modem working?
112. You've plugged in a USB drive, but it doesn't automatically mount. How would you manually mount the USB drive and access its contents?
113. You need to burn a data CD on a GNU/Linux system. What tools and commands would you use to write data to a CD?
114. The system is failing to boot up properly after a recent update. What steps would you take to diagnose and fix boot issues on a GNU/Linux system?
115. You need to configure a GNU/Linux system to connect to a secure corporate network over VPN. How would you set up and test the VPN connection?
116. You want to play MP3 files on a GNU/Linux system, but the necessary multimedia player is not installed. How would you install and configure a music player to handle MP3 files?
117. You need to edit a spreadsheet and a text document on a GNU/Linux system. What applications would you use, and how would you install them if they are not already present?
118. You want to set up an email client on your GNU/Linux system to send and receive emails. What steps would you follow to configure an email client?
119. You need to copy files from an external hard drive and also from a remote server. What commands and tools would you use for these tasks?
120. You want to install and play a popular game that's available for GNU/Linux. How would you go about installing and running the game?
121. You need to create an audio CD from a set of MP3 files on a GNU/Linux system. What tools and commands would you use to burn the CD?
122. The graphical user interface (GUI) on your GNU/Linux system isn't displaying correctly. How would you configure X Windows to resolve display issues?
123. You've connected a new monitor to your system, but X Windows doesn't detect it automatically. What steps would you take to manually configure and detect the new display?
124. You need to compile and install software from source code on a GNU/Linux system. What are the general steps involved in this process?
125. You want to install a precompiled software package using the package manager. What commands and procedures would you use to install the software?
126. You need to set up an SMTP server using Postfix on your GNU/Linux system. What are the basic configuration steps to get Postfix up and running?
127. You need to configure Courier to handle IMAP and POP3 email services. How would you configure Courier to manage these email protocols?

128. You want to set up a webmail interface using SquirrelMail. What are the steps involved in installing and configuring SquirrelMail?
129. You need to set up a basic web server using Apache. What are the initial configuration steps to get Apache serving web pages?
130. You want to enable PHP support on your Apache web server. How would you install and configure PHP to work with Apache?
131. You need to enable Perl CGI scripts on your web server. What steps are necessary to configure Apache to support Perl CGI scripts?
132. You need to set up file sharing between GNU/Linux and Windows systems using Samba. How would you configure Samba for file and authentication services?
133. You want to share files between GNU/Linux systems using NFS. What are the steps involved in setting up and configuring NFS for file sharing?
134. You need to configure Squid as a proxy server for HTTP and HTTPS traffic. What are the configuration steps to set up Squid for these services?
135. You need to set up a network printer on your GNU/Linux system. What are the steps to install and configure the printer so that it's available to all users on the network?
136. What command would you use to verify if a newly installed sound card is detected by the system?
137. How would you adjust the display resolution for a newly connected high-resolution monitor?
138. What steps would you follow if a newly installed network card fails to connect to the network?
139. What configuration file would you edit to set up a dial-up modem on a GNU/Linux system?
140. What command would you use to manually mount a USB drive that does not auto-mount?
141. What command is used to burn a data CD using wodim on a GNU/Linux system?
142. Which command would you use to view detailed boot messages to diagnose boot issues?
143. What tool or command would you use to set up a VPN connection on a GNU/Linux system?
144. What command would you use to install vlc, a multimedia player that supports MP3 files?
145. What package would you install to get LibreOffice for editing documents and spreadsheets?
146. What is a common command to install Thunderbird for managing email on a GNU/Linux system?
147. Which command would you use to copy files from a remote server to your local machine?
148. What would you do to install a game available for GNU/Linux through Steam?
149. What command would you use to create an audio CD from MP3 files using cdrtools?
150. What file would you edit to change settings for X Windows display issues?

151. What command helps you identify and configure a newly connected monitor in X Windows?
152. What are the general steps to compile and install software from source code on GNU/Linux?
153. What command would you use to install a software package from a binary package on Debian-based systems?
154. What configuration file would you edit to set up SMTP services with Postfix?
155. What files would you edit to configure Courier for handling IMAP and POP3 services?
156. What is the main configuration file to edit after installing SquirrelMail for web mail services?
157. What command starts the Apache web server after installation?
158. What command would you use to install PHP and enable it for Apache?
159. What module would you enable in Apache to support Perl CGI scripts?
160. What is the primary configuration file for setting up Samba file sharing?
161. What command would you use to export shared directories in NFS?
162. What is the main configuration file to edit for setting up Squid as a proxy server?
163. What tool would you use to configure and manage printers on a GNU/Linux system?
164. How would you compile a C source file example.c into an executable named example using gcc?
165. What command would you use to link an object file main.o with a static library libmath.a to produce an executable main?
166. How would you compile a C program app.c to generate a statically linked executable app using gcc?
167. What command would you use to create a shared library libutils.so from utils.c using gcc?
168. What gdb command would you use to start debugging an executable named program?
169. How would you open an executable program for debugging with ddd?
170. What valgrind command would you use to analyze memory usage and detect leaks in the program test?
171. What command would you use to make a Bash script script.sh executable?
172. How would you use sed to replace the first occurrence of "foo" with "bar" in the file text.txt?
173. What awk command would you use to print the third column from a file data.txt?
174. You have a C++ program main.cpp that depends on a header file utils.h and a source file utils.cpp. The utils.cpp file has been compiled into an object file utils.o. How would you compile and link main.cpp with utils.o to create an executable named myprogram using g++?
175. You are developing a project that needs to use the libmath.a static library and libnetwork.so dynamic library. You have a source file app.c that requires these libraries. What command would you use to compile and link app.c into an executable named app?

176. You need to compile a C program server.c into a statically linked executable named server to ensure that all necessary libraries are included in the binary. What gcc command would you use to achieve this?
177. You have a source file mathlib.c that you want to compile into a shared library named libmath.so. What command would you use to create this shared library using gcc?
178. You are debugging an application app and need to inspect the value of a variable count when the program hits a specific line. What gdb commands would you use to set a breakpoint at line 42 and print the value of count?
179. You are using ddd to debug an executable myapp. You want to step through the code line by line and watch the value of a variable status. How would you proceed in ddd to accomplish this?
180. You have a program memory_test that you suspect has memory leaks. How would you use valgrind to detect and report any memory leaks in memory_test?
181. You need to write a Bash script backup.sh that creates a tarball of the directory /home/user/docs and names it backup.tar.gz. What commands should be included in backup.sh to accomplish this task?
182. You have a configuration file setting. conf with multiple lines, and you need to change all occurrences of "localhost" to "127.0.0.1". What sed command would you use to perform this replacement?
183. You have a CSV file data.csv where each line contains three fields separated by commas. You want to extract and print the second field of each line. What awk command would you use to achieve this?
184. What is the role of the X server in the X Window System architecture?
185. How do you create a basic Qt application that opens a window with the title "Hello World"?
186. What is the purpose of the gtk_init() function in a Gtk+ application?
187. How would you open and read the contents of a file named data.txt in Python?
188. What environment variable would you set to include a directory /home/user/bin in the system's PATH?
189. What function in the Qt framework is used to translate strings in a Qt application for localization purposes?
190. What is a popular open source alternative to Microsoft Office for word processing and spreadsheets?
191. You are developing a graphical application and need to understand how the X Window System manages the display of windows. Describe the role of the X server, X clients, and X protocol in this architecture.
192. You are tasked with developing a simple Qt application that should have a button. When the button is clicked, it should display a message box with the text "Button Clicked!". Outline the steps and provide a code snippet to achieve this using Qt.
193. You are developing a Gtk+ application and need to create a window with a label that says "Welcome to Gtk+!" and a button. When the button is pressed, the label text should change to "Button Pressed!". Describe how you would implement this in Gtk+.

194. You are writing a Python script to process a list of numbers read from a file numbers.txt. The script should calculate and print the average of these numbers. How would you write the Python code to accomplish this task?
195. You need to run a script named run.sh from any directory on your system. What steps would you take to ensure that the run.sh script is executable and accessible from any location?
196. You are developing a Qt application that needs to support multiple languages. How would you configure the application to load and display translations based on the user's locale?
197. You are looking for an open source alternative to Adobe Photoshop for image editing. What open source software would you recommend and why?

♦♦♦